United Methodist Church of Geneva
211 Hamilton Street
Geneva, IL 60134

Beside
Still Waters

C. H. SPURGEON

Beside
Still Waters

Words of Comfort
for the Soul

Roy H. Clarke, Editor

THOMAS NELSON PUBLISHERS
NASHVILLE

Library of Congress Cataloging-in-Publication Data

Spurgeon, C. H. (Charles Haddon), 1834-1892
    Beside still waters / Charles H. Spurgeon; compiled and edited by Roy H. Clarke.
    p.   cm.
    ISBN 0-7852-0678-7
    1. Suffering—Religious aspects—Christianity. 2. Devotional calendars. 3. Consolation. I. Clarke, Roy H., 1930- . II. Title.
BV4909.S65 1999
242' .4—dc21   98-35026
                                        CIP

Printed in the United States of America

6 7—04

Preface

Charles Haddon Spurgeon is my avocation. I have read over two thousand of his sermons, outlining and analyzing more than a thousand. In them I found a field of precious gems: more than three hundred vignettes promising hope, comfort, and encouragement.

Spurgeon pointed out that people often come into the house of God heavily loaded with the thoughts of their daily vocations, the pressures of business, and the burdens of family life. The farmer remembers the fields that need plowing. The merchant sees unpaid bills fluttering before his eyes. Others are unable to forget a sick wife or ailing children. For these, he said, the preacher must have suitable leverage in his sermon to lift folk from the earth to which they cling and elevate them a little nearer heaven.

As Spurgeon looked into the eyes of hurting and bewildered parishioners, he often responded with words of comfort. These passages are characterized by Spurgeon's rare ability to put deep truths into simple language with rich, warm, spiritual tones. As I identified and updated these vignettes into clear, contemporary language, I shared them with the adult Bible classes that I taught, and they proved a mighty blessing. Spurgeon's words can reach across the years and speak to today's hurting, struggling, bewildered, and depressed people. His answers are still valid.

As Thielicke observed, "It is evidence of the substance and excellent form in Spurgeon's sermons that, removed from the situation in which they were originally preached and from the magnetism of Spurgeon's personality, they lose little in print. They are still a bubbling spring whose water needs no filtering or treatment. It is impressive that even though Spurgeon wrote and preached over a century ago, his words are still fresh and fragrant."

Spurgeon's ability to offer hope and healing was best expressed by Russell Conwell. "No man in this [19th] century has ever healed so many people as Mr. Spurgeon. Although he was not a physician, and never wrote prescriptions, Spurgeon felt that there was an unexplained mystery about the whole matter. Yet he asserted that there was power connected with prayer that should be used when people were in pain and could be relieved by it."

Though now regarded by some as the Prince of Preachers, Charles Haddon Spurgeon knew well the humbling effect of rejection and sickness in his own life. From the time he came to his London pulpit at the age of nineteen, he was the butt of cruel jokes in the press and the object of scorn from other clergy. Depression was a frequent and perverse companion. He suffered from gout, a disease that produces tortuous misery, and pain hounded him the last twenty years of his life.

During his ministry, the Asiatic cholera epidemic scourged London, and many people died daily. Tuberculosis was rampant and incurable. Most surgery was performed without anaesthesia. The debtor's prisons were full—business failures were common. In London alone, one hundred thousand children wandered in destitution, headed for jails or early graves. As a dedicated pastor, Spurgeon drove all over south London to visit and minister.

Spurgeon's trials and afflictions drew him closer to Jesus Christ and to his people. He knew their distress. His spirit was so sensitive to the feelings and needs of his congregation that he ultimately came to think as they thought and feel as they felt. Spurgeon seemed able to enter fully into their disappointment, success, depression, pain, anxiety, and fear of death. This gave him the insight to love and minister to a hurting and bewildered people. The selections in this book reveal Spurgeon ministering to the hurting, lifting them out of their trials and drawing them a little closer to heaven.

This volume of promising pictures is a faithful, careful, revision that, like a classic piece of furniture, has been lovingly restored. As with two of my other books, *Morning and Evening*, updated and *The Treasury of David*, updated, the text has been completely modernized into contemporary English, with biblical quotations identified and converted to the New King James Version. The three hundred and sixty-six vignettes in this collection use texts from sixty-four of the books of the Bible.

Readers may approach this book in any of several different ways. Every selection is complete on a separate page. Each selection is tied to a specific Scripture reference that appears at the top of the page. These references are listed in biblical sequence. Thus readers may

- Dip into the book at random, searching for treasures that speak to them where they are;
- Incorporate the book into a daily devotional plan, reading one selection a day for a full year;
- Seek out selections tied to favorite Scripture verses or a Bible book being studied;
- Explore the thirty categories in the Topical Index in the back of the book for a list of selections related to special problems in their lives;
- Simply begin at the beginning and read straight through to Charles Haddon Spurgeon's farewell at

the end of the last selection.

Whichever approach you choose, you will be amazed at the fresh inspiration and comfort provided by Spurgeon's thoughts penned more than 100 years ago!

Roy H. Clarke
Ponte Vedra Beach, Florida
September, 1998

This book is lovingly dedicated to my sister,
Elaine Clarke Hiscock

DO NOT BE AFRAID. *Genesis 15:1*

The Lord came to Abram in a vision, saying, "Do not be afraid, Abram. I am your shield, your exceedingly great reward" (Gen. 15:1). These words were spoken shortly after Abram had given his nephew Lot the choice of territories. Lot chose what appeared to be the best, Jordan's well-watered plain. Abraham, however, looked to the kingdom of God and His righteousness. Thus, he lost nothing.

Then the Lord appeared and seemed to say, "Your nephew Lot trusted in what he could see. He followed the leaning of his own judgment and chose what seemed best for his immediate advantage. Abram, do not be afraid, you will not lose, for I am your shield and your exceedingly great reward. You have chosen the good part, and it will not be taken from you. Do not worry."

The patriarch might have responded, "O LORD, You are the portion of my inheritance and my cup; You maintain my lot. The lines have fallen to me in pleasant places; yes, I have a good inheritance" (Ps. 16:5-6).

Beloved, you have seen others suffer losses, and it has probably depressed you. Regardless of what happens, do not be alarmed. God is your defense and refuge in the day of your trouble (Ps. 59:16). You will be most secure in Him. You may have losses and afflictions, but they will not overwhelm you. You will be kept by God's power. He will deliver you out of every trial and affliction. He will be your shield and your exceedingly great reward.

EXPECT TRIALS TO MULTIPLY. *Genesis 22:1*

God does not put heavy burdens on weak shoulders. God educates and tests our faith by trials that increase in proportion to our faith. God expects us to do adult work and to endure adult afflictions only after we have reached a mature status in Christ Jesus. Therefore, beloved, expect your trials to multiply as you proceed toward heaven.

Do not think that as you grow in grace your path will become smoother and the sky calmer and clearer. Quite the contrary. As God gives you greater skill as a soldier of the cross, He will send you on more difficult missions. As He more fully equips your ship to sail in storms, He will send you on longer voyages to more boisterous seas, so that you may honor Him and increase in holy confidence.

You would think that in Abraham's old age—after he had come to the land of Beulah, after the birth of Isaac, and especially after the expulsion of Ishmael—he would have had a time of rest. But "it came to pass after these things that God tested Abraham" (Gen. 22:1). Let Abraham's story warn us to never plan on a rest from trials this side of the grave.

The trumpet still plays the notes of war. You cannot sit down and put the victory wreath on your head. You do not have a crown. You still must wear the helmet and carry the sword. You must watch, pray, and fight. Expect your last battle to be the most difficult, for the enemy's fiercest charge is reserved for the end of the day.

BLESSED BEYOND MEASURE. *Genesis 22:17*

The greatest blessing God gives is His presence. If I could choose any of life's blessings, I certainly would not ask for wealth, because wealth cannot bring freedom from pain, concern, or anxiety. I certainly would not ask for popularity, because there is no rest for the world's leaders. My choice, my highest honor, would be to have God with me always.

When God is with us, there is no difference between Nebuchadnezzar's fiery furnace (Dan. 3:19) and a comfortable bed. It does not matter! We will be happy in either. If God is with us, if His divine love surrounds us, then we carry our own atmosphere and residence wherever we travel, and we can say with Moses, "Lord, you have been our dwelling place in all generations" (Ps. 90:1).

The individual who can say this is full of heaven, full of God, and blessed beyond measure. This is the privilege of all who truly believe in Jesus, of all who come out from the world, and of all who, like Abraham, live a life of faith (Gen. 12:4). Bow your head, believer, and let the Lord God pronounce this blessing, "I will bless you."

If you are sorrowing, suffering, weary, or burdened, receive this blessing from God's own mouth, "I will bless you."

If you are poor, despised, or slandered, this blessing is not shortened. Take it with you, and go on your way rejoicing.

3

THE LORD'S PRESENCE. *Genesis 28:16*

The Puritans believed in an ever-present God. Oh to be able to feel God everywhere, in the little as well as the great, in our rising up and our sitting down, in our going out and our coming in. I cannot imagine a life more blessed or a spirit more related to the spirit of the glorified than the mind and heart of the person who lives in God, who knows and feels that God is ever-present.

If you are in personal danger, or in the midst of a storm, or facing illness, and if you hear a voice saying, "Surely the Lord is in this place," you will be perfectly at rest. The anxious air grows pure if He is there. Lightning cannot strike you, or if it does it will be joy. The storm cannot devour you, nor can the hungry ocean engulf you, or if one does it is happiness if God is there. There is no need to fear. Nervousness is wickedness when "the eternal God is your refuge, and underneath are the everlasting arms; He will thrust out the enemy from before you" (Deut. 33:27).

You may be in great poverty. Your walls may be bare and your furnishings scant. And still you may say, "Surely the Lord is in this place." Remember the old Christian's exclamation, "What, all this and my God present with me?" Better to have poverty and feel His presence than to own the world's riches and not know that He is here.

Some of you are in deep affliction. Your difficulties are so great that you do not know where things will end, and you are deeply depressed. But remember, "Surely the Lord is in this place."

Some of you are called to some extraordinary duty and do not feel strong enough. Follow that call, for surely the Lord is in that place. He will help you.

THE GOD OF BETHEL. *Genesis 31:13*

Sometimes in deep depression, in the midst of the darkest shadows, Christ appears and seems sweeter than He ever was before. When all the created streams have run dry, then the everlasting fountain bubbles up with a pure and cooling stream. Remember those occasions and the circumstances that made them cheerful, and say, "This God, even the God of Bethel, is still my God." If I am in trouble, if I am lonely, if I am brought so low that literally I have nothing but a doorstep for my pillow, if I should lose house, home, and friends and be left like an orphan with no one to shelter me, oh God of Bethel, You who cover my head and protect my spirit, You will still be with me.

The God of Bethel is a God who concerns Himself with the things of earth. He is not a God who shuts Himself up in heaven; He is a God who has a ladder between heaven and earth (Gen. 28:12). "In my distress I called upon the Lord, and cried out to my God; He heard my voice from His temple, and my cry came before Him, even to His ears" (Ps. 18:6). God numbers our wanderings. He puts our tears in His bottle (Ps. 56:8).

"Seeing that we have a great High Priest who has passed through the heavens, Jesus the Son of God, let us hold fast our confession. For we do not have a High Priest who cannot sympathize with our weaknesses, but was in all points tempted as we are, yet without sin. Let us therefore come boldly to the throne of grace, that we may obtain mercy and find grace to help in time of need" (Heb. 4:14-16).

GOD HAS MADE ME FORGET. *Genesis 41:51*

D o you feel marked for sorrow? Are you the target of the arrows of affliction? Are you punished more than others? Do not sorrow. The arrows of affliction are sent by covenant love to prepare you for a special work that will yield a great blessing from your Heavenly Father.

The day will come when you will be grateful for every blow, even grateful for the bitter pangs of unkindness from friends. Joseph's brothers hated him (Gen. 37:4), and they sold him into slavery (Gen. 37:28). "The archers have bitterly grieved him, shot at him and hated him" (Gen. 49:23). Yet see the reward, for Joseph had exclusive blessings: "His bow remained in strength, and the arms of his hands were made strong by the hands of the Mighty God of Jacob" (Gen. 49:24). The abundance of God's revelation is usually accompanied by a thorn in the flesh (2 Cor. 12:7).

Grief notwithstanding, there will be born to you, as there was to Joseph, a Manasseh, for God will make you forget all your labor. And there will be an Ephraim, for God will make you fruitful in the land of your affliction (Gen. 41:51-52).

Instructed by affliction, you will become a comforter to the afflicted.

ALL ... ARE AGAINST ME. *Genesis 42:36*

When racked with physical pain, we need the Comforter. Some pain can be endured, but the sharp fangs of certain pains push into the marrow of our nature and horribly bore their ways through the brain and the spirit. For such pains, much grace is needed.

When your head throbs, when your heart palpitates, when your system is upset, it is natural to say with Jacob, "All these things are against me." We complain of providence, but this is the time to apply the promise with power. "Fear not, for I am with you; be not dismayed, for I am your God. I will strengthen you, yes, I will help you, I will uphold you with My righteous right hand" (Is. 41:10).

When pain gives every sign of increasing, when we wait for the surgeon with his dreaded knife, if we are to be sustained under suffering that makes the flesh shudder, we need the upholding gentleness of God. "Fear not, for I am with you." This promise, like the nightingale's song, is most sweet when heard in the night season.

IN THE END, NOTHING TO FEAR. *Genesis 49:33*

Unless the Lord comes quickly, we will soon leave this body and expect to gather up our feet. We may expect to breathe our last and like our fathers go to meet our God (Gen. 49:33). But do not let sorrow dim your eye. Do not let fear trouble your spirit, because death is vanquished. We have no reason to fear. Courage, Christian soldiers, for you are encountering a vanquished enemy.

If your Master had been defeated, you might expect to be blown like chaff before the wind. But the power by which He overcame, He lends to you. Awaken all your powers to the conflict and strengthen them with the hope of victory. Remember this: the Lord's victory is your guarantee of victory, because if the Head conquers the members cannot be defeated. You must conquer for Christ has conquered. The Holy Spirit is in you. Jesus Himself has promised, "Lo, I am with you always, even to the end of the age" (Matt. 28:20).

Are you afraid to die? Does the grave alarm you? Do not fear, for you cannot die. "Christ is risen from the dead, and has become the first fruits of those who have fallen asleep. . . . For as in Adam all die, even so in Christ all shall be made alive" (1 Cor. 15:20, 22). Oh, the comfort of the gospel.

Allow me to say this: If your trust is in Jesus, there is nothing in the Bible to make you afraid. Nothing in the Bible, did I say? There is nothing in heaven, nothing on earth, and nothing in hell to make you fear, if your trust is in Jesus Christ. Jesus said, "Because I live, you will live also. At that day you will know that I am in My Father, and you in Me, and I in you" (John 14:19-20).

8

LAID ASIDE FOR A TIME. *Exodus 3:1*

This is counsel for you who are temporarily laid on the shelf. Some of God's best workers have been laid aside for long periods. Moses was forty years in the desert, doing nothing but tending sheep. One greater than Moses, our blessed Savior, was thirty years doing—I will not say nothing, but certainly doing no public work.

When you are retired or inactive, prepare for the time when God will again use you. If you are put on the shelf, do not rust; pray that the Master will polish you, so that when He uses you again you will be fully ready for the work.

While you are laid aside, I want you to pray for others that are working. Help them and encourage them. Do not get into that peevish, miserable frame of mind that grudges and undervalues other's efforts. Some people, when they cannot do anything, do not like anybody else to work. Promise that if you cannot help, you will never hinder. Spend time in prayer, that you may be fit for the Master's use.

At the siege of Gibraltar, when the fleet surrounded it and determined to storm the old rock, the governor fired red-hot shot down on the men-of-war. The enemy did not care for the governor's warm reception. Think how it was done. Here were gunners on the ramparts firing away, and every garrison soldier wanted to join them. What did those who could not fire a gun do? They heated the shot. And that is what you must do.

Your pastor is the master gunner, so heat the shot for him with your earnest prayers. When you see your friends working for God, if you cannot join them, say, "Never mind. If I can contribute nothing else, my prayers will heat the shot."

THIS IS THE BREAD. *Exodus 16:15*

Dear friend, you and I are greatly pardoned. Look at Calvary, and if you can see through your blinding tears, behold the sacrifice. "He has appeared to put away sin by the sacrifice of Himself. And as it is appointed for men to die once, but after this the judgment, so Christ was offered once to bear the sins of many" (Heb. 9:26-28).

Today, we are journeying through the wilderness toward Canaan. We have great pressing needs. We are poverty itself, and only All-sufficiency can supply us. We need a great abundance of food. The heavenly bread lies around the camp, and we may take our fill (Ex. 16:16). We require rivers of living water, and Jesus gives us a fountain springing up into everlasting life (John 4:14).

We have great demands, but Christ has great supplies. Between here and heaven, we may have greater wants than we have yet known. But all along the journey, every resting place is ready; provisions are laid up, good cheer is stored, and nothing has been overlooked. The commissary of the Eternal is absolutely perfect.

Do you sometimes feel so thirsty for grace that you could drink the Jordan dry? More than a river could hold is given to you, so drink abundantly, for Christ has prepared a bottomless sea of grace to fill you with all the fullness of God. Do not be frugal. Do not doubt your Savior. Do not limit the Holy One of Israel. Be great in your experience of His all-sufficiency. Be great in your praises of His bounty, and in heaven you will pour great treasures of gratitude at His feet.

Rest in God's Prfesence. *Exodus 33:14*

Nothing can harm you if God is your refuge. David said, "You are my rock and my fortress" (Ps. 31:3), and every believing child of God may claim the same promise.

"God is our refuge and strength, a very present help in trouble, therefore we will not fear, even though the earth be removed, and though the mountains be carried into the midst of the sea; though its waters roar and be troubled, though the mountains shake with its swelling" (Ps. 46:1-3). "My presence will go with you, and I will give you rest" (Ex. 33:14). May these inexpressibly precious promises be fulfilled in your life today.

What could your heart desire or your mind conceive beyond the blessedness of these assurances? God's presence and God's rest is a ring of finest gold set with the choicest pearl. This blessing is worthy of God, and only His boundless love could proclaim it.

Think these promises over. Chew on them as food for your soul. Let the Holy Spirit speak these words with power and your innermost soul will be satisfied with the best of heaven's food:

Enough, my gracious Lord,
Let faith triumphant cry;
My heart can on this promise live,
Can on this promise die.

THE LORD YOUR GOD. *Leviticus 11:44*

In the worst of times our great consolation is God. The very name of our covenant God, "The LORD your God," is full of good cheer. "The LORD your God" is Jehovah, the Self-existent One, the unchangeable One, the ever-living God, who cannot change or be moved from His everlasting purpose (Heb. 7:24).

Child of God, whatever you do not have, you have a God in whom you may greatly glory. Having God, you have more than all things, for all things come from Him. If everything was blotted out, He could restore it by His will. He speaks and it is done. He commands and it does not move. Blessed are you if the God of Jacob is your help and hope (Ps. 146:5). The Lord Jehovah is our righteousness and everlasting strength (Is. 26:4). Trust Him forever. Let the times roll on; they cannot affect our God. Let troubles run like a storm; they will not come close because He is our defense. Jehovah is as much your God as if no other person in the universe could use that covenant expression.

All His wisdom, all His foresight, all His power, all His immutability—all of Him is yours.

Let us rejoice in our possession. Poor as we are, we are infinitely rich in having God. Weak as we are, there is no limit to our strength since the Almighty Jehovah is ours. "If God is for us, who can be against us?" (Rom. 8:31). Sorrowful one, rejoice! If God is yours, what more do you need?

He is our God by our own choice of Him, by our union with Christ Jesus, and by our experience of His goodness. By the spirit of adoption, we cry, "Abba, Father" (Rom. 8:15).

HIS PEACE WILL COME. *Numbers 6:26*

My dear believer, you must totally trust the Lord in everything and concerning everything. "Trust in Him at all times" (Ps. 62:8). Trust in the shadow of His wings (Ps. 91:4). Trust in the light of His countenance (Rev. 1:16).

Some have only learned to trust the smile of His face, but they must also learn to trust the blows of His fist. God brings us to that! "No," you say, "I can never come to that." But surely you can! Did not one of old say, "Though He slay me, yet will I trust Him" (Job 13:15)? This is precisely what we mean.

God's children undergo a variety of experiences. Today your heart is a place of sacrifice, tomorrow a battlefield. In turn, your soul is a temple and a threshing floor. But what-ever your ups and downs, you will never be removed from your ordained and appointed place. By the grace of God, you are where you are and where you shall be. You will never be effectually removed from the Lord. Infinite love holds you.

Since you trusted in the Lord there have been times when you felt that you did not receive the expected support and comfort. And yet it came. Will you now leave Him and look elsewhere? God forbid! At the very worst, our gospel is better than the world at its best. I would rather drink the dregs of Christ's wine vat, when the berries are sour, than swallow the sweetest wine of the vintage of unbelief. Believe the gospel, whether or not it yields immediate comfort. We would sooner be God's dogs than the devil's darlings.

"The LORD lift up His countenance upon you, and give you peace" (Num. 6:26).

A DESERT LAND. *Deuteronomy 32:10*

Dear believer, if you are in trouble, the voice of that trouble is designed to draw you nearer to God. God has favored you, favored you with an extraordinary means of growth in grace. To use Rutherford's simile, "He has put you down in the wine cellar in the dark. Now begin to try the well-refined wines on the lees (Is. 25:6). He has brought you to a sandy desert. Now begin to seek the treasures that are hid in the sand."

Believe that the deepest afflictions are always neighbors to the highest joys. The greatest possible privileges lie close to the darkest trials. The more bitter your sorrow, the louder your song at the end. There is a reason, and that reason faith may discover and experience may live on.

Our afflictions are the highway that leads us closer to God. Our troubles are a fiery chariot to bring us to God. Our afflictions, wave upon wave, will drive our souls nearer heaven. It is a blessed thing when God's judgments bring us closer to Him.

May God bless you, my tested friend.

HE PROVIDES STRENGTH. *Deuteronomy 33:25*

There is strength promised for you, for "as your days, so shall your strength be" (Deut. 33:25). You must not excuse yourself from the battle because you are weak, for the Lord strengthens the feeble. "Have you not known? Have you not heard? The everlasting God, the LORD, the Creator of the ends of the earth, neither faints nor is weary. His understanding is unsearchable. He gives power to the weak, and to those who have no might He increases strength. Even the youths shall faint and be weary, and the young men shall utterly fall, but those who wait on the LORD shall renew their strength; they shall mount up with wings like eagles, they shall run and not be weary, they shall walk and not faint" (Is. 40:28-31).

You cannot serve Him in your strength. You can only serve Him in the strength He gives as you need it. Here, take the bread, take the fish, and feed the thousands. Never say that it is not enough (Matt. 14:17). He will multiply both the bread and the fish as it is broken and consumed. There will be more than you need.

Listen, you who profess to be in Christ, you who love Him, you who have a work to do. God will give you the necessary strength and grace.

SURROUNDED BY GOD. *Deuteronomy 33:26*

God surrounds His children. We dwell in Him. "There is no one like the God of Jeshurun, who rides the heavens to help you, and in His excellency on the clouds. The eternal God is your refuge, and underneath are the everlasting arms; He will thrust out the enemy from before you" (Deut. 33:26-27). These verses show that the Lord is above, around, and underneath His saints. "LORD, You have been our dwelling place in all generations" (Ps. 90:1). We are as surrounded by You as the earth is surrounded by the atmosphere:

> Within Thy circling power I stand,
> On every side I find Thy hand;
> Awake, asleep, at home, abroad,
> I am surrounded still with God.

The eternal God is your dwelling place and your rest, and underneath are the everlasting arms. A parallel passage is, "His left hand is under my head, and His right hand embraces me" (Song 2:6). The soul has come to its resting place in God and is supported by divine strength. The heart has learned to live in Christ Jesus and to lean on Him day and night.

We are like Noah's dove, weary and about to drop into the destroying waters. But Noah puts out his hand, takes her, and draws her into the ark (Gen. 8:9). The dove found a refuge that surrounded and upheld her. The hands covered her on all sides.

The hand of God sustains those who dwell in the secret place of the Most High and abide under the shadow of the Almighty. I will say of the Lord, "He is my refuge and my fortress; my God, in Him I will trust" (Ps. 91:1).

18

IN DAYS OF TRIALS. *Deuteronomy 33:27*

Some of you are enduring deep affliction. In your extraordinary trial, remember the depth of divine faithfulness. You may be unable to comprehend why, but I urge you to believe in the firmness and stability of divine affection. You will have comfort in proportion to your trials. If you have shallow sorrows you will receive shallow graces. If you have deep afflictions you will obtain deeper proof of God's faithfulness.

I could lay down and die when I think of life's trials, but like Sarah (Gen. 21:6) I recover and laugh when I remember that the eternal God is our refuge and that underneath are the everlasting arms (Deut. 33:27). God will not fail. God will not take away His hand until He has finished His purpose concerning us.

Great trials bring great promises. Much afflicted one, there are great and mighty words that are not meant for saints of easier experiences. You will drink from the deep golden goblets reserved for those giants who can drink a great portion of wormwood, but God will also supply deep drinks of the well-refined wines on the lees (Is. 25:6).

Trials greatly enlarge the soul. Thus I do not want, in my better mind, to escape great trials, since they involve great graces. If my strength shall be as my days (Deut. 33:25), then let my days be long and dark, for my strength will be mighty, God will be glorified, and I will be blessed. I earnestly urge every tested Christian to dwell on this truth, for it may be a great comfort.

There is love, immortal and unchanging love, in heaven toward you, which will never grow cold. You will be helped. God would sooner cease to be than cease to be faithful. Be of good courage, for today He will strengthen your heart.

BE COURAGEOUS. *Joshua 1:7*

God's tender love for His servants makes Him concerned about our inner feelings. Some think it a small matter for believers to be troubled with doubts and fears. God does not, and He wants us free from cares and doubts. When depressed, we are victims of a terrible sickness. Do not trifle with this disease. Take it immediately to our beloved Physician. Our Lord does not want us to remain sad. It was a law of King Ahasuerus that no one could enter the king's court dressed in mourning. This is not the law of the King of kings. We may come sorrowing, but He puts "the garment of praise for the spirit of heaviness" on us (Is. 61:3).

Christians should be courageous. We glorify the Lord when we endure trials in a heroic way. If we are fearful, we dishonor our God. This disease of doubtfulness and discouragement is an epidemic that could spread among the Lord's flock. One depressed believer can make twenty souls sad.

If you do not keep your courage, Satan will be too much for you. Let your spirit be joyful in God your Savior. "The joy of the LORD is your strength" (Neh. 8:10), and no fiend of hell can make progress against you. Moreover, labor is easy to those of a cheerful spirit; success waits on cheerfulness. The ones who work while rejoicing in God and believing with all their hearts have success guaranteed.

If you sow in hope, you will reap in joy. Therefore, "be strong and very courageous."

A CITY OF REFUGE. *Joshua 21:13*

It may be that I am speaking to a sad one who is suffering from mental depression. Some of us are prone to that condition. I have sometimes envied those good people who are never excited with joy and consequently are seldom or ever depressed. "Along the cool, sequestered vale of life they hold the even tenor of their way." Happy people! At the same time, when I rise as with eagle's wings in joyful rapture, I feel right glad to be capable of the blissful excitement. Yet if you soar to the skies, you are apt to drop below sea level. He that can fly, can fall. Elijah, after he had slain the prophets of Baal, fled into the wilderness from Jezebel (1 Kin. 19:1-4).

If you are so constituted that you rise and fall, if you are a creature who can be excited and then depressed, and worse still, if you happen to have been born on a foggy day and swallowed so much fog that you have found it shading your spirit ever since, then you can only be strong by faith. If you are one of those plants that seldom bloom with bunches of bright flowers, but if you have blossoms hidden and concealed, do not be uneasy. If you are never happy and seldom able to call yourself joyful, the only cure for your depression is faith.

Settle this in your heart. "Whether I am up or down, the Lord Jesus Christ is the same. Whether I sing or sigh, the promise is true and the Promiser is faithful."

Believe in Him, though you see no flashes of delight or sparkles of joy. You are safe because you are in the City of Refuge and not because you are healthy or ill. If you will stand firm in Christ Jesus, even in your weakness you will be made strong.

MANMADE GODS. *Judges 18:24*

Earthly comforts are loaned. They are not gifts, for all that we possess is God's property. He has only lent them, and what he lends He has a right to take. We hold possessions and friends on a lease that can be terminated at the Supreme Owner's option. Therefore, do not complain when God takes His own. In a world where thorns and briars grow, it is natural that some sharp points will pierce you.

The world swarms with thieves, deceivers, and slanderers, with losses in business, crosses in our expectations, false or fickle friends, and with sickness and death. Little wonder our joys are stolen. Our Master warns that our habitation is not theft-proof. "Do not lay up for yourself treasures on earth, where moth and rust destroy and where thieves break in and steal" (Matt. 6:19).

Beloved, because these calamities may be expected, let us be prepared. Hold all things loosely. Hold them as though you did not have them. Look at them as fleeting; never expect them to remain. Never make mortal things your gods. If you do, your heart will be broken when they are taken, and you will cry with Micah, "You have taken away my gods which I made" (Judg. 18:24).

GLEANING GOD'S RICHES. *Ruth 2:2*

Troubled and depressed Christian, come and glean this morning in the broad field of promise. Here are abundant and precious promises to meet your exact needs.

Take this one. "A bruised reed He will not break, and smoking flax He will not quench" (Is. 42:3). Does this meet your need? Here is a reed that is weaker than weakness itself, yet He will not break it. Perhaps you are like the smoking flax, from which no light or warmth can come, still He will not quench you. He will blow with His sweet breath of mercy until He fans you into a flame.

Would you glean another ear? "Come to Me, all you who labor and are heavy laden, and I will give you rest" (Matt. 11:28). What soft words! Your heart is tender, and the Master knows it. He speaks gently to you. Will you obey and come to Him now?

Take another ear of corn. " 'I will help you,' says the LORD and your Redeemer, the Holy One of Israel" (Is. 41:14). How can you be afraid when you have this wonderful assurance?

You may gather ten thousand golden ears like these! "I have blotted out, like a thick cloud, your transgressions, and like a cloud your sin" (Is. 44:22). Or this, "Though your sins are like scarlet, they shall be as white as snow. Though they are red like crimson, they shall be as wool" (Is. 1:18). Or this, "The Spirit and the bride say, 'Come!' And let him who thirsts come. Whoever desires, let him take the water of life freely" (Rev. 22:17).

Our Master's field is full and rich. The precious promises lie in front of you. Gather them. Make them your own. Grasp these sweet promises. Thresh them by meditation. Feed on them with joy.

23

THE PILLARS OF THE EARTH. *1 Samuel 2:8*

It is a high privilege to rest in God when danger or pain strikes. The doctor has said that you have to undergo surgery, and there is every probability that your disease and weakness will increase and that you will be bedridden for a considerable time. Do not fret; that will not help. Do not fear the future; that will not improve your condition. Put yourself (this is your privilege) in the keeping of those dear hands that were pierced for you. Surrender to the love of that heart which was pierced to purchase your redemption.

The rest that the Holy Spirit gives under the worst conditions is wonderful. Martyrs have sung at the stake! They have rejoiced on the rack! Bonner's coal-hole at Fulham, England, where the martyrs were locked up, was a wretched place to spend a winter's night. Still the martyrs sang there, and it was the sweetest singing this side of heaven. Bonner said, "Contempt on them that they should make such a noise." But they told him that he, too, would make such a noise if he was as happy as they were. When you trust in God, you have sweet rest in danger or pain. Oh, to be in God's hand. What a place—in the hands of God!

There are myriads of stars, and there is the universe itself. The stars do not fall because God's hands uphold their everlasting pillars (1 Sam. 2:8). If we are in God's hands, we are where all things rest; we are home and we are happy. We have left the creature's nothingness and entered into the Creator's all-sufficiency. Beloved friend, get there. Hurry to get there, and from this moment live in God's hands.

HE WILL GUARD OUR FEET. *1 Samuel 2:9*

The way is slippery and our feet are feeble, but the Lord will guard our steps. If we give ourselves by obedient faith to be His holy ones, He will Himself be our guardian. Not only will He give His angels charge to keep us (Ps. 91:11), but He Himself will preserve our way.

He will guard our feet from falling, that we do not stain our garments, wound our souls, or cause the enemy to blaspheme.

He will guard our feet from wandering, that we do not go into paths of error, ways of folly, or courses of the world's customs (Ps. 32:8).

He will guard our feet from swelling due to weariness, blistering, or the roughness and length of the way (Deut. 8:4).

He will guard our feet from being cut, and our shoes will be iron and bronze (Deut. 33:25). Even if we step on swords or on deadly serpents, we will not bleed or be poisoned (Mark 16:18).

He will also pluck our feet out of the net (Ps. 25:15). We will not be entangled by the deceit of our malicious and crafty foes.

With such a promise as this, let us run without weariness and walk without fear. He who guards our feet will do it effectively.

Speak, LORD. *1 Samuel 3:9*

S peak, LORD, for Your servant hears" (1 Sam. 3:9). You may not know which of two opportunities to choose. Some friends have urged you to follow one plan and some have urged you to follow the other. If you have used your best judgment and have endeavored to direct your steps according to the Word of God, you will receive an answer. God will give you distinct guidance.

Take your difficulty to the God of wisdom and spread your situation before Him. Divest your own will and solemnly desire to know God's will. Then expect, by some means or other, for God has different ways of doing it, to have an answer from the Most High. Make this your prayer, "Speak, LORD, for Your servant hears."

In our daily lives, we need to acknowledge God fully. We need to acknowledge Him in the common transactions of daily living. If we do not, we may, like the Israelites with the Gibeonites, be betrayed in the simplest transaction and deceived to our lasting injury (2 Sam. 21:9).

Domine dirige nos, "Lord direct us," is a good motto not only for the City of London, but also for the citizens of heaven. This is my advice: Take your difficulty to God in prayer and say, "Speak, LORD, for Your servant hears." Do not ask God to confirm your opinion; ask Him to make your opinion conform to His truth.

Follow the simple Word of God as you find it. Let the Holy Spirit flow on the sacred page, and as you read you will hear the Master say, "This is My Word." He will make it come to your soul with power. You will have no doubt when your heart cries, "Speak, LORD, for Your servant hears."

THE LORD HAS HELPED US. *1 Samuel 7:12*

God is with you wherever you go. On land or by sea, day or night, you never can be alone. It is impossible to journey out of your Father's dominions (Ps. 139:8). You may dwell here or there, or you may live in a mansion or a hovel, and still you will be in your heavenly Father's great house. His house is enormous. "In My Father's house are many mansions" (John 14:2).

God will provide all necessary things. You have had some hard pinches. You have suffered the bitterness of widowhood, or you are poor and the supply you receive is scant. Still, you are alive. Your food has been given to you and your water is sure (Is. 33:16). Your clothing is worn but not worn out. Thus far the Lord has helped you (1 Sam. 7:12). Jehovah-Jireh has been your song; the Lord has provided.

Little birds in the winter morning sit on bare branches and sing. Snow covers the ground, and they cannot tell where their breakfast will come from. Still, they sing and God provides. Seldom do you see a sparrow that died of hunger; generally, the birds of heaven are fed. Jesus said, "Look at the birds of the air, for they neither sow nor reap nor gather into barns; yet your heavenly Father feeds them. Are you not of more value than they?" (Matt. 6:26).

Perhaps you would like to live in a cage and be regularly fed and have a pension. I believe that caged birds die earlier than those that are taken care of by God. So it is better to trust in the Lord than place your confidence in others. He has not, and He will not, let you want. Take His words as your assurance, "Trust in the LORD, and do good; dwell in the land, and feed on His faithfulness. Delight yourself in the LORD, and He shall give you the desires of your heart" (Ps. 37:3-4).

AFTER HIS OWN HEART. *1 Samuel 13:14*

When your faith endures many conflicts and your spirit sinks low, do not condemn yourself. It was David in haste who said, "I am cut off from before Your eyes" (Ps. 31:22). Yet there is David now in the blessed heavenly choir, for even here on earth he was a man after God's own heart (1 Sam. 13:14).

There is a reason for your season of heaviness. Great soldiers are not made without war. Skillful sailors are not trained on the shore. It appears that if you are to become a great believer, you will be greatly tested. If you are to be a great helper to others, you must pass through their trials. If you are to be instructed in the things of the kingdom, you must learn from experience. The uncut diamond has little brilliance, the unthreshed corn feeds no one, and the untried believer is of little use or beauty. There are great benefits to come from your trials and depression.

Many people have a comparatively smooth path through life, but their position is not the equal of the tested believer. The one who is much plowed and often harrowed will thank God if the result is a larger harvest to the praise and glory of God by Jesus Christ. If your face is now covered with sorrow, the time will come when you will bless God for that sorrow. The day will come when you will see great gain from your losses, your crosses, your troubles, and your afflictions:

From all your afflictions His glory shall spring,
And the deeper your sorrows the louder you'll sing.

THE BATTLE IS THE LORD'S. *1 Samuel 17:47*

I may be addressing some godly people who are terribly distressed. You believe that God will bring you out of your affliction. Maintain that faith, and if deliverance does not come for a long time, maintain it still. Can you lean on the Lord? Can you grasp the Invisible? Can you forget all other helpers? Can you hold His hand and let everything else go? If so, you glorify God and you will be delivered!

If you must have your own bow and sword, then the battle depends on you, and you cannot plead God's promises. Put the bow aside, hang the sword on the wall, and go to Him who is better than bow and sword. Rest in Him, and He will gloriously work so that His name is magnified and you are blessed.

I pray that the Holy Spirit will apply this truth to your heart. Oh for grace to rest in the Lord and wait patiently for Him! In His time and in His way He will work out your deliverance. Nothing will stop Him. Remember, "The battle is the LORD's."

THEY SHALL SHARE ALIKE. *1 Samuel 30:24*

Are you sick? Has the vigor you felt in the bright days of health failed? Are you suffering pain, weariness, or exhaustion? Are you house-bound? Are you so restricted that there is little you can do?

You wish that you could serve the Lord. You dream of that pleasure, but you are denied the privilege. Willingly would you run, readily would you work, and gladly would you testify. You devoutly wish that you could do some personal ser-vice in your Master's cause.

I want to encourage you with the reminder that the law of the Son of David is the same as the law of David himself. You know David's law about those who went to battle; some were incapable of action and David left them with the supplies. "You are weary and ill," he said to them. "Stay in camp and take care of the supplies while we go and fight."

After the battle, the men who fought claimed all the spoils, saying, "These people have done nothing but lie around the camp. They will not have a share of the spoils."

But King David immediately said, "My brethren, you shall not do so with what the LORD has given us, who has preserved us and delivered into our hand the troop that came against us. For who will heed you in this matter? But as his part is who goes down to the battle, so shall his part be who stays by the supplies; they shall share alike" (1 Sam. 30:23-24).

The law of the Son of David is equally gracious. If sickness, age, or infirmity detains you, if you are unable to enter active service, if you would fight if you could, and if your heart is in it, you will have an equal share with the best and the bravest of those who, in the armor of God, encounter and grapple with the adversary.

WAITING FOR MERCY. *2 Samuel 7 :15*

The old proverb says:

> No sweat, no sweet:
> No pains, no gains:
> No mill, no meal.

It is the same in heavenly things. God's usual rule is to make us pray before He gives the blessing and to make us fervently pray before great mercies are given. When God makes us knock at mercy's gate, it is a great blessing. When we plead with God and have not realized success, we become more earnest and more intent and our hunger increases. If we obtained the blessing when we first asked, we would not have a sense of mercy's value. Standing outside mercy's gate, we grow more passionately earnest in our pleading. First we ask, then we seek, and finally we plead with cries, tears, and a broken heart.

I never would have been able to comfort anguished seekers if I myself had not been kept waiting for mercy. I have always felt grateful for distress because of the results afterward. Many saints whose experiences are published could never have written those books if they had not waited hungry and thirsty and full of soul sorrow. The spade of agony digs deep trenches to hold the water of life.

If the ships of prayer do not speedily return, it is because they are heavily loaded with blessings. When prayer is not immediately answered, it will be all the sweeter when the answer arrives. Prayer, like fruit, is ripened by hanging longer on the tree.

If you knock with a heavy heart, you will soon sing with the joy of the Spirit. Therefore, do not be discouraged because the door is still closed.

IT IS ENOUGH! *1 Kings 19:4*

It is difficult for a young person to understand why Elijah could be so dreadfully depressed as to pray, "It is enough! Now, LORD, take my life" (1 Kin. 19:4). As we grow older and more experienced, our trials multiply and our inner life enters difficult conflicts. Because we are in similar places, we better understand why God allowed His ancient servants to be put in these situations. There is relief in discovering that we are walking paths that others have traveled.

We understand Elijah's attitude on Mount Carmel when he said, "I alone am left" (1 Kin. 18:22), and we comprehend why he executed the prophets of Baal (1 Kin. 18:40). If we are puzzled as to why he got under a juniper bush (1 Kin. 19:4) or hid in a cave (1 Kin. 19:13), we understand the reasons when we ourselves get under the juniper and remember that Elijah once sat there. When we hide in a cave, it is a comfort to remember that this great prophet also did.

Perhaps you have prayed Elijah's prayer. One saint's experience is instructive to others. Many of the psalms—called Maschil, or instructive psalms—record the writer's experiences and become our textbooks.

If the Holy Spirit will guide me, I may be able to say something to help. You do not know how much there is to live for. Nevertheless, God has such blessings in store that your mouth will be filled with laughter and your tongue with singing. The Lord has done great things for you, and you will be glad (Ps. 126:2-3). Be of good courage. Strengthen your heart and wait on the Lord until He comes. May His blessing be with you forever!

A STILL SMALL VOICE. *1 Kings 19:12*

In our religious services, we too often rely on carnal force and energy. We hope that if we make enough noise, create enough excitement, and stir and agitate, we will be identified with the power of God.

How does God touch our hearts? Our heavenly Father generally uses a soft, tender, gentle, quiet, calm, and peaceful—still, small—voice. Softly and gently, the Holy Spirit works like the breath of spring dissolving icebergs and melting glaciers. After winter has taken every stream by the throat and held it fast, spring sets it free. No hammer or file is heard as the icy bonds fall off; only the soft south wind blows, and all is life and liberty.

So it is with the work of the Holy Spirit when He comes into the soul. He can be a mighty rushing wind (Acts 2:2), for He comes according to His own sovereign pleasure. Yet when He brings the peace of God, He usually descends as the dove (Matt. 3:16) or as the dew from heaven—all peace, all gentle, and all quiet.

Satan can set the soul on fire with agony, doubt, fear, and terror. Then the Spirit comes in tender love and reveals Christ the Gentle One. He sets up the Savior's cross and speaks peace, pardon, and salvation. This is what we want and need: the work of the Spirit of God coming in His own manner of living love.

HE MADE THE IRON FLOAT.   *2 Kings 6:6*

The borrowed axe head was hopelessly lost underwater. The honor of the prophetic band was threatened because the name of their God would be compromised. Against all expectations, the iron rose from the stream's bed and floated. "The things which are impossible with men are possible with God" (Luke 18:27).

A few years ago a Christian I knew was called to a project that far exceeded his ability. It was so difficult that the very idea of attempting it bordered on the absurd. Yet he was called, and his faith rose to the occasion. God honored that faith, and unexpected aid was sent: the iron floated.

Another member of the Lord's family was in a disastrous financial situation. He would be able to meet all of his obligations and much more if he could sell part of his estate. When it did not sell, he was placed under great pressure. In vain he sought the help of friends, but then faith led him to the unfailing Helper and the trouble was averted. "God enlarged his path under him, so his feet did not slip" (2 Sam. 22:37). The iron floated.

A third individual had to deal with a friend who was terribly depraved. He taught, warned, invited, and interceded. But the stubborn spirit would not relent. Then came an agony of prayer and soon a blessed answer from heaven. The hard heart was broken. The iron floated.

Beloved, what is your desperate problem? What heavy trial hangs over you? Bring it to the mercy seat. The God of the prophets lives. He lives to help His saints, "that you may lack nothing" (1 Thess. 4:12). Believe in the Lord of hosts! Approach Him. Plead the name of Jesus. The iron will float.

You will see the finger of God working miracles for His people. "According to your faith let it be to you" (Matt. 9:29). And, once again, the iron will float.

CHARIOTS OF FIRE. *2 Kings 6:17*

Jesus speaks of the angels that His Father would send. "Do you think that I cannot now pray to My Father and He will provide Me with more than twelve legions of angels?" (Matt. 26:53). Think of the seraphs at the disposal of the Man of Sorrows. They are swift of wing, quick of hand, and wise of thought. They are the Son of Man's messengers, Jesus' servants.

Jesus speaks of "twelve legions"—I suppose one for each of the eleven disciples and himself. A legion in the Roman army was a minimum of six thousand soldiers; twelve times six thousand would come in answer to a wish from Jesus. No, that is not correct, for He says, "More than twelve." There is no limit to the available resources of the Christ of God. Thousands of thousands would fill the air if Jesus willed it. Remember this, even in His humiliation Jesus was Lord of all things, including the unseen world and its armies. The more clearly you perceive this, the more you will admire the all-conquering love that took Him to death on the cross.

Pause here. Remember the angels are also at your call. You have only to pray, and "He shall give His angels charge over you, to keep you in all your ways. In their hands they shall bear you up, lest you dash your foot against a stone" (Ps. 91:11-12). We do not think enough of these heavenly beings, yet they are sent to minister to the heirs of salvation. Like Elijah's servant, if your eyes were opened you would see the mountain full of horses and the chariots of fire all around the servants of God (2 Kin. 6:17). Let us learn from our Master to reckon on forces invisible.

Do not trust what is seen and heard. Respect the spiritual agencies that escape the senses and are only known to faith. Angels play a far greater part in matters of providence than we think. God can raise up friends for us on earth, and if He does not, He can find us abler friends in heaven.

SEEK MY FACE. *2 Chronicles 7:14*

There are nests among the stars where God's saints dwell, yet many are content to creep like worms in the dust. Oh for grace to break through the clouds and enter the pure blue sky of Christ's fellowship! We, however, are cold as ice when we should be like molten metal burning our way through all opposition. We are like the barren Sahara when we should be blooming like the Lord's garden. He has said, "Pray and seek My face." Yet our hearts refuse to say, "Lord, Your face I will seek." When we do not listen to His gentle call, trials come to make us obey.

Sickness is one such trial. Many Christians drag about in a diseased body or are suddenly thrown on a sick bed to toss night and day in pain and weariness. This is God's medicine, and when it arrives remember that it was not sent to kill but to heal. As a file removes rust, sickness frequently removes our heart's deadness. The diamond has to be cut, but that cutting increases its value, and so it is with the believer.

My friend, if you will not come to God, He will send you to a sick bed that will carry you to Him. If you will not come running, He will make you come limping. If you will not come while you are healthy, He will make you come when you are sick. But you will come and, if by no other means, sickness will be the black chariot in which you finally ride.

THE EYES OF THE LORD. *2 Chronicles 16:9*

I testify that in some of my many sicknesses I have been able to see the reason as plainly as I can see that two times two equals four. Even when we cannot see the reason, God knows why.

Your sickness, pain, grief, depression, and all sorts of trials are often sent to prevent sinning. It ties you fast, like a horse with a heavy weight on its leg. Someone asked the horse's owner, "Why do you put a weight on such a fine horse. It seems a pity."

"Well," replied the owner, "I would rather weight him down than lose him. He jumps fences, and this is the only way we can keep him in the pasture." So, my friend, you might be weighed down because the Lord does not want to lose you. He would sooner have you suffer here than permit you to suffer forever in hell.

A Quaker felt an irresistible impulse to get out of bed and ride to a neighboring town. He stopped at a house where he saw a light upstairs. He knocked and knocked and knocked again. Finally a man came to the door and asked what he wanted at that time of night. The Quaker replied, "Perhaps, friend, thou canst tell me, for the Lord has sent me to thee. But I do not know why."

"Come upstairs," said the man. "I think I can tell you." He had fixed a rope to hang himself, but God had sent His servant to prevent the crime.

Such striking providence may not happen to us, but it does happen to some to prevent sinning. "The eyes of the LORD run to and fro throughout the whole earth, to show Himself strong on behalf of those whose heart is loyal to Him" (2 Chr. 16:9).

THE BATTLE IS GOD'S. *2 Chronicles 20:15*

Receive a fresh assurance of God's goodness, "Do not be afraid nor dismayed because of this great multitude, for the battle is not yours, but God's" (2 Chr. 20:15). May the Holy Spirit bear witness to this sweet promise. May He strengthen and comfort you, and may you be delivered even before deliverance comes.

The main business is to be saved from the fear of trouble. If you are quiet, calm, and assured, you are really saved from the trial's sting. The trial is nothing if it does not sting your soul. If your heart is not troubled, then there is no trouble. All the poverty and all the pain in the world would not prevail if the evil of it did not enter your soul.

In the twentieth chapter of 2 Chronicles, Judah received actual deliverance. When they came to face their foes, there were none, for they were all dead (2 Chr. 20:24). In the same manner, God will deliver you. In answer to prayer, He will be your defense; therefore praise His name.

He delivered you when you went out to meet the great army of your sins. You saw that Christ had put them away and your heart danced. You could say, "There is therefore now no condemnation to those who are in Christ Jesus, who do not walk according to the flesh, but according to the Spirit" (Rom. 8:1). He has slain our sins and they can curse us no more.

This is the case with a great many troubles that have appeared to overwhelm you. When you come to them, they disappear. They have been removed as you have advanced. Now you have nothing to do but praise the name of the Lord.

SUPPORT FROM ON HIGH. *Ezra 4:14*

Here is a gracious fact: "We receive support from the palace" (Ezra 4:14). Both the upper and the lower springs from which we drink are fed by the great King's eternal goodness. In every moment we have been supplied with food and clothing.

Sometimes we have been reduced to a pinch. Then through our infirmity, fermented with the irritability of our unbelief, we ask, "What shall we eat? What shall we drink? What shall we wear?" (Matt. 6:31). Still we have lived in the land and we have been fed. It has been especially gratifying to receive a loaf of bread from our Father's hand. You have known poverty, but there has been a special sweetness in the daily bread that has been sent in answer to prayer. Although we do not drink water from the rock (Ex. 17:6) or find daily manna (Ex. 16:4), God's providence still produces the same results, and we are fed and satisfied.

Looking back, many of us can say, "My cup runs over. Surely goodness and mercy shall follow me all the days of my life" (Ps. 23:5-6). Thus, even in daily living we believe that we have been supported from the King's palace.

It is in spiritual things that our continued experience of the King's goodness is most noticed. Our strength has been renewed like the eagle's (Is. 40:31). We have had huge wants and bottomless depths of need. Yet, great God, the treasures of Your grace have been everlasting mines, as deep as our helpless miseries and as boundless as our sins.

In looking back on the way the Lord our God has led, we can sing of the beginning, and we can sing of the middle, and we believe we shall sing of the end. Through it all we have been supplied from the King's palace in both earthly and spiritual things.

THE JOY OF THE LORD. *Nehemiah 8:10*

There is a bottomless well of delight for every Christian who fellowships with God. When we enter God's love, it enters us. When we habitually walk with God, our joy is like the Jordan at harvest; our banks overflow.

Do you know what it means to walk with God—Enoch's joy (Gen. 5:22)? Do you know what it means to sit at Jesus' feet—Mary's joy (Luke 10:39)? Do you know what it means to lean your head on Jesus' bosom—John's familiar joy (John 13:23)? Fellowship with the Lord is not mere talk. We have known this fellowship in affliction. We have known this fellowship in the solitude of many nights of broken rest. We have known this fellowship beneath discouragement, under sorrow, and in all sorts of ills. We reckon that one drop of Christ's fellowship is enough to sweeten an ocean of trials. Just to know that He is near, to enjoy His presence and to see His gleaming eye, 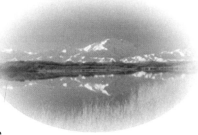 would transform even hell into heaven.

The animals in the meadow do not know the far-reaching thoughts of Him who counts the number of the stars and calls them all by name (Ps. 147:4). The unsaved cannot even guess at the things God has prepared for those who love Him (1 Cor. 2:9). God reveals this to believers by His Holy Spirit.

Fellowship with the Father and with His Son Jesus Christ is the joy of the Lord. The habit of fellowship is the life of happiness.

YOU PRESERVE THEM ALL. *Nehemiah 9:6*

Nothing is impossible with the Lord. Learn something of His power. All the power in the universe came from God. It still comes from Him, and at His command this world would immediately cease. Whatever force there is in inanimate nature, it is God at work. He sets the wheel of nature in motion, and at His command it would cease. Whatever mental faculty there is in cherub, seraph, angel, or humanity, it flows from His creative energy.

If Jehovah wills, the enormous planets that revolve around the sun would rush in wild confusion to inevitable destruction. The law of gravity, which holds all things in place, would be instantly broken if He withdrew the force that makes the law a power. If Jehovah withdrew there would be no coherence among the atoms; they would dissolve into non-existence and leave the universe void.

This is power so great that we cry with Nehemiah, "You alone are the LORD; You have made heaven, the heaven of heavens, with all their host, the earth and everything on it, the seas and all that is in them, and You preserve them all. The host of heaven worships You" (Neh. 9:6).

Our great God can do all things without help. He needs no assistance! Indeed, there could be no such aid, since all power is from Him alone. Creatures do not contribute to His strength. Creatures only testify of Him, revealing the power that they borrowed from Him. To achieve any purpose He asks none to be His ally, for He does as He wills.

THE BANQUET. *Esther 5:4*

The Lord's right arm is uplifted to preserve the saints. His wisdom watches for their good, and His heart of love beats with constant affection. The entire Godhead bows to protect the chosen. We have the promise, "He shall deliver you from the snare of the fowler and from the perilous pestilence. He shall cover you with His feathers, and under His wings you shall take refuge" (Ps. 91:3-4).

Our God is both the sustenance and the preservation of His people. Is there a wind that does not bring us blessings? Is there a wave on any shore that does not bring us good? The huge wheels of providence as they revolve are full of eyes (Ezek. 1:18) that look toward God's chosen.

"All things work together for good to those who love God, to those who are the called according to His purpose" (Rom. 8:28). Do you see it? If your eyes are opened you will. "There are horses and chariots of fire all around" (2 Kin. 6:17). Invisible spirits of superior race are servants to God's beloved children. Heaven's hosts are ready for our defense. We need not fear. Our needs are large, but the supplies are greater. Our daily dangers are enough to provoke anxieties, but the Lord's eternal preservation puts those anxieties to rest.

Blessed Lord, we are poor feeble infants, but when we lie on Your bosom we feel mighty in Your strength. We are penniless beggars, but when we feast at Your table we would not change our position for the banquets of Esther or the feasts of Solomon (1 Kin. 10:5). It is our bliss to be nothing and to find our all in You. Amen.

THE LORD GAVE. *Job 1:21*

The trial of our faith usually comes in the form of affliction. Our jealous Lover uses tests to see if He has our heart.

You say, "Lord Jesus, I love You. You are my best beloved."

"Well," says the heavenly Lover, "if it is so, then your precious child will become sick and die. What will you say then?" If you are truthful in what you have said concerning your supreme love for Jesus, you will give up your darling at His call and say, "The LORD gave, and the LORD has taken away; blessed be the name of the LORD."

The more He loves you, the more He will test you. I remember Samuel Rutherford writing to a lady who had lost five children and her husband, "Oh, how Christ must love you! He would take every bit of your heart to Himself. He would not allow you to reserve any of your soul for any earthly thing." Can we stand the test? Can we let everything go for His sake?

My Lord sometimes comes to me in this fashion. He says, "I have made you to trust Me these many years. I have supplied the needs of your works by liberal friends. But I am about to remove a generous helper." When I go to the grave of this friend, the suggestion dogs me, "Who is to provide for the orphanage and the college after other dear friends are buried? Can you trust God then?" Blessed be the name of the Lord, this fiery trial has never even left the smell of smoke on me.

If every earthly prop were knocked away, could you stand by the lone power of your foundation? God may not send you this trial, but He will send you a sufficient amount of trials to let you see if your faith is truth or talk.

THE LORD HAS TAKEN AWAY. *Job 1:21*

Some of us have suffered great physical pain that bites into our spirits and causes depression. Others have suffered heavy financial losses and been deprived even to the point of extreme hardship.

Are you complaining against the Lord for this? I pray not! The Lord has been pruning you, cutting off your best branches; you seem to be continually tormented with the knife. Just suppose that your loving Lord has caused this; suppose that from His own hand all your grief has come, every cut and every gash. If this is true, put your finger to your lips and be quiet until from your heart you are able to say, "The LORD gave, and the LORD has taken away; blessed be the name of the LORD" (Job 1:21).

Recently I sat in the garden with my friend and secretary. We were in perfect health, rejoicing in the Lord's goodness. We were happy as we sat there reading the Word of God and meditating. Dare we think of being so happy? Within five days I was stricken with disabling pain, and worse, far worse, he was called upon to lose his wife. Here is our comfort: the Lord has done it. The best rose in the garden is gone. Who has taken it? The Gardener. He planted it and watched over it, and now He has taken it. Does anyone weep because of that? No! Everyone knows it is best that He should come and gather the garden's finest.

Are you deeply troubled by the loss of your loved one? Remember, the next time the Lord comes to your part of the garden, He will only gather His flowers. Would you prevent Him from doing this, even if you could?

ACCEPTING ADVERSITY. *Job 2:10*

Our memory of God's goodness is often crushed by pain. When you suffer sharp pain, or weary aches, or a high fever, you tend to forget the days of health and strength. You only remember the sharp intervals of weakness and sorrow.

When you stand over the grave of a loved one, you are likely in the loss to forget the loan. When a dear one is taken, a precious loan has been called by its Owner. We ought to be grateful to have been allowed to borrow the comfort. We should not complain when the Owner takes what He kindly lent—the husband or wife of all these years, the child who nestled in your embrace, the friend that you enjoyed for half a lifetime, the brother who was such a comfort all his days. When these loved ones are gone, do not look at their going, but thank God that you had them. Bless a taking and a giving God, who only takes what He gave. We live too much in the present. We strike a mark of oblivion across the happy past, and we look with dread on the unknown future. We dwell on the trouble of the present and forget the Lord's mercy.

You are growing old and feeble, and you cannot do what you once did. But bless the Lord for your years of vigor. Your mind is weak, but bless God that there was a time when you could serve Him without fatigue.

Perhaps your funds are low and you are afraid of poverty. Be grateful that you have had enough and to spare for many long years. Perhaps you are now sad. Recall the days when you praised the Lord on the high-sounding cymbals and stood on the high places of earth. Do not let memory fail because of the present crushing sorrow. May the Holy Spirit help your infirmities and bring His lovingkindness from past years to your memory.

IN SIX TROUBLES. *Job 5:19*

Remember what God has done for you and then say, "Jesus Christ is the same yesterday, today, and forever" (Heb. 13:8). When you are praying, if you cannot see that He is comfortable towards you today, recall that He was yesterday. If there is no present manifestations of divine favor, remember the past. He has been gracious. Can you tell how gracious? He has abounded towards you in lovingkindness, tenderness, and faithfulness. He has never been a wilderness or a land of drought to you. Well then, if in six troubles He has delivered you, will you not trust Him for seven? (Job 5:19). If you get to sixty troubles, will you not trust Him for sixty-one?

We say that we ought always to trust someone until they deceive us. We reckon someone honest until we find otherwise. Let it be so with God. Since we have found Him good, faithful, true, kind, and tender, let us not think badly of Him now that we have come into difficult straits. Come to Him and say, "Are You our God? Did You not bring us 'up out of the horrible pit, out of the miry clay' (Ps. 40:2)? Surely, then, You will not leave us now."

The wonders God can do! He loves us to state our difficulty, that when He gets us out we will well remember the condition we were in.

After pleading the promise and confessing our condition, we may say, "Lord, if help does come, it must come from You. It cannot come from anywhere else, so we look to You. We believe help will come. Though we do not know how it will come, we are looking to You. Though we do not know when, we are looking to You. Though we do not know what You would have us to do, still we are looking to You. Our eyes may be full of tears, but they are on You."

Yet will I trust Him. *Job 13:15*

A child of God is not expected to be a stoic, for God's grace takes away the heart of stone. When we endure trials, we feel the pain. Do not ask to be made hard and callous, for this is not how grace works. Grace makes us strong to bear trials, but we still have to bear them. Grace gives us patience and submission, not stoicism. We feel, and we benefit by the feeling. There are some who will not cry when God chastens, and there are some who will not yield when God strikes. Do not be like them! Be content to have Job's suffering heart (Job 1:21). Feel the bitter spirit and the anguish of soul which racked that blessed patriarch.

My dear friend, when grief presses you to the dust, worship there! Remember David's words, "Pour out your heart." But do not stop there; finish the quotation. "Pour out your heart before Him." Turn your heart upside down, empty it, and let every drop run out. "Pour out your heart before Him; God is a refuge for us" (Ps. 62:8).

When you are bowed down beneath a heavy burden of sorrow, worship and adore God there. In full surrender to His divine will, say with Job, "Though He slay me, yet will I trust Him" (Job 13:15). This kind of worship subdues the will, arouses the affections, stirs the whole mind, and presents you to God in solemn consecration. This worship sweetens sorrow and takes away its sting.

I SHALL SEE GOD. *Job 19:26*

The promises elevate life, but they greatly cheer and gild with glory the deathbed. Ah, how delightful it is to die with a promise on the lips, feeling it in the heart. It may be a lonely cottage—the stars may come out and look through the tiles, the bed's covering may be ragged, and all the surroundings poverty-stricken. But the one who lies there can say, "I know that my Redeemer lives, and He shall stand at last on the earth; and after my skin is destroyed, this I know, that in my flesh I shall see God" (Job 19:25-26).

Those that can rejoice in the promise of the resurrection and of the life to come die grandly. Their bed is changed into a throne. Their little room, despite its poverty, becomes a palace chamber. The child of God, who seemed so poor before, is now perceived to be a peer of heaven's royalty, soon to take possession of the heritage appointed from before the foundation of the world.

Yes, the promises have been precious to us in their influence on our minds. I am sure I can say they are precious because of their priceless value to our souls. There are passages of Scripture that are carved on our hearts. All of you possess some little secret treasures that bring heart-moving memories. I have seen a mother go to a secret drawer to look at a little pair of woolen shoes and sit down and weep for hours. The little feet that wore those shoes are now laid motionless in a lap of earth. I have seen a friend look at a ring, a little plain gold ring that he wears on his finger, and as he looked at it he wept. There was once a dear hand on which that ring was fondly placed in happier days.

In just that way, some of the promises of God have been so rich and so connected with family memories, with personal trials and personal mercies, that they are unutterably precious.

My Eyes Shall Behold. *Job 19:27*

Happy are the prosperous who can hear God's voice in the tinkling of the sheep bells from an abundant flock, who can hear Him in the lowing of cattle that cover their fields and in the loving voices of their precious children.

A word of caution! Prosperity is a painted window that shuts out much of God's clear light. Only when the blue, crimson, and gold tinge is removed will the glass be restored to transparency.

Adversity takes away the tinge, the color, and the dimness, and then we see our God. In the absence of other goods, the good God is better seen.

In prosperity, God is heard, and that is a blessing. In adversity, God is seen, and that is a greater blessing. Sanctified adversity quickens spiritual sensitivity. Sorrow after sorrow will wake the spirit and infuse a delicacy of perception that perhaps will not come in any other way. I purposely said perhaps, for I believe that some choice saints are favored to reach God by smoother ways. But I think they are few. Most of us are so coarse that we need melting to attain that sacred softness by which the Lord God is joyfully perceived.

Child of God, if you are suffering as much as Job, and if your suffering permits you to see the Lord with a spiritually enlightened eye, be thankful for the sorrowful process. Who would not go to Patmos if one might see John's visions (Rev. 21)? Who would not sit with Job in the ashes to cry, "In my flesh I shall see God, whom I shall see for myself, and my eyes shall behold" (Job 19:26-27)?

THE MERE EDGES OF HIS WAYS. *Job 26:14*

Your troubles and sorrows are sent according to the Lord's thoughtful purpose. It is in His fixed intent and thoughtfulness that the real character of an action lies. A person might do you a good turn, but if it were accidental, you would not be overwhelmed with gratitude. When a friend's kind action is the result of deliberation, you are far more thankful.

Remember, there is never a thoughtless action on God's part. His mind goes with His hand. His heart is in His action. He thinks so much of His people that "the very hairs of your head are all numbered" (Luke 12:7). He thinks not only of the great things, but also of the little things that are incidental to the great things, such as the number of hairs on your head.

Every affliction is timed and measured. Every comfort is sent with a loving thoughtfulness that makes it precious. The Divine Mind exercises great thoughtfulness toward the Lord's chosen. Nothing happens as the result of a remorseless fate. All your circumstances are ordered in wisdom by a living, thoughtful, and loving God.

Our heavenly Father knows what He is doing. Even when His way appears to be involved and complicated and we cannot untangle the threads, the Lord sees all things clearly. His breadth exceeds the range of our vision; His depth baffles our profoundest thought. "Your way was in the sea, Your path in the great waters, and Your footsteps were not known" (Ps. 77:19).

When we are overwhelmed with wonder, we are humbled by the reminder, "Indeed these are the mere edges of His ways, and how small a whisper we hear of Him!" (Job 26:14).

BOUND IN FETTERS. *Job 36:8*

Dear friend, doubts and fears are more common in work and business than in sickness. I do not know how you have found it, but "when I am weak, then I am strong" (2 Cor. 12:10). Before trouble comes, many believers are silent and their heart toward the Lord is heavy, but when providence clips their wings or puts them in a cage, they sing sweetly. Then their faith revives, their hope returns, their love glows, and they sing God's praises in the fire.

Dear friend, have you found that trouble cuts the cords that tie you to earth? When the Lord takes a child, there is one less cord to fasten you to this world and another band to draw you toward heaven. When money vanishes and business goes wrong, we frequent the prayer meeting, the prayer closet, and the Bible. Trials drive us from earth. If all went well, we would begin to say, "Soul, relax." But when things go amiss, we want to be gone. When the tree shakes, the bird flies away. Happy is the trouble that loosens our grip of earth.

After a few days of sharp pain on a sick bed, you will not love life so much. You will begin to say, "Let me be gone." Now you can understand why David said, "My heart and my flesh cry out for the living God" (Ps. 84:2). Making our flesh cry out after God is difficult. But if you turn the screw a little further and stretch it on the rack a little more, then the dumb earthborn flesh will cry to be gone and leave the pain and sickness behind.

53

THE CORDS OF AFFLICTION. *Job 36:8*

When you are in trouble, do not expect to perceive any immediate benefit. In hard pain, I have tried to see if I have grown a bit more resigned, or more earnest in prayer, or more absorbed in fellowship with God. But I confess that I have never been able to see the slightest improvement, because the pain distracts and scatters my thoughts.

Severe trouble in a true believer has the effect of loosening the soul's roots earthward and tightening the heart's anchor-hold heavenward. How can we love a world that has become so dismal? Why should we seek grapes that are bitter? Should we not ask for the wings of a dove to fly to our dear country and be at rest forever?

Afflictions clip our wings with regard to earthly things, and we cannot fly from our dear Master's hand. Yet the same affliction makes our wings grow with regard to heavenly things. We are feathered like eagles. A thorn is in our nest, and we catch the soaring spirit. We spread our wings toward the sun.

Affliction frequently opens truths to us and opens us to the truth. Experience unlocks truths that were closed. Many passages of Scripture will never be made clear by the commentator, for these must be expounded by experience. Many a verse is written in a secret ink that must be held to the fire of adversity to make it visible. Affliction plows and opens our hearts, so that into our innermost nature the truth penetrates and soaks like rain into the plowed land.

Affliction, when sanctified by the Holy Spirit, brings much glory to God through the believer's experience with the Lord's faithfulness.

TWICE AS MUCH. *Job 42:10*

Many people imagine that God has a great deal to do with their prayer closet but nothing to do with their pantry. If this were so, life would be dreadful. We should see as much of the Lord's hand on the kitchen table as on the communion table. The same love that spreads the table when we commemorate our Savior's dying love also spreads the table to provide our daily bread. Learn to see God in everything. Learn to praise Him for all that you have.

It may be that you have suffered a financial loss. Dear friend, the Lord can restore your loss. When Job lost everything, God readily restored his losses (Job 42:10). "Yes," you say, "but that was a remarkable case." Still we have a remarkable God, and He still works wonders.

Consider the matter, for it was remarkable. Job lost all his property. It was equally remarkable that he got it all back. Surely, if God can scatter, He can gather. If God could scatter Job's large holdings, He could, with equal ease, restore it.

We see God's destructive power. We do not, however, always see His building power. Yet it is more consistent with God's nature to give and not to take. It is more like Him to caress rather than to chastise.

I think that it was a strange work with God to take all of Job's property and bring him to deep distress. When the Lord again enriched His servant Job, however, He was doing what He delights to do. God's happiness is most clearly seen when He is distributing the bounty of His love.

Can you look at you own circumstances in this light? It is more likely that God will bless and restore rather than chasten. He can restore your wealth, your health, and even more.

MARVELOUS LOVINGKINDNESS. *Psalm 17:7*

What deep depression some of us have had! We have gone to the bottom of the mountains, and the bars of the earth seemed to hold us there. We feel as John Fawcett's hymn puts it:

> My soul, with various tempests tossed,
> Her hopes overturned, her projects crossed,
> Sees every day new straits attend,
> And wonders where the scene will end.

But after just one glimpse of God's everlasting love, we are near God's right hand.

Pray for this experience: "Show Your marvelous lovingkindness" (Ps. 17:7). He will do it! He will bring you up, out, and through—not necessarily in the way you would like to come, but in the best way.

"Commit your way to the LORD, trust also in Him, and He shall bring it to pass" (Ps. 37:5). Always expect the unexpected when you are dealing with God. Look to see in God and from God what you never saw before. When you are dealing with Him who is omnipotent, faithful, and true, the things that seem utterly impossible will be those most likely to happen.

God grant you grace, dear friend, to use this meditation and these verses as the means of deliverance from deep trouble.

YOU GAVE IT TO HIM. *Psalm 21:4*

God will give us much more than we ask. Abraham asked God that Ishmael might live before him. He thought, "Surely this is the promised heir. I cannot expect Sarah to have a child in her old age. God has promised me an heir. It must be Hagar's child." So he said, "Oh, that Ishmael might live before You!" (Gen. 17:18). God granted Abraham that request, but He still gave him Isaac and all the blessings of the covenant.

There is Jacob. He kneels to pray and asks the Lord to give him bread and clothing (Gen. 28:20). What did God give him? When he returned to Bethel he had thousands of sheep and camels and much wealth (Gen. 32:3). God had heard, and He did exceedingly abundantly above what he asked (Eph. 3:20).

It is said of David, "He asked life from You, and You gave it to him—length of days forever and ever" (Ps. 21:4). Yes, God gave not only length of days, but also a throne for his sons throughout all generations. David sat before the Lord, overpowered with the Lord's goodness.

"Well," you ask, "is that true of New Testament prayers?" Yes, it is. They brought a paralytic to Jesus and asked Him to heal him. He said, "Son, be of good cheer, your sins are forgiven you" (Matt. 9:2). He had not asked for that, had he? No, but God gives greater things than we ask.

Hear that poor dying thief's humble prayer, "'Lord, remember me when You come into Your kingdom.' And Jesus said to him, 'Assuredly, I say to you, today you will be with Me in Paradise'" (Luke 23:42-43). He had not dreamed of such an honor.

Once you ask, you will have what you never asked for and never thought to receive.

HE TRUSTED IN THE LORD. *Psalm 22:8*

Faith teaches us to look for the end of every trial and to know that this trial works together for good if we love God, if we are the called according to His purpose (Rom. 8:28). Faith teaches us to depend on God's power during trials. Thus, we no longer stumble but rise above our afflictions.

Believer, if you are anxious, careworn, and worried, it cannot do you any good. It reflects no honor on your great Father. Pray for faith to transfer your back-breaking load to the great Burden bearer. If your burden is lightened, your strength is multiplied. If you are content with the divine will, it is better than increased riches, because wealth does not bring peace, and prosperity gives no joy in the Lord.

Whatever burden faith finds, it casts it on God in prayer. We begin with God in the morning, seeking His help to do our work well. At His hands, we seek guidance and prosperity from hour to hour. We pray to prevent doing wrong to others or suffering wrong from them. We ask Him to keep our temper and to preserve our spirit while we are in the world.

Believers, go to God with the matters of each day. Look for the morning dew to fall and for God to be your constant shield. At night before you rest, empty the day's gathered troubles and fall into a happy sleep. Thus, we sweetly live, trusting our Lord with everything and finding Him always near.

In all this, our Savior's example leads us, and His love within our hearts draws us. "He trusted in the LORD, let Him rescue Him; let Him deliver Him, since He delights in Him" (Ps. 22:8).

GOD'S ATTENTIVENESS. *Psalm 22:24*

God is so great and mighty that all things are little to Him. There are worlds so enormous that human reckoning cannot estimate their size; the stars are so numerous that we have to leave them uncounted. Yet all these must be as a drop in a bucket to Him. Since all things are little to Him, it follows that nothing is more than little to God.

If divine observation and care is extended to creatures, then it must be given to the insignificant and the weak. Why? When compared with Him everything is insignificant and weak.

If you want proof that the Lord considers the lesser things, look at creation. The great and mighty God displays His greatness as much in tiny objects as in magnificent worlds that He has fashioned. Myriads of creatures play in a single drop of water, and in each drop omnipotence is readily seen. For each of these creatures, so small that they can only be observed by a microscope, God finds food and puts life-force in every part of their organization. God sees to everything that concerns a gnat or a fly as surely as He watches over seraphim and cherubim. He guards the earth's worms and the brook's minnows.

Since He does this, He will deal tenderly with you, for He will despise none that seek Him. He who takes care of gnats and flies will hear your prayer. "He has not despised nor abhorred the affliction of the afflicted; nor has He hidden His face from Him" (Ps. 22:24).

Some of you have been in deep waters through pain, poverty, and bereavement. Loved ones and friends have forsaken you—but not God. He will hear the prayer of the humble heart. God will not forsake you. He is very near in your distress.

MY SHEPHERD. *Psalm 23:1*

Give me ten million dollars, and one reversal of fortune may scatter it. Give me a spiritual hold on the divine assurance that "the LORD is my Shepherd; I shall not want" (Ps. 23:1), and I am set for life. I cannot go broke with this stock in my hand. I can never be bankrupt with this security.

Do not give me ready cash; give me a checkbook and let me withdraw what I need. This is how God works with the believer. God does not immediately transfer the inheritance; He lets us draw what we need out of the riches of His fullness in Christ Jesus. "The LORD is my Shepherd; I shall not want." What a glorious inheritance! Walk up and down it. Rest on it. It will be a soft downy pillow for you to lie on.

Climb the creaking staircase of your house, lie down on your hard mattress, wrap yourself in a blanket, and look out for the winter of hard times. But do not say, "What shall I do?" Just hum, "The LORD is my Shepherd; I shall not want." This will be the hush of a lullaby to your soul, and you will soon slumber peacefully.

Business people, go to your office and review your wearisome books. You say, "How about my business? These prices will ruin me. What can I do?" Analyze your accounts and enter this against your fears: "The LORD is my Shepherd; I shall not want." Write that in your checkbook. It is better than pounds and pence, than gold and silver. Now see what your new balance is.

If you disregard this truth—"The LORD is my shepherd; I shall not want"—you know nothing about its preciousness. If you grasp it, you will find this promise is like Chianti wine, which the ancients said flavored the lips of those that tasted it.

I SHALL NOT WANT. *Psalm 23:1*

Do you want more faith, more love, more holiness, and more fellowship with your Savior? Beloved, the Lord is your Shepherd (Ps. 23:1). He will give you these blessings if you just ask. But He often answers in an unexpected manner. Many of God's answers come in black-edged envelopes. Yet, remember this, they will come.

If you want peace, joy, and sanctification, they will be given because God has promised them. The Lord is your Shepherd, and you shall not want.

I often think of that great promise—I do not know where there is a larger one—that "no good thing will He withhold from those that walk uprightly" (Ps. 84:11). "No good thing!" It is a mercy that the word good is there. If it had said, "He will withhold nothing," we might ask for many things that would be bad for us. But it says, "No good thing!"

Spiritual mercies are good. They are more than good. They are the best, and you may well ask for them. If no good thing will be withheld, certainly the best things will be given.

Ask then, Christian, for He is your Shepherd, and you will not want. He will supply your need. He will give you whatever you require. Ask in faith, never doubting, and He will give you what you really need.

HE LEADS ME. *Psalm 23:3*

We wish for many things that we do not really need, and there is no promise that we will have all we wish for. God has not promised anything more than what we need. But He will give us that.

Lift up your head. Do not be afraid. God is with you. He will turn darkness into light and bitter into sweet. All the way, He has led you. And all the way, He will lead you. Let this be your constant joy.

He is your Shepherd. You will not lack what is absolutely necessary. Whatever you really require, you will be given it by your tender Father's lavish hand. Believer, this is your estate, your inheritance, your annual income, your yearly living: He is your Shepherd, and you shall not want (Ps. 23:1).

What is your income? "It varies," you say. Oh, but your spiritual income is always the same, for the Lord is your Shepherd, and you shall not want. It is my income, and it is your income. It is the income of the poorest pauper who has an interest in God's grace. It is the income of the believing orphan who has no other friend. It is the orphan's fortune, for the Lord is his Shepherd, and he shall not want. It is the widow's inheritance, for the Lord is her Shepherd, and she shall not want. It is the believer's share, the believer's portion, and the believer's blessing.

The Lord is our Shepherd. We shall not want.

THROUGH THE VALLEY. *Psalm 23:4*

Yea, though I walk through the valley of the shadow of death, I will fear no evil; for You are with me; Your rod and Your staff, they comfort me" (Ps. 23:4). I intended to keep this choice promise in reserve until I came near the river Jordan. Then in my last hour, I hoped to enjoy its sweetness. But the other day I needed this heavenly loaf, and I ate it.

Children are told that they cannot have their cake and eat it too, but this rule does not apply to God's comforts. You can have a promise and enjoy it, too. Several days ago, when a trial howled around me, I ate the honey out of this verse. Its sweetness is still there, and no doubt I will enjoy this promise again when I come near death's gate. The blessed Holy Spirit has already sealed it to my soul with rich and full comfort. Would to God that every believer who is burdened and depressed might find it precious.

Although this promise has an inexpressibly delightful application to the dying, it is also for the living. If you are depressed by any difficult trial, then you are walking through the valley of death-shade; I urge you to repeat this promise, and may the Lord help you to feel its truth. "Yea, though (even now) I walk through the valley of the shadow of death, I will fear no evil; for You are with me; Your rod and Your staff, they comfort me."

The words are not in the future tense; they are not reserved for a future moment, so use them now. Do not let this song lie on the shelf until your last day. Sing it all the days of your life.

YOU ARE WITH ME. *Psalm 23:4*

Are you anguished because sickness is undermining your health? Do not be afraid. His Holy Spirit teaches you to sing, "Yea, though I walk through the valley of the shadow of death, I will fear no evil; for You are with me; Your rod and Your staff, they comfort me. You prepare a table before me in the presence of my enemies; You anoint my head with oil; my cup runs over. Surely goodness and mercy shall follow me all the days of my life; and I will dwell in the house of the LORD forever" (Ps. 23:4-6).

Go, tell the Lord of His own promise, and you will look forward to death without fear and be able to sing:

Knowing as I am known,
How shall I love that
word,
And oft repeat
before the throne,
Forever with the
Lord!
That resurrection
word,
That shout of victory,
Once more, forever with the Lord!
Amen—so let it be.

THE TROUBLES OF MY HEART. *Psalm 25:17*

It is wonderful how difficulties flee in the face of Omnipotence. The sick, who have been given up by the physician, often recover. It is, perhaps, God's mercy that the physician gave up. When you reach the end, God has only begun. The old proverb, "Man's extremity is God's opportunity," is certainly true. If God wills it, fevers fly and diseases disappear. As a soldier obeys the commander, God says to Death, "Go," and it goes, or "Come," and it comes.

It is the same in our circumstances. Often, days open dark with gathering clouds and yet end with a bright sunset. I should not wonder that some of you in looking back are quite surprised with your current situation. This morning I was talking with a gentleman who said, "I cannot tolerate waste in my home, and this is the reason: if ever there was a poor wretch who lived on hard times and envied a dog its piece of bread, it was me. But now God has been pleased to prosper me, and I often look back on that season of poverty and thank Him for having helped me through it." You see, dear friend, God can turn the wheel; He can make the bottom spoke the upper one, and He can do it all in a few days.

Though sin and sorrow rests like a double burden on your body and soul, go to Him and say, "Turn Yourself to me, and have mercy on me, for I am desolate and afflicted. The troubles of my heart have enlarged; bring me out of my distresses! Look on my affliction and my pain, and forgive all my sins" (Ps. 25:16-18).

LOOK ON MY AFFLICTION. *Psalm 25:18*

I have suffered as much pain as most. I also know as much about depression as anyone. Still, my Master's service is a blessed service. Faith in Him makes my heart leap for joy. I would not change places with the healthiest, wealthiest, or most eminent if I had to give up my faith in Jesus Christ. It is a blessed thing to be a Christian.

I visited a beloved sister from my congregation, she was dying with consumption, and death was near. I never spent a happier hour. She could scarcely speak, but what she said was full of sacred joy. She is in heaven now, and heaven was in her then. "I am so much closer," said she, "to the better land. I have fewer of these hard breaths to fetch and fewer of these hard pains to bear. I shall soon be where Jesus is." She talked as freely about dying and going home as I talk about going to my house for dinner.

Before she died, she felt as if she was going through a river. She said that she was in the midst of it and that floods were around her. In an interval of consciousness, she said, "I am going up the other side. The waters are shallower. I am climbing the other bank. Jesus is coming for me! I can hear the music of heaven." Her heart seemed overpowered with some sweet mystic melody that reached her inner spirit. "I can hear them sing! I can hear them sing! When Jesus comes, don't keep Him waiting for me. Don't wish me to stop. Let me go."

It does my soul great good to see the Lord's people depart this life. I grieve that they are taken away to heaven, for we want them here. But I thank God for the evidences of His hope and love.

YOU HAVE BEEN MY HELP. *Psalm 27:9*

In difficult times, a choice of options is not necessarily a benefit. While we are making our selection, the danger may overtake us. While the fox is considering which way to run, the hounds seize him. While the patient is seeking a second opinion, the disease proves fatal. It is good to have only one source of help, provided that help is all we need.

Believers are in that exact condition. We must trust God or remain without hope. We dare not look to others, for we have discovered their incompetence. We cannot rely on ourselves, for we have learned by bitter experience the folly of self-confidence. We are compelled to look to the Lord alone.

Blessed is the wind that drives the ship into the harbor. Blessed is the wave that washes the sailor onto the rock of safety. Blessed is the distress that forces us to rest in our God. This was David's condition when he wrote, "You have been my help; do not leave me nor forsake me, O God of my salvation" (Ps. 27:9).

David looked to God alone. Throughout David's experiences, the Lord's goodness shone like the polestar of his life's voyage. Thus David set his sight on the one sure guiding light and trusted in the God of his salvation.

Today, may our prayer be, "You have been my help; do not leave me nor forsake me, O God of my salvation. Amen."

WAIT. *Psalm 27:14*

The psalmist says, "Wait on the LORD; be of good courage, and He shall strengthen your heart. Wait, I say, on the LORD!" (Ps. 27:14). There is no real danger. You are safe while God lives, while Christ pleads, and while the Holy Spirit dwells in you.

Do not be fearful and unbelieving. "Wait on the LORD; be of good courage." Wait on the Lord as a beggar waits for a handout. We have gone to God's door, knocked, waited, and obtained gracious answers. Wait, but knock as you wait. Knock, but with fervent pleading and strong confidence, for the Lord Himself waits to be gracious. Agonize in desire. Make the door of mercy resound again and again with your resolute blows. The Lord is good to those who wait on Him. He will answer you in due time, and you will never be sent away empty-handed. It is your Father's business to provide for you. His name is Jehovah Jireh.

It is your Father's business to preserve you. He has given His angels charge over you, to keep you in all your ways. In their hands they shall bear you up, lest you dash your foot against a stone (Ps. 91:11-12).

It is our Father's business to mark the future. Our eyes are dim. We cannot see tomorrow. But our Father knows all about tomorrow, and He will be ready for whatever happens.

Therefore, I wait on Him. I raise no questions. I expect great mercies. Blessed are you if you also wait on Him.

WAIT, I SAY, ON THE LORD. *Psalm 27:14*

I have this to say. If I should never preach again, if this might be the last discourse I should ever deliver in this world, I would wish to make this my final testimony. There is a joy in religion that I never dreamed of. He is a good Master whom I have served. It is a blessed faith that He has given me, and it yields such blessed hope that

> "I would not change my blessed estate
> For all the world calls good or great."

If I had to die like a dog and there was no hereafter, I would still prefer to be a Christian, or to be the humblest Christian minister, to being a king or an emperor. I am persuaded there are more delights in Christ, yes, more joy in one glimpse of His face, than is to be found in all the praises of this harlot-world and in all the delights that it can yield in its sunniest and brightest days. I am persuaded that what He has been until now, He will be to the end. And where He has begun a good work, He will carry it on.

Sinners, Christ's cross is a hope that we can die by. It can take us down to the grave without a fear; it can make us rejoice when we are in the swelling waters of Jordan. It can fill us with delight when we are bowed down with physical pain or nervous distress. There is that in Christ which can make us triumph over the gloomiest terrors of grim death, that make us rejoice in the darkest of storms that can blacken the grave.

Trust, trust in the Lord, because both our testimony and that of all His people is that He is worthy to be trusted. "Wait on the LORD; be of good courage, and He shall strengthen your heart; wait, I say, on the LORD" (Ps. 27:14).

I WILL INSTRUCT YOU. *Psalm 32:8*

A believer may seek from God the qualifications for a particular vocation. Laborers may appeal to God for strength. Artists may ask God for skill. Students may seek God for help to accelerate their intellect. David was a great warrior, and he attributed his valor to God, who trained his hands for war and his fingers for battle (Ps. 144:1). We read about Bezalel and how God filled him with wisdom, understanding, and knowledge to design artistic works in gold, silver, bronze, jewels, and wood (Ex. 35:30-35).

If you pray about your work, I am persuaded that you will be helped. If you are not fully qualified, pray every morning for God to help you to be careful and observant. He has promised, "As your days, so shall your strength be" (Deut. 33:25). A mind that trusts in the Lord is in the best condition to acquire knowledge and understanding.

It is well to be clever, but being pure is essential. I would like you to be masters of your trades, but I am even more concerned that you would be honest, truthful, and holy.

My dear friend, engaged in service or business, go to your heavenly Father and ask Him to lead you in a smooth path (Ps. 27:11). Ask Him to uphold your steps that you may not slip (Ps. 17:5). Ask Him to instruct and teach you in the way you should go. Ask Him to guide you with His eye (Ps. 32:8).

Rest assured. He will order all your ways, that your daily calling will not hinder your heavenly calling, or your conduct belie your profession. Act both in your trade and in your calling as Christ would have acted had He been in your place. Hang this question on your wall, "What would Jesus do?" Then think of another, "How would Jesus do it?" What He would do and how He would do it is always the best guide.

I WILL GUIDE YOU. *Psalm 32:8*

Like a shepherd, God supplies our needs (Ps. 23:1). Some of you know for certain that God is your provider. Your trials have been so difficult that if it had not been for heaven's action you would never have been delivered. You have sunk so deep in poverty that family and friends have stayed away. You knew there was only one arm that could have lifted you.

Perhaps you have been reduced to such conditions that all you could do was pray. You wrestled at the throne and sought an answer, but it did not come. You used every effort to extricate yourself, but darkness covered your way again and again; you tried until hope vanished. Adding vows to your prayers, you said in agony, "Oh God, if You will deliver me this time, I will never again doubt You."

Look back on the path of your pilgrimage. You may be able to count as many blessings as there are mile markers, blessings piled up with oil poured on them—places where you said, "The LORD has helped me." Look through your diary to see time after time when perils and demands were so great that no earthly source could help and you felt compelled to witness that there is a God—a God who guides your path and is acquainted with all your ways (Ps. 32:8).

You have received deliverance in many marvelous ways from so unseen a hand, from so unlikely a source, and under circumstances foreign to your wishes. Yet the deliverances were so perfect, so complete, and so wonderful that you have been obliged to say, "The LORD is my shepherd" (Ps. 23:1). You now see this title stamped on all your mercies.

The Shepherd leads the sheep where He pleases, and you can be certain that He will lead them according to His will.

NO UNDERSTANDING. *Psalm 32:9*

You who are the King's favorites will sometimes suffer a twitch of pain, or a little trial in business, or some slight affliction. There may be something that your loving Lord would have you purge, something displeasing to Him or dangerous to you. Search and look for the faintest hint.

He promises, "I will instruct you and teach you in the way you should go; I will guide you with My eye." But He adds, "Do not be like the horse or like the mule, which have no understanding" (Ps. 32:8-9). If you do not obey the motion of God's eye, the hints become stronger and more painful. Notice how the psalmist proceeds, "Do not be like the horse or like the mule, which have no understanding, which must be harnessed with bit and bridle, else they will not come near you." God does not want to bit and bridle you; He wants to guide you with His eye. If you refuse this gentle guidance, then it will come stronger from the bridle and the bit. If one severe trial does not sanctify you, expect another more rigorous.

I am afraid that most of us are children; we cause our Father to chasten frequently. Oh that the breath of His Word may make enough fire to melt our hearts to repentance!

THE LORD HEARD HIM. *Psalm 34:6*

"The poor man cried out, and the LORD heard him" (Ps. 34:6). The man was alone, and the only one who heard him was the Lord. Yes, the Lord, Jehovah of Hosts, the All-glorious, heard his prayer. God stooped from His eternal glory and gave attention to this cry.

Never think that a praying heart pleads to a deaf God. Never imagine that God is so far removed that He fails to notice our needs. God hears prayer and grants His children's desires and requests.

We can never pray earnestly until we believe that God hears prayer. I have been told, "Prayer is an excellent exercise, highly satisfying and useful, but nothing more. Prayer cannot move the Infinite Mind." Do not believe so gross a lie or you will soon stop praying. No one prays for the mere love of the act. Amid all the innumerable actions of divine power, the Lord never ceases to listen to the cries of those who seek His face. This verse is always true, "The righteous cry out, and the LORD hears, and delivers them out of all their troubles" (Ps. 34:17). What a glorious fact! Truly marvelous!

This is still Jehovah's special title: the God who hears prayer. We often come from the throne of grace as certain that God heard us as we were sure that we had prayed. The abounding answers to our supplications are proof positive that prayer climbs above the regions of earth and time and touches God and His infinity. Yes, it is still true, the Lord will hear your prayer.

A BROKEN HEART. *Psalm 34:18*

Many in this world live with broken hearts. A broken limb of any kind is bad, bruised and wounded flesh is hard to bear. But when your heart is crushed or broken, or when your spirit trembles, you are depressed and utterly wretched. You are dreary company. Others get away from you like the herd leaves the wounded deer to bleed and die alone. People instinctively avoid the company of those who are habitually gloomy. Their own desire for happiness leads people to escape from the miserable.

Those who are taught by God will help the brokenhearted, but human sympathy is soon worn out because of its inability to help. You can set a limb and the bone will grow, but what can you do with a broken or crushed heart? Not liking to attempt the impossible and not caring to be continually baffled, it seems natural even to good people to avoid the depressed. Thus, the sad are doomed to sigh, "Loved one and friend You have put far from me, and my acquaintances into darkness" (Ps. 88:18).

When people comfort the depressed, they often become bitter by their conscious failures. They criticize until the poor tortured creature cries out in agony, "Miserable comforters are you all!" (Job 16:2). The trials of the brokenhearted are difficult because they are often despised and avoided.

Happy is it for them that "the LORD is near to those who have a broken heart, and saves such as have a contrite spirit" (Ps. 34:18).

THE LORD DELIVERS. *Psalm 34:19*

Are you in great trouble? If you have a trial that you cannot share or a trouble that, if you did share, no one could help, then go and spread it before the Lord. Remember His words, "Many are the afflictions of the righteous, but the LORD delivers him out of them all" (Ps. 34:19).

Go and tell Him that He has spoken and that He has pledged Himself to deliver you out of all your afflictions. Be sure of this, God will be as good as His Word.

My brothers and sisters, may God help us to look to Him.

How precious. *Psalm 36:7*

God loves His people. If you are a believer in Christ Jesus, trusting only in His merits, God loves you as surely as He is God. There is no question about the matter. His divine love is yours as certainly as His power is displayed in creation.

Set God's lovingkindness before your eyes. Think of His faithfulness! God's lovingkindness never pauses. It is as constant as the flight of time. Never a moment but there has been love for that moment. Never an hour but there has been that hour's portion of lovingkindness.

You have often forgotten the Lord, but He has never forgotten you. You have failed ten thousand times, but He has never failed you. If He had dealt with you justly and not graciously, He would have long ago divorced you from His heart, but you are as precious to Him now as ever. And you will be precious to Him when heaven and earth shall pass away. So why not seek to serve Him constantly? Let every day have its duty, and let each day's duty be your pleasure and privilege to serve Him. Do not receive without giving.

God's sovereign goodness comes without a pause. There are no miscarriages in divine grace. Never let any forgetfulness, negligence, or delay be in your gratitude or in the obedience that springs from it. In your health, in your sickness, in your wealth, in your poverty, in your joy, and in your sorrow, may your theme be God's lovingkindness and helpfulness.

Do not forsake me. *Psalm 38:21*

We frequently pray that God will not forsake us in our hours of trials and tests. We need, however, to use this prayer all the time. There is not a moment in our life that we can do without His constant upholding. Whether in light or in darkness, in fellowship or in temptation, we need to pray, "Do not forsake me, O LORD." "Hold me up and I shall be safe" (Ps. 119:117). A little child learning to walk needs the hand of her mother. The ship without a captain drifts from its course. We cannot make it without continued aid from above.

Pray, "Do not forsake me, O LORD." Father, do not forsake Your child, or I will fall by the hand of the enemy. Shepherd, do not forsake Your lamb, or I will wander from the safety of the fold. Great Vineyard Keeper, do not leave your plant, or I will wither and die. "Do not forsake me, O LORD," now or at any moment of my life.

Do not forsake me in my joys, lest they fully engage my heart. Do not forsake me in my sorrow, lest I murmur against You. Do not forsake me during repentance, lest I lose the hope of pardon and fall into despair. Do not forsake me in the days of my strongest faith, lest my faith degenerate into presumption.

Do not forsake me. Without You I am weak; with You I am strong. Do not forsake me. My path is dangerous and full of snares. I desperately need Your guidance.

The hen does not forsake her chickens. Cover me with Your feathers, and under Your wings I will take refuge (Ps. 91:4). "Be not far from me. Trouble is near and there is none to help" (Ps. 22:11). "Do not leave me nor forsake me, O God of my salvation" (Ps. 27:9). Amen.

His bed of illness.   *Psalm 41:3*

The Holy Peace of God's Suffering Child is one of the finest sermons that can ever be preached. A sick saint is often used by God far more than the most eloquent preacher. When people see how willingly you submit to the divine will, how patiently you endure painful operations, and how God your Maker gives you songs in the night (Job 35:10), you are greatly used.

I visit people who have been bedridden for years, whose influence extends over the entire parish. They are known as poor holy women or as old Christian men. I get more from talking with these people for half an hour than I derive from all the books in my library. Yet these saint thought they were doing nothing.

Look at your situation in this light. You can praise God on your bed; you can make your room as vocal for God as any pulpit. Let true religion be your life, and then your life will be true  religion. This is how it ought to be. "Whether you eat or drink, or whatever you do, do all to the glory of God" (1 Cor. 10:31). As the stream of your common life flows obscure and unobserved, be holy and courageous, and you will find that "they also serve who only stand and wait." You, who can do no more than simply sit at Jesus' feet and listen to His words, will not be neglected or overlooked. This is a service for Him that He appreciates.

LORD, BE MERCIFUL. *Psalm 41:4*

When your heart throbs and flutters, when your swollen limb seems as if it were laid on an anvil and beaten with red hot hammers, when the pain goes through you again and again until you cry out in agony, and when the tears unwillingly fall from your eyes, pray this prayer, "LORD, be merciful to me" (Ps. 41:4).

I have found that when medicine fails, or when sleep is chased away, or when pain becomes unbearable, it is good to appeal directly to God. I say, "Lord, I am Your child. Will You allow Your child to be tortured with pain? Did You not say, 'As a father pities his children, so the LORD pities those who fear Him' (Ps. 103:13)? Therefore, Lord, be merciful to me."

I can honestly assert that I have found immediate relief and remission of extreme pain in answer to a simple appeal to my Father. I know that many of you have had a similar experience.

When hurting with severe physical pain, you will find that quiet resignation, holy patience, and childlike submissiveness will enable you to pray, "LORD, be merciful to me." This often brings better relief than anything that the most skilled physician can prescribe. You are permitted and encouraged to act this way. When the rod falls heavy, look up into your Father's face and say, "LORD, be merciful to me."

I SHALL YET PRAISE HIM. *Psalm 42:5*

Sorrow deserves sympathy. But when believers refuse to be comforted, they act like the world. When a Christian is beyond comfort over the loss of creature goods, God's name is degraded. Surely the professed truths never entered the soul.

If the furnace is hot, let your faith be strong. If the burden is heavy, let your patience endure. Acknowledge that He who lends has the right to reclaim. As you bless the giving, bless the taking.

There are times when the brightest-eyed Christians can hardly brush the tears away. Strong faith and joyous hope subside into a fear that is scarcely able to keep the spark of hope and faith alive. In times of gloom, when your soul is overwhelmed, grasp the promise and rejoice in the Lord. Although it is not always easy, cry with David, "Why are you cast down, O my soul? And why are you disquieted within me?" (Ps. 42:5). Question the cause of your tears. Reason until you come to the psalmist's conclusion, "Hope in God, for I shall yet praise Him" (Ps. 42:5).

If you can believe God in the midnight of your soul, then you have ten times more cause to rejoice than to sorrow. If you can lie humbly at Jesus' feet, there are more flowers than thorns ready to spring up in your path.

Companions in tribulations, do not give in to hopeless sorrow. Salute with thankfulness the angel of hope, for you shall yet praise Him.

Our Refuge.   *Psalm 46:1*

When your trials were so severe that you were forced to flee to God, did you find this statement true? His door was never closed. He never said, "Go elsewhere." He never upbraided you for presumption when you came. When you hid in Him, it was a blessed retreat. When you entered your closet, shut the door, and hid with God, you had perfect peace.

Look at the little chicks under the hen. See how they bury their heads in the feathers of her warm bosom. Hear their little chirps of perfect happiness as they nestle under their mother's wing. "He shall cover you with His feathers, and under His wings you shall take refuge; His truth shall be your shield and buckler" (Ps. 91:4). Have you found this to be true?

My happiest hours have not been days of pleasure but nights of sorrow. When all waters are bitter, the cup of divine consolation is all the sweeter. For brightness, do not give me sunshine, give me the Lord's superior glory, for it lights up affliction's darkness. Happiness does not depend on success in business or being applauded by one and all. The only thing necessary for happiness is for the Lord to smile on you. It is not essential to be in good health or even naturally cheerful. God gives the truest health in sickness and the most tender joy in depression.

"God is our refuge and strength, a very present help in trouble" (Ps. 46:1). It has been many days since we first went to Him, and we have been many times since, but He has never failed. To know Him is life eternal. To know Him is solid peace. No calamity can destroy that peace.

WE WILL NOT FEAR. *Psalm 46:2*

The very hairs of your head are all numbered" (Matt. 10:30). This verse literally means what it says. God's wisdom and knowledge are so great that He even knows the number of hairs on your head. His providence descends to the minute dust particles in a summer storm. He numbers the gnats in the sunshine and the fish in the sea. He controls the massive planets that shine in the heavens, and He deals with the teardrops that trickle from your eyes. He who supports the dignity of His throne in the splendor of heaven maintains it in the depths of the dark sea. There is nothing above, under, or around you that is not determined by His counsel and will.

I am not a fatalist, but I strictly hold to the doctrine that God has decreed all things that come to pass and that He rules over all things for His glory and good. What have we to fear? The unbeliever looks at the lightning and is apprehensive, but the Christian believes that it follows a predestined path, and he contemplates it with confidence. At sea, when the waves dash against a ship and toss it to and fro, some panic because they think that this is all chance. But believers see order in the waves. They hear music in the wind and are at peace because the tempest is in God's hand. Why then should we fear?

In all this world's convulsions, in all temporary distress and danger, we can remain calm, collected, and boldly say with confidence, "I know God is here and all this is working for my good." "Therefore we will not fear, even though the earth be removed, and though the mountains be carried into the midst of the sea; though its waters roar and be troubled, though the mountains shake with its swelling" (Ps. 46:2).

Think on these things.

CALL UPON ME. *Psalm 50:15*

Oh Lord, You see how great my trouble is! It is heavy. I cannot carry it, and I cannot get rid of it. It follows me to bed, and it will not let me sleep. When I rise, it is still with me. I cannot shake it off. My trouble is unusual. Few are as afflicted as I am. Please give me extraordinary help, for my trouble is crushing. If you do not help, I will soon be broken! This is good reasoning and good pleading.

Turn your adversity to advantage. Go to the Lord this moment and say, "Lord, do you hear me? You have commanded me to pray. I, though I am evil, would not tell anyone to ask me for something unless I intended to honor their request. I would not urge them to ask for help if I meant to refuse it."

When God tells you to call on Him, He will deal compassionately with you. You are not urged to pray in the hour of trouble to experience deeper disappointment. God knows that you have trouble enough without the added burden of unanswered prayer. The Lord will not unnecessarily add even a quarter of an ounce to your burden. When He tells you to call on Him, you may call on Him without fear of failure.

So plead the time, plead the trouble, plead the command, and then plead with God. Speak reverently, but with belief, "Lord, it is You Yourself to whom I appeal. You said, 'Call upon Me in the day of trouble; I will deliver you' (Ps. 50:15). So Lord, by Your truth, by Your faithfulness, by Your immutability, and by Your love, I, a poor sinner, heartbroken and crushed, call on You in the day of trouble. Help me. Help me soon, or else I die."

If I were in trouble, I would pray like David, Elijah, or Daniel in the power of this promise, "Call upon Me in the day of trouble; I will deliver you, and you shall glorify Me."

HE SHALL SUSTAIN YOU. *Psalm 55:22*

In order to apply this remedy, rather than just describe it, by the help of God's Holy Spirit I will mention some fears and cares that can only be relieved by leaving them with God. "What shall I eat, what shall I drink, what shall I wear? With no opportunity to earn a living, without friend or patron to assist me, what shall I do?"

You are a Christian, you must use all diligence, for that is your duty. If God will help you, do not mingle fretfulness with diligence, or impatience with suffering, or distrust with trials. Remember what Jesus sweetly said, "Look at the birds of the air, for they neither sow nor reap nor gather into barns, yet your heavenly Father feeds them. Are you not of more value than they? Which of you by worrying can add one cubit to his stature? So why do you worry about clothing? Consider the lilies of the field, how they grow; they neither toil nor spin, and yet I say to you that even Solomon in all his glory was not arrayed like one of these. Now if God so clothes the grass of the field, which today is, and tomorrow is thrown into the oven, will He not much more clothe you, O you of little faith?" (Matt. 6:26-30).

"Therefore do not worry, saying, 'What shall we eat?' or 'What shall we drink?' or 'What shall we wear?' For after all these things the Gentiles seek. For your heavenly Father knows that you need all these things. But seek first the kingdom of God and His righteousness, and all these things shall be added to you" (Matt. 6:31-33). Use your most earnest effort and humble yourself under the mighty hand of God. If you cannot do one thing, do another. If you cannot earn your bread by the sweat of your brain, do it by the sweat of your brow. Then, if every door is still shut, "Trust in the LORD, and do good. . . . Delight yourself also in the LORD, and He shall give you the desires of your heart" (Ps. 37:3-4).

GIVE GOD YOUR BURDEN. *Psalm 55:22*

The failure of companies, frequent bad debts, changes in the market, financial pressure, and sudden panic cause a world of trouble. Our credit system makes it difficult for a Christian to conduct business in the sober substantial fashion that a tender conscience prefers. "Owe no one anything" (Rom. 13:8). If that could be woven into the economic system, it would cure ten thousand ills.

If you have a business so extensive that you do not sleep at night, if you toss on your bed thinking about employees that may have robbed you, or about the cargo that is at sea, or about the deflated prices of your large inventory, then I say to you, "Are you sure that you have used your best prudence, wisdom, effort, and attention?" Well then, what else can you do?

Suppose you weep all night. Will that keep your ship from sinking? Suppose you could cry your eyes out. Will that make your employees honest? Suppose you could worry until you could not eat. Would that raise the value of your inventory? If you were to say, "Well, I have done all that is to be done, and now I will leave it with God," one would think that you might have the full use of your senses to attend to your business and to get a good night's sleep. But you fritter away your senses and commit blunders that multiply your troubles, both in waking and sleeping.

We say, "Leave well enough alone." I say to you, "Leave ill alone; leave them both alone." Then with the hand of prayer in everything, with thanksgiving, let your requests be made known to God (Phil. 4:6). Then with the other hand, the hand of faith, trust in the heavenly Father and lift the load off your shoulders and let the entire weight be left with your Eternal God. "Cast your burden on the LORD."

A SHELTER FOR ME. *Psalm 61:3*

It is a wonderful fact that if others forsake us, God never does. To each of His redeemed people He says, "I will never leave you nor forsake you" (Heb. 13:5). Often, people are false. They forsake friends when those friends fall into poverty. Oh the tragedies of some of these cruel forsakings! May you never know them. These so-called friends knew their friends when their clothing was new, but how sadly their eyesight fails as the clothing becomes tattered. They knew them extremely well when they sat at their table and shared their generous hospitality, but they do not know them now that they knock at their door for help in time of need.

Matters have changed and friends that once were cherished are now forgotten. In fact, the man almost pities himself to think that he is so unfortunate as to have a friend who has failed him. There is no pity because he is so occupied in pitying himself. In hundreds, thousands, and tens of thousands of cases, as soon as the gold has gone, the pretended love has gone. When the dwelling changes from the mansion to the cottage, the friendship that once promised to last forever suddenly disappears.

Believer, God will never leave us because of poverty, regardless of how low we are brought. Scant may be your food. You may have hard work to provide things honest in the sight of all. You may sometimes have to look and look again and wonder how you will be able to escape your present difficulty. When all your friends have turned their backs, when acquaintances have fallen from you like leaves in autumn, under His bounty you will find "a shelter." When these other hands are shut, His hands will still be outstretched in lovingkindness and tender mercy to help and deliver the soul of the needy.

TRUST IN HIM. *Psalm 62:8*

A frequent form of weakness is depression. It is so common in English churches that it is as much a national disorder as tuberculosis. It is not so common as it was, but it is still more than I could wish. We are not as happy and frivolous as our Irish neighbors, and we are not quite so adventuresome as our transatlantic friends. I am afraid, as Englishmen, we have a natural tendency to become depressed. I feel it myself, and in the circle where I move it is not uncommon.

Depression is not a virtue; it is a vice, and I am heartily ashamed of myself for falling into it. Yet I am sure that there is no remedy for it like a holy faith in God. Asaph of old was subject to this weakness. He said to himself, "Why are you cast down, O my soul? And why are you disquieted within me" (Ps. 42:5)?

What was the medicine he took? "Hope in God, for I shall yet praise Him for the help of His countenance" (Ps. 42:5). That was the remedy.

David prescribes it when he says, "Trust in Him at all times, you people; pour out your heart before Him; God is a refuge for us" (Ps. 62:8).

Depression hamstrings you. It makes you weak in conflict, when you should be like a well-trained athlete struggling with your foe. Christian, beg your Lord to increase your faith in Him. When you get more faith you will rise superior to that weakness.

I REMEMBER YOU. *Psalm 63:6*

In trouble, God's children turn to their Father. It is their newborn nature to seek Him. The believing heart is like the needle in a compass. You may turn it with your finger, but when you withdraw the pressure it will turn toward its pole. The force of trials, the demands of business, or an overpowering lethargy can make us indifferent to our highest love, but this cannot continue because our only rest is in God.

These busy days leave little time for meditation, yet there is no exercise more nourishing to faith, love, and grace. A transient thought of God may greatly bless, just as a touch of the Savior's garment healed a woman (Matt. 9:21-22). When we meditate, we lean on His embrace and enjoy the full fellowship of His love. David said, "I remember You on my bed, I meditate on You in the night watches" (Ps. 63:6). Oh for more meditation! It would mean more grace and more joy. May you and I find pleasure in our sleepless hours and enter into close fellowship with Him through heavenly meditation.

Private meditation and devotion should be a dialogue between your soul and God. The Lord speaks to us through Scripture, and by prayer we speak to Him. When prayer is not urgent, read your Bible and hear His voice; then you will usually find it in your heart to pray. Speak to Him as you would speak to a friend. When you have expressed all your thoughts, let the Lord speak again, and realize His presence.

If half of our conversations with friends were silenced and our talks with God were multiplied ten times, it would be well for us.

From God's goodness. *Psalm 68:10*

All God's gifts are prepared in advance and reserved for needs foreseen. He knows our future needs, and out of the fullness of Christ Jesus He provides from His goodness. You may therefore trust Him for all your future needs. He has infallible foreknowledge about every one of them. He can say to you in any condition, "I knew that you would need this."

A traveler journeying across a desert may pitch the tent only to find that some essentials were not brought along. "Ah," says the traveler, "I did not foresee this. If I could start this journey over, I would bring these necessary items." God has foreknowledge of all that His wandering children require. When those needs arise, the supplies are ready. It is goodness that He has prepared for the poor in heart. Goodness, and goodness only. "My grace is sufficient for you" (2 Cor. 12:9). "As your days, so shall your strength be" (Deut. 33:25).

Is your heart heavy? God knew it would be. The comfort your heart wants is treasured in the sweet assurance of our text. You are poor and needy, but He knows your need and has the exact blessing you require. Plead this promise, believe it, and you will obtain fulfillment.

Do you feel that you were never so consciously vile as you are now? The crimson fountain is still open with all its former power to wash your sins away.

You will never be in a position where Christ cannot help you. There will never be a bind in your spiritual life where Jesus Christ will not be equal to the emergency. Your history is foreknown and provided for in Jesus Christ.

Has His promise failed? *Psalm 77:8*

When you are in distress, take a promise and see if it is true. If you have nothing to eat, take this promise: "Bread will be given him, his water will be sure" (Is. 33:16). When there is nothing in the kitchen, say, "I will see if God will keep this promise." If He does, do not forget it. Set it down in your diary, or mark it in your Bible. Be like the old saint who put T and P beside the promises. She told her pastor that it meant tried and proven. When she was again in distress, she believed that God would help.

There is a promise that says, "Resist the devil and he will flee from you" (James 4:7). Take that and prove it! When you have, make a mark and say, "This I know is true, for I have proven it." There is nothing in the world that can confirm faith like proof.

"What I want," said one, "are the facts." So it is with Christians. We want facts that make us believe. The older you grow, the stronger your faith should be. Then you will have many more facts to buttress your faith and compel your belief in God. When you reach seventy years, what a pile of evidence you will have accumulated if you have kept a record of all of God's providential goodness and lovingkindness.

I can bear willing testimony to His faithfulness. Not one good thing has failed of all that the Lord has promised! Every example of God's love should make us believe Him more. As we see the fulfillment of each promise, it compels us to say, "God has kept His promises and will keep them to the end."

The worst is that we forget. Then we will have no more faith than when we started, for we will have forgotten God's repeated answers. Though He has fulfilled the promises, we have buried them in forgetfulness.

Has God forgotten? *Psalm 77:9*

Have you indulged the idea that under your present trial, whatever it may be, God will desert you? My dear widowed sister, do not fear that the Lord will forsake you now that your husband is dead. My friend with heavy business losses, do you believe the Lord will help? Did He love you when you were dead in sins? Did He choose you before the foundation of the world (Eph. 1:4)? Is He going to desert you now? Do you think you will ever have to ask, with the psalmist, "Has His mercy ceased forever? Has His promise failed forevermore? Has God forgotten to be gracious? Has He in anger shut up His tender mercies?" (Ps. 77:8-9).

If you talk that way, ask the Lord why He ever began His work of love on you if He did not intend to finish it. Or was it His intention to forget you? If that was His intention, would He have ever started with you? He knew all that would happen and all that you would do. Nothing is a surprise to Him. Known to the Lord from the beginning were all your trials and all your sins. Nevertheless, He still loved you. In the foresight of all that was to happen, do not think that He will now or ever forget you. He will not! If He so loved you, even when you were dead in sins, will He deny you anything that is for His glory and your good?

You have been praying, but you fear that the mercy asked will never come. If He loved you when you were a mass of corruption, will He not answer your prayers now that He has made you an heir of heaven? Beloved, be of good comfort. Do not let depression or unbelief cross your mind. He loves you so much that He has made great sacrifices for you. He blesses you daily, and He will not be in heaven without you.

No good thing withheld. *Psalm 84:11*

Just as God provided Elijah with bread, meat, and water by the brook Cherith (1 Kin. 17:3-4), He can provide for you. Is your supply of meal running low? Is your flask of oil almost empty? Then where is the God of Elijah? He is still with His Elijahs. And He is still with the widows, just as He was with the widow of Zarephath (1 Kin. 17:14).

Do you think that God is dead? Has it crossed your mind that Divine Providence is a failure? Do you feel that God is unable to provide for His own? Do not think that! If you do, your unbelief will prove a punishment. It will break that meal barrel. It will dash that oil flask to pieces. If you waiver, you will receive nothing from the Lord. But if you keep strong in faith, you will find that Jehovah Jireh—the Lord will provide—is still His name.

"The Lord God is a sun and shield; the Lord will give grace and glory; no good thing will He withhold from those who walk uprightly" (Ps. 84:11). God can help us to have such confidence in Him that we shall find the Lord God of Elijah supplies our daily needs and feeds us until we want no more.

Sing this song, you tried and tested ones, sing it now:

> The Lord my Shepherd is
> I shall be well supplied;
> Since He is mine and I am His,
> What can I want beside?

A MULTITUDE OF ANXIETIES. *Psalm 94:19*

Some of you are perplexed with a multitude of anxieties about your life. You do not know what to do. One plan was suggested, and for a time it seemed the best action. But now you have doubts. You are bewildered and you cannot see Providence's clue. You are lost in a maze. Indeed, at this moment, you are depressed.

You have tried various ways and methods to escape your present difficulty. But you have been disappointed and are distracted. Your thoughts have no order; they drag you in opposite directions. The currents meet and twist as if you were in a whirlpool.

My perplexed friend, remember the children of Israel at the Red Sea. The sea was before them, rocks were on either side, and the cruel Egyptians roared in the rear. Imitate Israel's actions. "Do not be afraid. Stand still, and see the salvation of the LORD, which He will accomplish for you today" (Ex. 14:13). You reply, "I cannot be quiet. I am agitated, perturbed, perplexed, tossed, and distracted. What shall I do?"

"In the multitude of my anxieties within me, Your comforts delight my soul" (Ps. 94:19). Turn your eyes to the deep things of God. Cease from an anxious consideration of seen things, which are temporary, and gaze by faith on things that are eternal.

Remember, your way is ordered by a higher power than your will and choice. The eternal God has fixed your every step. All things are fixed by the Father's hand. He who loved us from before the foundations of the world has immutably determined every step of our pilgrimage.

It is a blessed thing, after you have been muddling and meddling with your anxieties, to throw your burdens on the Lord and leave them there.

A LESSON FROM THE BIRDS. *Psalm 104:17*

We are all to some measure, I suspect, dissatisfied with our lives. The great majority are always on the fly. They never settle; they never light on any tree to build their nest. They are always fluttering from one tree to another; this tree is not green enough, that one is not beautiful enough, this one is not picturesque enough. They are always on the wing and never build a peaceful nest.

Luther compared the Christian's contentment to a little bird in the tree: he fed himself tonight, but he does not know where tomorrow's breakfast is. He sits there while the wind rocks the tree; he shuts his eyes and puts his head under his wing and sleeps. When he wakes in the morning, he will sing:

> Mortals cease from toil and sorrow;
> God provideth for the morrow.

Few can say, "I want nothing else. I want but little here. I am satisfied. I am content." You who are apprentices are sighing until you become journeymen. You who are journeymen are groaning to be masters. Masters are longing to retire. We are like sailors who never get to port, like arrows that never reach the target.

Dear friend, what would your future be if you did not have Christ? Even if it is bitter and dark, it does not matter as long as Christ your Lord sanctifies it and the Holy Spirit gives you courage, energy, and strength.

LIGHT IN THE DARKNESS. *Psalm 112:4*

The upright will have days of darkness, sickness, sorrow, poverty, and depression. Their wealth may take wings and fly away, and even their righteousness may be cruelly suspected by all. Clouds may lower around them, but their gloom will not last forever, because in due time the Lord will bring light.

As surely as a good person's sun goes down, it will rise again. If darkness is caused by depression, the Holy Spirit will give comfort. If there is financial loss or personal bereavement, Christ's presence will give solace. If there is cruelty and malignity, the Lord's sympathy will give support.

It is as ordinary for the righteous to be comforted as it is for the day to dawn. Wait for the light; it will surely come. If our heavenly Father in our last hour puts us to bed in the dark, it will be morning when we awake.

HE BEHOLDS ALL THINGS. *Psalm 113:6*

God dwells so high that to observe heavenly things He must humble Himself. He must come down to view the skies and bow to see what angels do. What must His condescension be! He observes the humblest of His servants on earth and makes them sing for joy, like Mary when she said, "He has regarded the lowly state of His maidservant" (Luke 1:48).

Wonderful are Isaiah's words, "For thus says the High and Lofty One who inhabits eternity, whose name is Holy: 'I dwell in the high and holy place, with him who has a contrite and humble spirit, to revive the spirit of the humble, and to revive the heart of the contrite ones'" (Is. 57:15).

Heathen philosophers could not believe that the great God observed the small events of human history. They pictured Him dwelling in serene indifference to all the needs and woes of His creatures.

"Their rock is not like our Rock" (Deut. 32:31). We have a God who is high above all gods, yet He is our Father, knowing what we need before we ask Him. He is the Shepherd who supplies our needs. He is the Guardian who counts the hairs of our heads. He is the tender and considerate Friend who sympathizes with us in all our grief. Truly, our condescending God should be praised wherever He is known.

FROM THIS TIME FORTH. *Psalm 115:18*

"We will bless the LORD from this time forth and forevermore" (Ps. 115:18). Our praise will never end. "From this time forth and forevermore" includes eternity. We praise Him not in our strength but in the strength of grace. That strength will never be exhausted; it will be renewed day by day.

If God takes you to the sick bed, if every limb becomes a mass of pain, if every nerve is a highway for crowds of pain to travel, keep on praising Him. Continue to bless, praise, and magnify His name.

Even death cannot stop us from blessing God; it will only increase the heavenly choir and sweeten the harmony. We shall love the Lord more and praise Him better when our souls can speak without being hindered by our lips. Then we shall speak in a nobler and sweeter language before the throne of God:

> My God, I'll praise Thee while I live,
> And praise Thee when I die,
> And praise Thee when I rise again,
> And to eternity.
>
> Then in a nobler, sweeter song,
> I'll sing Thy power to save,
> When this poor lisping, stammering tongue,
> Lies silent in the grave.

I FOUND TROUBLE. *Psalm 116:3*

Believer, you are not exempt from trials, but you have sufficient grace for any trouble. God's choicest love letters are sent in black-edged envelopes. The envelope frightens us, but if we know how to break the seal we will find riches for our soul. Great trials are the clouds from which God showers great mercies. Frequently, when the Lord has an extraordinary mercy to send, He employs His rough and grizzled horses to drag it to our door. The smooth rivers of ease are usually navigated by little vessels filled with common commodities, but a huge ship loaded with treasure crosses deep seas.

Learn from David's experience. "I found trouble and sorrow. Then I called upon the name of the LORD: 'O LORD, I implore You, deliver my soul'" (Ps. 116:3-4). When the sorrows of death surround you, pray! When the pains of hell grab you, pray! When you find trouble and sorrow, pray! Everything else that prudence and wisdom suggests is to be done in a time of difficulty, but none are to be relied on by themselves. "Salvation is of the LORD" (Jon. 2:9), whether it be salvation from troubles or salvation from sins.

When you have done all, trust in God as though you had done nothing. "Unless the LORD builds the house, they labor in vain that build it; unless the LORD guards the city, the watchman stays awake in vain" (Ps. 127:1). In all things pray. Rest assured that if at this moment you are in the same dilemma as David, prayer will bring you out. Prayer is the universal remedy subduing every disease. Prayer unlocks the treasures of God and shuts the gates of hell. Prayer extinguishes the violence of flames and closes the mouths of lions. Prayer overcomes heaven and bends omnipotence to its will. Just pray, believer, and, in the name of the Well-Beloved, answers of peace must be given.

THE DEATH OF HIS SAINTS. *Psalm 116:15*

God did not allow the psalmist to die; He delivered his soul from death. This indicates that this psalm was to remind Jewish families about the mercies received by anyone who was seriously ill and then restored to health.

The Lord values the lives of His saints and often spares them when others perish. Saints will not die prematurely; they will be immortal until their work is done. When their times comes to die, their deaths will be precious. The Lord watches over their deathbeds, smooths their pillows, sustains their hearts, and receives their souls.

Those who are redeemed with the priceless blood are so cherished by God that even their deaths are precious to Him. The deathbeds of the saints are precious to the church, and she often learns much from them. They are precious to believers who treasure the last words of the departed. But they are most precious to the Lord Jehovah, who views the triumphant deaths of His gracious ones with sacred delight.

If we have walked before Him in the land of the living, we need not fear to die before Him when the hour of our departure arrives.

DEAL BOUNTIFULLY. *Psalm 119:17*

David takes great pleasure in acknowledging his duty to God, and he counts it joy to be in God's service. He pleads because a servant has some influence on a master. Yet in this case, the wording eliminates a legal claim, for he seeks a favor and not a reward. Let my wages be according to Your goodness and not according to my merit. Reward me according to Your liberality and not according to my service. "My father's hired servants have bread enough and to spare" (Luke 15:17). He will not let one of His household perish with hunger. If the Lord will only treat us as He treats the least of His servants, we will be deeply content. All His true servants are sons, princes of the blood, heirs of life eternal.

David's great needs required a bountiful provision, and his little desert could never give such a supply. Thus, he throws himself on God's grace and looks to the Lord and His great goodness for the great things he needs. He begs for heavy grace, like the one who prayed, "Oh, Lord, You must give me great mercy, or no mercy, for little mercy will not help me."

Without abundant mercy, David could not live. It takes great grace to keep a saint alive. Even life is a gift of divine bounty to such undeserving ones as we. Only the Lord can keep us alive, and it is mighty grace that preserves the life we have forfeited by sin.

It is right to want to live. It is proper to pray to live, and it is just to ascribe prolonged life to God's favor. Spiritual life, without which natural life is mere existence, is also to be sought from the Lord's bounty. It is the highest work of divine grace, and in it God's bounty is gloriously displayed. The Lord's servants cannot serve Him in their own strength. They cannot even live unless His grace abounds toward them.

NIGHT THOUGHTS. *Psalm 119:55*

When we hear the night songs of revelers, we have evidence that they do not keep God's Law. But the quiet thoughts of the gracious are proof positive that the Lord's name is precious to them. We may judge both people and nations by their songs. The singing and thinking of the righteous show their love for God, and whether they lift their voices or sit in silence, they are the Lord's. Blessed are those whose night thoughts are memories of the eternal light. They will be remembered by their Lord when the night of death comes.

Are your night thoughts full of light because they are full of God? Is His name the natural subject of your evening reflections? If so, it will give tone to your morning and noonday hours.

Or do you give your mind to the fleeting cares and pleasures of this world? If so, it is little wonder that you do not live as you should. No one is holy by chance. If we have no memory for Jehovah's name, then we are not likely to remember His commandments. If we do not think of Him secretly, we will not obey Him openly.

BEFORE I WAS AFFLICTED. *Psalm 119:67*

The way to a stronger faith usually lies along the rough path of sorrow. Only as faith is contested will faith be confirmed. I do not know if my experience is similar to all of God's people, but all the grace I have received in comfortable and easy times could lie on a penny. The good that I have received from sorrow, grief, and pain is incalculable. What do I not owe to the hammer and the anvil, the fire and the file? What do I not owe to the crucible and the furnace, the bellows that flamed the coals and the hand that thrust me into the heat? Affliction is the best bit of furniture in my house. It is the best book in a minister's library. We may wisely rejoice in various trials, knowing that the testing of our faith produces patience (James 1:2-3). And through this we are exceedingly enriched and our faith grows strong.

An old Puritan said that if you go into the woods and are very quiet, you will not know whether there is a partridge, or a pheasant, or a rabbit in it. But when you move or make a noise, you soon see the living creatures. They rise or they run. When affliction comes into your soul and makes a disturbance and breaks your peace, your graces rise. Faith comes out of hiding and love leaps from its secret place.

I remember Mr. William Jay saying that birds' nests are hard to find in the summer, but that anyone can find a bird's nest in the winter. When all the leaves are off the trees the nests are highly visible. Often in prosperity, we fail to find our faith. Yet when adversity comes, the winter of our trial bares the branches, and we immediately see our faith.

"Before I was afflicted I went astray," said David, "but now I keep Your word." He found that his faith was really there by keeping God's Word in the time of affliction.

I HAVE BEEN AFFLICTED. *Psalm 119:71*

There is no teaching or ministry even by the best taught servant of God that can do as much good as a sanctified experience. You must learn under that blessed schoolmaster, Mr. Affliction. It is good to go to his school, for the lessons are beneficial. One of his scholars wrote, "Before I was afflicted I went astray, but now I keep Your word. . . . It is good for me that I have been afflicted, that I may learn Your statutes" (Ps. 119:67, 71).

We receive our sweetest comforts in the time of trouble. I know that there are kisses from Jesus' lips for His tested children that He does not give to those who are without trial. "He will feed His flock like a shepherd; He will gather the lambs with His arm, and carry them in His bosom" (Is. 40:11). I would love to be a lamb and ride close to His heart. He will "gently lead those who are with young" (Is. 40:11). Sometimes it is well for us to feel pain and weakness, that we may have more gentle leading from the tender Shepherd.

The great Rutherford said that when Christ put him down in the cellar of affliction, he knew that He kept His wine there. Rutherford groped about until he found the bottles, and then he drank and was relieved. There is rich wine of comfort in the lowest cellars of affliction when Christ puts us there. The joys of heaven will be sweeter because of our trials. We often sing:

> Sweet affliction,
> Thus to bring my Savior near.

Christ is superlatively sweet. The next sweetest thing is His dear cross. He is most precious. The love-pats of His pierced hands are the proof.

A PRESCRIPTION FOR AFFLICTION. *Psalm 119:92*

I may be speaking to some dear child of God who is suffering a personal affliction. You would consider it an intrusion for another to interfere, so I will not intrude, for it would only increase your grief.

My affliction is an expression that bears a marked emphasis; it has a tone entirely its own. I do not know if I am more struck with its pity or its silence. At the sound of such words, a stranger might be touched with its pity, but a friend would shrink from prying into the secrets of a heart that so delicately conceals bitterness.

The one and only thing the psalmist wants to share is the prescription that soothes his pain and sustains his spirit, "Unless Your law had been my delight, I would then have perished in my affliction. I will never forget Your precepts, for by them You have given me life" (Ps. 119:92-93). On mature reflection, the psalmist realizes that he would have perished in affliction if it had not been for a certain comfortable and delightful reflection from God's Word.

At any time, you and I may be exposed to a similar mental or spiritual depression through one of those numerous sorrows that enters the Christian's life. There are plenty of miry places on the way to heaven, and so it is wise to inquire diligently how this psalmist passed through them. I like to hear how a believer has been comforted, for that comforts me. I take a deep interest in the simple tale of any prisoner whose bonds the Lord has loosened. It would be a choice pleasure to join the songs of thanksgiving that warble from the lips of the grateful suppliants whose cries the Lord has heard.

GOD NEVER SLUMBERS. *Psalm 121:3*

God is everywhere, in every place, in every time. His eyes never sleep. His hands never rest. He is in the city traffic as well as the wilderness. Every place feels His footstep. Every time trembles at His presence.

It is a great comfort to discern God in all our trials. Do not say that these are evil times—no times are evil when God is there. His presence scatters all that is harmful. Do not think that evil circumstances have happened. They may seem greatly evil, but these clouds will break in blessings on your head. If you can see that your troubles are sent from God, it will change them from wasps that sting to bees that gather honey.

A present God! I cannot suggest a theme to make you more courageous. You will find it exceedingly helpful and comforting to discover God in the unimportant things. If we had a God for only great things and not also for little things, we would be miserable. Blessed be our heavenly Father. He that wings an angel, guides a sparrow. He that rolls a world along, molds a tear and marks its track when it trickles from your eye.

God is in the motion of a grain of dust as much as He is in the revolutions of the planets. God is in the sparkling of a firefly as truly as He is in the flaming comet. God is in your home, in your bedroom, in your office, and in your shop. Recognize God in every little thing.

"He shall give His angels charge over you, to keep you in all your ways. In their hands they shall bear you up, lest you dash your foot against a stone" (Ps. 91:11-12). Why? Lest you fall from a mountain peak? No, lest you dash your foot against a stone. A great Providence keeps us safe.

THE LORD ON OUR SIDE. *Psalm 124:1*

If you are a true child of God, you will go through deep waters, and trials will chill you to the bone. Trials will seem to sweep you off your feet, take away your foothold, and carry you along their rapid currents. You must expect trials.

After you have endured them, do not delude yourself with the promise of relief. When one trouble has gone, another will come. It will probably be of a different character, and it will probably require the exercise of a different kind of grace and watchfulness. Instead of being in the water, you will be in the fire. You will not be chilled then; you will be heated like metal melting in a furnace. The fierce flames will be around you.

There are certain trials that would rapidly overwhelm our faith and consume us if we did not have a secret source of divine, omnipotent strength. If it were not true that the Lord sits enthroned at the flood and as King forever (Ps. 29:10), the rivers would long ago have overwhelmed us. If it were not that He makes the flaming fire His messenger and the burning heat His servant, we would be utterly consumed (Is. 43:2).

You may expect that between here and heaven, if you have not met with it yet, you will have enough trouble to destroy you unless the Lord is your Helper. Most of us can sing with the psalmist, "If it had not been the LORD who was on our side . . . then the waters would have overwhelmed us, the stream would have gone over our soul" (Ps. 124:1, 4).

YOU ANSWERED ME. *Psalm 138:3*

No proof is so convincing as experience. No one doubts the power of prayer after receiving an answer of peace. It is the distinguishing mark of the true and living God that He hears and answers the pleas of His people. The gods do not hear or answer. Jehovah is the God that hears and answers prayer.

There was a special day in David's life when he cried more fervently than usual. He was weak, wounded, worried, and weary. Like a child, he cried to his Father. It was a bitter, earnest, and eager prayer, as natural and as plaintive as the cry of a baby, and the Lord answered it!

Can there be an answer to a cry, to an inarticulate wail of grief? Yes, for our heavenly Father is able to interpret tears and cries. He replies to their inner sense in a way that fully meets the case. The answer came the day the cry ascended. Prayer rises to heaven rapidly and mercy returns to earth quickly.

The statement of this verse is one that all believers can make. When it can be substantiated with facts, we should boldly proclaim it, for it is to God's glory. Well might David say, "I will worship," when he felt bound to say, "You answered me." We cannot forsake the Lord, for He has heard our prayers.

God knows all my ways. *Psalm 139:3*

If you were to remove from the Bible all the stories about afflicted men and women, all the psalm of the sorrowful, all the promises for the distressed, and all the passages for the children of grief, the Bible would be a small book.

It is clear not only that the poor and needy are observed by our great King (Ps. 139:3), but also that the Holy Spirit's pen has been greatly occupied in recording their affairs. You who are poor, needy, sick, and sorrowing: may the Lord comfort your heart. On that day, when history's great books are read, your story will appear, and God will get as great a glory out of what He has done for you as from any deeds of His love that are recorded in the Bible.

In the New Testament, our Lord Jesus Christ lived among the fishermen and peasants, and He called the poor to be His disciples. "God has chosen the foolish things of the world to put to shame the wise, and God has chosen the weak things of the world to put to shame the things which are mighty; and the base things of the world and the things which are despised God has chosen, and the things which are not, to bring to nothing the things that are" (1 Cor. 1:27).

When your situation is recorded on high, it will be worthwhile to be among the poor, the despised, and the sad, for you will magnify the dignity of our Lord.

Praying in the Holy Spirit, I say this to bless and cheer some depressed saint.

GOD IS EVERYWHERE. *Psalm 139:9*

Wherever you are, your heavenly Father watches over you. He looks on you as if there were no other created being in the entire world. His eye is fixed on you every moment.

You cannot banish me from my Lord. Send me to the snows of Siberia, and I will have the eyes of God on me. Send me to Australia, and He will visit me. Send me to the utmost verge of this globe, and I will still have God's eye on me. Put me in the desert, where there is not one blade of grass, and His presence will cheer me.

Let me go to sea in the howling tempest, with winds shrieking, the waves lifting their mad hands to the skies, and I will have the eye of God on me. Let me sink. Let my gurgling voice be heard in the waves. Let my body lie down in the caverns of the sea, and still the eye of God will be on my very bones. "If I take the wings of the morning, and dwell in the uttermost parts of the sea, even there Your hand shall lead me, and Your right hand shall hold me" (Ps. 139:9-10). And in the resurrection day, my every atom will be tracked in its wanderings.

The eye of God is everywhere. Providence is universal. God's eye is on your friends who are far away. If you have beloved ones moving, wherever they go, God will keep them.

Wherever you are, whatever your case, God will be with you. His eye is at the wedding, the funeral, the cradle, and the grave. In the battle, God's eye is looking through the smoke. The revolution of God's hand is managing the masses who have broken from their rulers. In the earthquake, Jehovah is manifested. In all seasons, always, in all dangers, and in all regions of the earth, there is the hand of God.

HE HEALS BROKEN HEARTS. *Psalm 147:3*

The Holy Spirit mentions this as a part of the glory of God and as a reason to declare His praise. The Lord is a Healer. He restores the brokenhearted. The leaders of the earth think that they are great through their loftiness. But Jehovah becomes great by His condescension. The Most High associates with the sick and the sorry, the wretched and the wounded. He walks the hospitals as the good Physician. His deep sympathy with mourners is a special mark of His goodness.

Few will associate with the depressed, but Jehovah chooses their company and stays until He has healed them with His comfort. He wants to handle and heal the brokenhearted. He applies the ointment of grace and the soft bandages of love. He binds the bleeding wounds of those convicted of sin. This is Godly compassion.

Well may those people to whom He has acted graciously praise Him. The Lord is always healing and binding. This is not new work for Him. He has done it from old. It is not a thing of the past, of which He is now weary, for He is still healing, still binding. Come, brokenhearts. Come to the Physician who never fails to heal. Show your wound to Him who tenderly binds them up.

THE LORD'S CHASTENING. *Proverbs 3:11*

Deep water conceals great treasure. Pearls lie there, and masses of precious things that make a miser's eye gleam like a star. Down deep are the wrecks of old Spanish galleons lost centuries ago. There they lie, huge mines of wealth. So it is with the deep judgments of God (Ps. 36:6). Wisdom is concealed there, treasures of love and faithfulness. If we could only understand that there is as much wisdom in some of God's deep afflictions as there is in the creation of the world. God afflicts His people artistically. His is never a random blow. Only marvelous skill lies in the Lord's chastening. Thus we are told, "Do not despise the chastening of the LORD, nor detest His correction" (Prov. 3:11).

Treasures are concealed in the great depths. We do not receive or even perceive the present and immediate benefit of some of our afflictions. Affliction in our youth may be intended for the ripening of our old age. Today's affliction may have no meaning for today; it may be designed for circumstances fifty years ahead.

Why then will you not let the Lord have time? Why are you in a hurry? Why do you perpetually ask, "Explain this now, and show me the present motive and reason." "A thousand years in Your sight are like yesterday when it is past, and like a watch in the night" (Ps. 90:4). The mighty God takes mighty time to work out His grand results. Therefore, be content to let the treasures lie at the bottom of the deep. Everything that is stored in the great deep of eternal purpose belongs to you. Rejoice in it. Let it lie there until God chooses to raise it for your spiritual enrichment.

WAYS OF PLEASANTNESS. *Proverbs 3:17*

You that are lowest on the scale of visible joy, you that are broken like a shipwreck, you that are a mass of pain, you that are in poverty, will you give your Lord a good word? Will you say, "Though He slay me, yet will I trust Him" (Job 13:15)?

At our worst, we are better off than the world at its best. Godly poverty is better than unhallowed riches. Our sickness is better than the sinner's health. Our depression is better than the earth's honors. We consider it better to suffer pain equal to the torture of death than bathe in sin's pleasures. We will take God at all the discount you can put on Him. You can have the world with all the compound interest that you are able to get from such a sham.

God's people sing. They are children of the sun, birds of the morning, and flowers of the day. Wisdom's "ways are ways of pleasantness, and all her paths are peace" (Prov. 3:17). We hear the full-toned, high-ascending music that never ceases. Its soft cadences are with us when darkness thickens on darkness and the heart is heavily oppressed.

Sorrowful, yet always rejoicing. Do you know this paradox? Some of us have known it for many years.

RICHES DO NOT PROFIT. *Proverbs 11:4*

When a Christian is permitted to grow rich, what a trial of faith is hidden in that condition! It is one of the severest of providential tests. Where I have seen one fail through poverty, I have known fifty who failed through riches. When our friends have a long stretch of prosperity, they should invite believers to offer special prayer that they may be preserved. Thick wet clay is heavy stuff to walk on, and when our feet slip into it, it adheres and makes traveling to heaven very difficult. If we do not cling to wealth, it will not harm us. But there is a lot of glue in money.

You who have no riches may yet find a test in your daily mercies. Your domestic comfort, that loving wife, or those dear children may tempt you to walk by sight instead of faith (1 Cor. 5:7). Even good health, or the absence of depression, or the help of friends and relatives may make you self-content and keep you from God.

To be in the dark, altogether in the dark, is a great thing for faith. Then you are sure that what you see is not seen of the flesh but is in very deed a vision of spiritual faith. To be under a cloud is a trial, but not one-half so much a trial as it is to always have the light of this world. We are so likely to mistake the light of carnal comfort for the light of God that it is well to see how we do without it.

THE FURNACE FOR GOLD. *Proverbs 17:3*

Gold is put into the furnace because it is gold (Prov. 17:3). It is useless to try to refine rubbish there. A first-rate diamond will undergo more cutting than an inferior one. The great Owner of heaven's jewels uses a sharper cutting machine on the most valuable stones. Our King desires that we have many facets to reflect the glory of His name.

You often think that Jesus does not care because He has not interposed with a great miracle. Gradually, you are getting poorer or becoming more afflicted in body. You had hoped for a miracle. My dear friend, sometimes God works a greater wonder when He sustains people in trouble than by delivering them. To let the bush burn with fire and not be consumed (Ex. 3:2) is a greater thing than quenching the flame and saving the bush.

Possibly, the hard suspicion that Jesus does not care takes another form. I do not ask the Lord to work a miracle, but I do ask Him to cheer my heart and apply the promises to my soul. I want His Spirit to visit me so that my pain may be forgotten in the delight of His presence. I want to feel the full assurance of the Savior's presence, that this present trial will be swallowed up in a far greater weight of joy (2 Cor. 4:17). Yet to my regret, the Lord hides His face, and this makes my trial all the heavier.

What a mercy that you can never sink lower than grace! When you come to your lowest point, God interposes. The tide turns when you reach the full ebb. The darkest part of night is farthest from the rising of sun. Believer, be of good courage.

WHEREVER HE WISHES. *Proverbs 21:1*

God knows what He intends. You and I begin with a plan, and we deviate from it when we see something better. With God, however, there is no defect of judgment that would require a change of plan, no defect that would drive Him from His first plan. With Him there is no shadow of turning (James 1:17). Depend on it. It would be an insult to the Supreme Intellect if we supposed that He worked randomly.

This is a truth: God has one boundless purpose that embraces all the things that He permits and ordains. Without denying free choice, we believe that God foresees the curious twisting of human will, and that He overrules all for His own purpose. God knows and numbers all of humanity's inclinations and devices; in the mighty sweep of His plan, He takes them all into account. He never swerves; what He has resolved to do, He will do. The settled purpose of His heart will stand forever.

The will of God must be done. Without effort, He molds all events into His chosen form. In the spheres of mind and matter, His dominion is absolute. "The king's heart is in the hand of the LORD, like the rivers of water; He turns it wherever He wishes" (Prov. 21:1). God can bend the thoughts of people as easily as we can turn on a water faucet.

Tested believer, the Lord will be as faithful to you as He has been to me. The Lord will not fail you. Do not be discouraged, "the eternal God is your refuge, and underneath are the everlasting arms" (Deut. 33:27). You will conquer. You will be delivered, and God will be glorified.

THE ROD OF CORRECTION. *Proverbs 22:15*

There are actions of providence that fill you with dismay. You not only have trouble within, but also, strange as it seems, trouble without. It partly arises from friends who say that you are mad for believing in Christ; would to God that they were bitten with the same madness. It also arises from circumstances over which you have no control. It is not unusual for God to wreck the vessel in which His people sail, although He fulfills His promise that not a hair of their heads will perish. Do not wonder if He causes two seas to meet around your boat, that there is nothing but a few boards and broken pieces of the ship left. If you have faith in Christ, He will bring you safe to shore.

It is not at all uncommon for the Lord to add the outward lashing of affliction to the inner scourging of conscience. This double scourging is meant for proud, stubborn hearts, that they may be humbly brought to Jesus' feet. For in us it may be said, as Solomon said of the child, "Foolishness is bound up in the heart of a child; the rod of correction will drive it far from him" (Prov. 22:15). God is bringing folly out of you by the sting of His rod.

"Blows that hurt cleanse away evil, as do stripes the inner depths of the heart" (Prov. 20:30). The Lord is making your wounds black and blue. I should not wonder if He will let them be infected until you say with Isaiah, "From the sole of the foot even to the head, there is no soundness in it, but wounds and bruises and putrefying sores; they have not been closed or bound up, or soothed with ointment" (Is. 1:6). It is then that eternal mercy will take advantage of your extreme distress and bring you closer to Christ.

APPLES OF GOLD. *Proverbs 25:11*

I seem to be standing increasingly alone, for many of my friends are melting away. My brothers, my comrades, and my friends are leaving me for the better land. We have enjoyed holy and happy fellowship in days of peace. We have stood shoulder to shoulder in the Lord's battle, but they are now melting away. One has gone and then another, and before I look around, another will have departed. I see them for a moment, and then they vanish from my gaze. They do not rise into the air like our Divine Master (Acts 1:9), but I am persuaded that they do rise. It is only the poor body that descends, and that descent is only for a little while. They rise to be forever with the Lord, and the grief is ours who are left behind.

Why this constant thinning of our ranks when the warfare is so difficult? Why are the finest removed? I am sad. I could best express myself in a flood of tears as I survey the line of newly dug graves, but I restrain myself and look on it in a clearer light. The Master is gathering His ripest fruit, and well does He deserve them. He is putting His apples of gold in settings of silver (Prov. 25:11).

When we realize that it is the Lord who desires them to be with Him (John 17:24), it dries our tears and makes us rejoice. We are no longer bewildered because we now understand why the dearest and best are going home:

> Father, I long, I faint to see
> The place of Thine abode;
> I'd leave Thine earthly courts and flee
> Up to Thy seat, My God.

TOMORROW. *Proverbs 27:1*

A Christian can look forward to tomorrow with joy. Tomorrow is a happy thing. It is one stage nearer glory, one step nearer heaven, one more mile sailed across life's dangerous sea, one mile closer to home.

Tomorrow is a fresh lamp of the fulfilled promise that God has placed in His firmament. Use it as a guiding star or as a light to cheer your path. Tomorrow the Christian may rejoice. You may say that today is black, but I say that tomorrow is coming. You will mount on its wings and flee. You will leave sorrow behind.

Look forward to tomorrow with ecstasy, because our Lord may come. Tomorrow, Christ may be on this earth. "Therefore you also be ready, for the Son of Man is coming at an hour you do not expect" (Matt. 24:44). Tomorrow, we may all be in heaven. Tomorrow, we may lean on Christ's breast.

Tomorrow, or perhaps before then, this head will wear the crown (James 1:12). This arm will wave the palm (Rev. 7:9). This lip will sing the song (Rev. 5:13). This foot will walk the golden streets (Rev. 21:18). Tomorrow, this heart will be full of immortal, everlasting, eternal bliss (Rev. 21:4). Be of good cheer, fellow Christian, tomorrow can have nothing negative for you.

"Do not boast about tomorrow, for you do not know what a day may bring forth" (Prov. 27:1); rather, comfort yourself with tomorrow. You have a right to do that. You cannot have a bad tomorrow. It may be the best day of your life, for it may be your last day on earth.

LEST I BE POOR. *Proverbs 30:9*

Adversity! Things are going wrong, or so you think. You have to give up that fine home with its lovely gardens and move into small rooms. You must cut expenses. Your income has shrunk terribly. You hardly know how you will support your loved ones.

Pray, "Uphold me according to Your word, that I may live; and do not let me be ashamed of my hope. Hold me up, and I shall be safe" (Ps. 119:116-117).

Use Agur's prayer, "Two things I request of You (deprive me not before I die): Remove falsehood and lies far from me; give me neither poverty nor riches—feed me with the food allotted to me; lest I be full and deny You, and say, 'Who is the LORD?' Or lest I be poor and steal, and profane the name of my God" (Prov. 30:7-9).

He that kept you when you were rich will not shun you now that you are poor. Ask Him to uphold you according to the promise. He is able to do it, and He is as willing as He is able.

ALL IS VANITY. *Ecclesiastes 1:2*

It may be well to make the best of both worlds, but of this poor world nothing can be made unless it is viewed in the light of another. This is a poor withering life at its best, for we will fade as a leaf. Unless we purposely live with a view to the next world, we cannot make much out of our present existence. The rotten rags of this poor world of time and sense can never be made into an array in which any Christian would care to dress.

At the same time, do not be frightened at the ugly form this life sometimes takes, for it is, after all, "a vapor that appears for a little time and then vanishes away" (James 4:14). Do not be overjoyed like the person who hoped to embrace a goddess and was deceived by a cloud. Sorrows over vapors are scarcely worth the tears, nor do their joys deserve a smile. Vanity and vapor are things that wise people set small store by. Children may be pleased with soap bubbles blown from a pipe, but adults who have put away childish things should not be greatly moved by the things of this life. They are only bubbles of less brilliance and less substance than those that delight a child.

"'Vanity of vanities,' says the Preacher; 'vanity of vanities, all is vanity'" (Eccl. 1:2). Let the lower lights burn dimly before your eyes, for they are mere sparks and soon quenched. Let us tightly grip the eternal and loosely hold the temporal. The jewels of eternity will glitter in our crowns when all things pass away. The trifles of this life are like flowers that children pick in the meadows; they wither in their hands as they carry them home.

A TIME TO DIE. *Ecclesiastes 3:2*

God has fixed the time of our death (Job 7:1). It is useless to dream of living here forever. A time of departure must come unless the Lord returns. If He returns before our departure, then "we who are alive and remain shall be caught up . . . in the clouds to meet the Lord in the air. And thus we shall always be with the Lord" (1 Thess. 4:17).

Here, diseases wait in ambush, eager to slay. But, "He shall cover you with His feathers, and under His wings you shall take refuge. . . . You shall not be afraid of the terror by night, nor of the arrow that flies by day, nor of the pestilence that walks in darkness, nor of the destruction that lays waste at noonday. A thousand may fall at your side, and ten thousand at your right hand; but it shall not come near you" (Ps. 91:4-7). We are immortal until our work is done. Then we shall receive our summons home.

If duty calls you into danger, if you have to nurse the contagious sick, do not hold back. You will not die by a stray arrow from death's quiver; only God can take your breath. Your death is not left to chance. It is determined by a heavenly Father's gracious will; therefore, do not be afraid. Now do not be reckless and rush into danger without reason, for that is madness. Yet never fear to face death when God's voice calls you into danger.

Here is comfort: If the Father of our Lord Jesus arranges all, then our friends do not die untimely deaths. Believers are not cut off before their time. God has appointed a time to harvest His fruit. Some are sweet, even in the early spring, and He gathers them. Others, like baskets of summer fruit, are taken while the year is young. Yet some remain until autumn mellows them. Be sure of this, each will be gathered in season. God has appointed the commencement, the continuation, and the conclusion of your mortal life.

THE HOUSE OF MOURNING. *Ecclesiastes 7:2*

My dear friend, you have been in "the house of mourning," and I have been there with you. This past week, we have seen so many funeral processions on our crowded streets that it begins to be common. Some of you may be saying, "No one has suffered as we have." Do not say this. The path of sorrow has been well-trodden. Many others have had their teeth broken with gravel (Lam. 3:16) and have drunk wormwood (Lam. 3:15). You are not alone.

Many have gone to the house of mourning to offer comfort. I can say from the deepest recesses of my soul that this week I have sorrowed almost as much as if I had been the real mourner. Often, I have gone directly from one deathbed to another. It is not pleasant, but it is rewarding. Do not be afraid to go to the house of mourning. Go and comfort those who hurt. It is imperative that every believer visit the sick. Go and help those who mourn and give them comfort. "Better to go to the house of mourning than to go to the house of feasting" (Eccl. 7:2).

In a little while, death may again be in our midst. If God appoints death to you, you will surely die. One way or another, you may soon be called "to go to the house of mourning." Do not be afraid, child of God, for the Holy Spirit will so reveal Jesus by your bedside that it will be a Bethel (Gen. 12:8).

LOOKING TO THE END. *Ecclesiastes 7:8*

The world lives for the present. The Christian lives for the future. You must have the cross or you will not receive "the crown of glory" (1 Pet. 5:4). You must wade through the mire or you will never walk the golden pavement (Rev. 21:21). Cheer up, Christian. Let this truth encourage you: "The end of a thing is better than its beginning."

See that creeping, contemptible worm that you want to sweep away? That is the beginning. See that insect with the gorgeous wings playing in the sunbeams and sipping at the flower bells. It is full of happiness and life. That is the end. That worm, that caterpillar, that maggot is you. You are to be content with that until you are wrapped in death.

You cannot tell what you will be like after death. All we know is this, "We are children of God; and it has not yet been revealed what we shall be, but we know that when He is revealed, we shall be like Him, for we shall see Him as He is" (1 John 3:2).

See that rough diamond on the jeweler's wheel? Carefully it is turned and cut on all sides, and it loses much that seems costly. Do you see it now? A glittering ray flows from the greatly cut diamond. Christian, compare yourself to such a diamond. You are one of God's jewels, and this is the time of cutting. You must endure it, so be of good courage. "Through faith and patience inherit the promises" (Heb. 6:12). "'They shall be Mine,' says the LORD of hosts, 'on the day that I make them My jewels'" (Mal. 3:17).

DO IT WITH YOUR MIGHT. *Ecclesiastes 9:10*

Listen to the people James describes: "Today or tomorrow we will go to such and such a city, spend a year there, buy and sell, and make a profit" (James 4:13). They have plenty of time. They can make a selection according to their pleasure and go where and when they like. They see themselves entering a city, and, with a prophetic glance, they are fully assured that they will "spend a year there." Of course, a year is a small matter for them; if they please, they will stay longer. They may allot themselves a lease for three, seven, fourteen years; at least they talk as if they could.

They are going into the city to "buy and sell." They are sure of that. They will not be laid up with sickness. They do not fear that accident or disease will keep them from the market or hinder them from actively transacting business. They are going to buy and sell, and such is their confidence that they feel sure to make a profit. The markets cannot fall below the price they have fixed in their minds. Neither will they have bad debts nor incur other losses, for they have decided that they will "make a profit."

They are self-made people, and they mean to go on making themselves until they put on the finishing stroke by adding a few more thousands. They have visions of making a fortune. Ah, you prophets, you are going to your graves. The tomb will be your only estate, grave clothes your only possession.

Let none of us talk of what we resolve to do at some future date. Let us, instead, look well to the present, for that is all the time we can be sure of, and there may be little enough of that. "Whatever your hand finds to do, do it with your might; for there is no work or device or knowledge or wisdom in the grave where you are going" (Eccl. 9:10). Thus said the wise man. Let the wise heed his counsel.

THE BANQUETING HOUSE. *Song of Solomon 2:4*

It is blessed praying when you lean on the Beloved. You feel that you cannot be denied. You have entered the King's court with your advocate, and you lay your prayer at the foot of the throne. Then the Prince Himself puts His seal and stamp of love on your requests.

This is the sweet way to be content while suffering. It is easy to suffer when Jesus makes your sickbed. This is the divine method, and believe me, no sacred work can continue unless you lean on the Beloved.

You who are in business, you with your families, or your shops, or your fields, or your enterprises, it will be poor living unless you lean on your Beloved in all things. If you can bring your daily cares, your domestic troubles, your family sicknesses, your personal infirmities, and your losses and crosses to Jesus, it will be easy and happy living. When the soul reclines in the embrace of divine love, it is as cool and comfortable as a royal banqueting house spread for a king's banquet, even when the furnace coals burn hot.

Saints, strive after more of this. We are such lovers of caring for ourselves that we want to set up our own accounts. We long to run when our legs are too weak; we aspire to stand alone when the only result can be a fall. Give up this yearning, which is our weakness. Be like a baby lying in its mother's arms. Let us be conscious that our strength is not in ourselves but in the dear embrace that holds us up.

THE RAIN IS OVER. *Song of Solomon 2:11*

The time is approaching when we will lie on our deathbeds. Oh long-expected day, come quickly! The best thing a Christian can do is die and be with Christ, for this is "far better" (Phil. 1:23) than life in the flesh. When we lie on our deathbeds panting out our life, we shall remember that the winter is forever past. No more of this world's trials and troubles are ours, for "the rain is over and gone" (Song 2:11). No more stormy doubts, no more dark days of affliction.

We have come to the land Beulah (Is. 62:4). We sit on beds of spices. We can almost see the celestial city on the hilltop, just the other side of death's narrow stream. "The time of singing has come" (Song 2:12). Angelic songs are heard in the sickroom. The heart sings, and midnight melodies cheer the quiet entrance of the grave. "Though I walk through the valley of the shadow of death, I will fear no evil" (Ps. 23:4). These words are sweet birds that sing in the groves by the side of the river Jordan.

The voice of the turtledove is heard in the land (Song 2:12). Calm, peaceful, and quiet, the soul rests in the consciousness that there is now no condemnation to those who are in Christ Jesus (Rom. 8:1). "The fig tree puts forth her green figs, and the vines with the tender grapes give a good smell" (Song 2:13).

You who are believers in Christ, look forward to death with great joy. Expect it as your springtime of life, the time when your real summer will come and your winter will be over forever.

LED BY A LITTLE CHILD. *Isaiah 11:6*

It may be, dear friend, that you are in trouble. If so, I pray that your affliction may be the black horse that mercy rides to your door. It is a sad, sad thing that the better the Lord deals with some people the worse they are. On the other hand, there are hearts that turn to the Lord when He afflicts them. When they drift into deep waters, when they can scarcely find bread to eat, when sickness attacks their bodies, and especially when their children are afflicted, they begin to think of God. Blessed is the discipline of the great Father in these cases. It is well for the troubled if trials bruise their hearts to repentance, for repentance leads them to seek and find pardon.

We read of a royal official's affliction (John 4:46-53). His child, a little boy whom he dearly loved, was sick with a deadly fever. No doubt he had tried all the known remedies and had sent for every physician that could be found. Then he heard of Jesus of Nazareth, who at Cana had turned the water into wine (John 2:9) and who had done many mighty works (John 21:25). In desperate hope and with eager petition, this royal official seeks Jesus. He might never have thought of seeking Jesus had it not been for his dear dying boy. It often happens that children do better work than angels accomplish, because they lead their parents to God and heaven.

Children wrap themselves around our hearts, and when we see their pain we are full of anguish. We cry, "God, spare my child! Lord, have mercy on my little one." The first prayers of many are brought by grief over dearly loved little ones. Is it not written, "a little child shall lead them" (Is. 11:6)?

So it was with this official. He was brought to Jesus by trouble, by anxiety over a child. He was brought to Jesus' mercy by affliction.

A BITTER DRINK. *Isaiah 24:9*

Earthly security is the worst foe of confidence in God. If I say, "Soul, you have many goods laid up for many years, take your ease, eat, drink, and be merry" (Luke 12:19), then the road of faith is barricaded. Adversity sets the barn on fire, and thus "the many goods laid up for many years" are gone and can no longer block the path of faith. Blessed axe of sorrow, clear a path to God by cutting down the thick trees of my earthly comfort.

When I say, "My mountain stands firm, I shall never be moved" (Ps. 30:6-7), the visible fortification, rather than the invisible protector, engages my attention. Then the earthquake shakes the rocks, the mountain is swallowed up, and I must fly to the immovable Rock of ages to build my confidence. Worldly ease is a great foe of faith. It loosens the joints of holy strength and snaps the muscles of sacred courage.

The balloon never rises until the ropes are cut, and affliction does this same sharp service for believing souls. When the wheat sleeps comfortably in the husks, it is useless; it must be threshed from its resting place before its value can be known.

I make this sad confession. When my soul is happy and things prosper, I do not live so near to God as I do in the midst of trials and depression. When the world's bread is sugared and buttered, we eat it until we become sick. Then the world changes our diet, filling our mouths with vinegar and making our drink bitter. The world's wells are full of sweet but poisonous water. We pitch our tents at the mouth of the well and drink until we forget the well of Bethlehem. When earth's waters become bitter like Marah's stream (Ex. 15:23), we turn away sick and faint. But this affliction brings us to our God, just as the barking dog drives the wandering sheep to the shepherd's hand.

EVERLASTING STRENGTH.   *Isaiah 26:4*

Some of you have passed through deep waters and have not drowned. Some of you have been sustained for forty years in the wilderness, and you should know God's faithfulness. Yet I am ashamed that you become disheartened and discouraged. But most of all, I am ashamed when you fall into depression, for I have been there myself.

When your vision is obscured, you walk in darkness and are greatly molested by doubts and haunted with fears. You can hardly grasp anything to believe in. It is in this season of acute distress, when the world has no comfort to offer, that God's Word can minister infinite delight as it soothes and heals the heart's sorrows. Surely He who has preserved you in all your previous distress will not desert you in your present adversities.

If you had not taken delight in God's Word, you would long ago have perished in your affliction. Look back, God has been sufficient, so what reason do you have to suspect that He will not befriend you to the end? It is a great comfort to stand on divine faithfulness. May the Holy Spirit help you grasp this delightful truth.

Rejoice in the faithfulness of God. You are not poor, for your Father is rich. You are not deserted, for God is with you. If only I could touch your heart and make you see how God is working for you even now. Surely you will be helped. "Trust in the LORD forever, for in YAH, the LORD, is everlasting strength" (Is. 26:4).

THE HOLLOW OF HIS HAND. *Isaiah 40:12*

Are you severely tested with cares, losses, and crosses? Are you dreading tomorrow? Is your business failing? Is a loss staring you in the face? Are you sorrowing over that precious child who lies in a little casket? Do you have a sick wife? Day by day, do you see fresh signs of the great loss that is certainly awaiting you?

My Master has sent me with His blessed precious promises, and they are more than sufficient to comfort every sorrowing saint. Beloved, remember everything that happens to you comes in the course of divine providence. Your loving heavenly Father has foreseen, foreknown, and, I venture to say, foreordained it all. The medicine that you have to drink is bitter, but the unerring Physician has measured the ingredients drop by drop and mixed them in a way that will best work for your highest good.

Nothing in this world happens by chance. Our great God has "measured the waters in the hollow of His hand, mea-sured heaven with a span and calculated the dust of the earth in a measure" (Is. 40:12). Our great God makes the clouds His chariot and He walks on the wings of the wind (Ps. 104:3). This same God cares for you with such special care that He has numbered the very hairs of your head (Matt. 10:30). He even puts your tears in His bottle (Ps. 56:8). You may rest assured that even those experiences that are causing much sorrow are in accord with His eternal counsel and decree.

I trust that these divine promises make you forget your misery and poverty.

FEAR NOT. *Isaiah 41:10*

In trouble, the Lord will always be near. If you have a Gethsemane, if you have to drink the bitter cup, the Lord will be with you. His presence will encourage you, and you will be able to say, "Nevertheless, not as I will, but as You will" (Matt. 26:39).

Do you say, "I am sick and depressed. I wish that I had more of life's comforts, but my resources are sadly limited?" Your Savior was tested in all points as you are (Heb. 4:15), but He always set the Lord before Him. Thus He was able to say, "O LORD, You are the portion of my inheritance and my cup; You maintain my lot. The lines have fallen to me in pleasant places; yes, I have a good inheritance" (Ps. 16:5).

Let everything go. If God is with you, you will be upheld. Let friends die one after another. Let earthly comforts fade like autumn leaves. If you set the Lord before you, there is fullness of joy in God's every attribute. There is heaven in every glimpse of Jesus' face, overwhelming bliss in every drop of Jehovah's everlasting love. You will not fail. You will not be discouraged. You will even sing His praises in the fiercest fires.

To you He says, "Fear not, for I am with you; be not dismayed, for I am your God. I will strengthen you, yes, I will help you, I will uphold you with My righteous right hand" (Is. 41:10). "When you pass through the waters, I will be with you; and through the rivers, they shall not overflow you. When you walk through the fire, you shall not be burned, nor shall the flame scorch you" (Is. 43:2).

I WILL STRENGTHEN YOU. *Isaiah 41:10*

When called to serve or to suffer, we take inventory of our strength and find it to be less than we thought and less than we need. Do not let your heart fail when you have this promise to fall back on, for it guarantees all that you can possibly need. God has strength omnipotent, and He can communicate that strength to you, and His promise is that He will do so. He will be the food of your soul and the health of your heart, and thus He will give you strength. There is no telling how much power God can put into a person. When divine strength comes, human weakness is no longer a hindrance.

Do we remember times of labor and trial when we received such special strength that we wondered at ourselves? In the midst of danger, we were calm. Under bereavement, we were resigned. In slander, we were self-contained. In sickness, we  were patient. The fact is that God gives unexpected strength when unusual trials come. We rise out of our feeble selves. Cowards play the hero, foolish ones have wisdom given them, and the silent receive in that moment what they shall speak.

My own weakness makes me shrink, but God's promise makes me brave. Lord, strengthen me according to Your Word.

I WILL HELP YOU. *Isaiah 41:10*

Yesterday's promise secured strength for what we have to do today, but this promise guarantees help when we cannot act alone. The Lord says, "I will help you." Strength within is supplemented by help from without. God can raise up allies in our warfare if it seems good in His sight. Even if He doesn't send human assistance, He Himself will be at our side, and this is even better. "Our august Ally" is superior to thousands of human helpers.

His help is timely, for He is a very present help in time of trouble (Ps. 46:1). His help is wise, for He knows how to give what is good for us. His help is effective, though futile is the help of friends. His help is more than help, for He carries all the burdens and supplies all the needs. "The LORD is my helper; I will not fear. What can man do to me?" (Heb. 13:6). Because He has already been our help, we feel confidence in Him for the present and the future.

Our prayer is, "LORD, be my helper" (Ps. 30:10).

Our experience is, "The Spirit also helps in our weaknesses" (Rom. 8:26).

Our expectation is, "I will lift up my eyes to the hills—from whence comes my help? My help comes from the LORD, who made heaven and earth" (Ps. 121:1).

Our song will be, "You, LORD, have helped me and comforted me" (Ps. 86:17).

YOU ARE MINE. *Isaiah 43:1*

Concerning spiritual and earthly things, to whom could we go but to Him who has been so good to us? Who else can supply our needs but Jehovah? Who can hold us up but God? Who can guide us but God? Who can keep us from falling into ruin but God? Who can, on an hour by hour basis, supply our desperate needs but God?

Our imaginations could not have conceived greater wealth than is ours in the covenant of grace. All things are ours, the gift of God. God being ours, the Infinite is ours, the Omniscient is ours, and the Omnipotent is ours. What a boundless, unfailing portion that always comes in due season.

Have you ever rested on Him and found Him to fail? Did you ever trust Him in vain? Are His promises false? Has He ever left you in deep waters? When you passed through the fire, did the flames burn you? Have you found your God to be a wilderness? Has He failed in the day of your difficulty?

"Fear not, for I have redeemed you; I have called you by your name; you are Mine. When you pass through the waters, I will be with you; and through the rivers, they shall not overflow you. When you walk through the fire, you shall not be burned, nor shall the flame scorch you. For I am the LORD your God" (Is. 43:1-3).

Beloved, our God has blessed and continues to bless, not by fits and starts but by a constant grace. He is a faithful friend. We are well supplied by our King.

I WILL BE WITH YOU. *Isaiah 43:2*

Jesus Christ is with you in every pang that rips your heart and in every pain that tears your body. Do you feel the sorrows of poverty? Jesus said, "Foxes have holes and birds of the air have nests, but the Son of Man has nowhere to lay His head" (Matt. 8:20). Are you sorrowing? "Jesus wept" at Lazarus' tomb (John 11:35). Have you been slandered and hurt? He said, "Reproach has broken My heart, and I am full of heaviness" (Ps. 69:20). Have you been betrayed? Remember, He had a friend who sold Him for the price of a slave (Matt. 26:15).

Every stormy sea that has tossed you has roared around His boat too. There is no adversity so dark, so deep, or so apparently pathless that you cannot discover the Crucified One's footsteps when you kneel. In the fires, in the rivers, in the cold night, and under the burning sun He cries:

> Fear not I am with you, O be not dismayed,
> For I am your God, I will still give you aid:
> I'll strengthen you, help you, and cause you to stand,
> Upheld by My gracious, omnipotent hand.
> When through the deep waters I call you to go,
> The rivers of sorrow will not overflow,
> For I will be with you, your trials to bless,
> And sanctify to you your deepest distress.
> When through fiery trials your pathway shall lie,
> My grace all-sufficient shall be your supply
> The flames shall not hurt you, I only design
> Your dross to consume and your gold to refine.

Free from the Flood. *Isaiah 43:2*

In losses, crosses, and troubles, you realize God's presence more conspicuously than ever. The Bible does not say that when you walk along the flowery path or rest on the soft green bank, "I will be with you." It does not say that when you walk on the close cut grass, which feels like a carpet under your feet, "I will be with you." I do not remember reading a Scripture promise like that. But God does say, "When you pass through the waters I will be with you" (Is. 43:2). He gives a special promise for a special time of trial. To meet the doubts of His troubled child, He says, "Fear not, for I have redeemed you; I have called you by your name; you are Mine" (Is. 43:1).

Our way to heaven lies through the flood, and through the flood we will go. God has ordained that no trouble, however great, and no persecution, however terrible, will stop the onward march of a soul predestined to eternal joy.

Suppose the river is deep and rapid and the torrent sweeps everything before it, still we shall go through it. We shall not be stopped or swept away because God has promised, "When you pass through the waters, I will be with you; and through the rivers, they shall not overflow you" (Is. 43:2).

FREE FROM THE FIRE. *Isaiah 43:2*

Believer, you will pass through the fire. But the Lord says that "when you walk through the fire, you shall not be burned, nor shall the flame scorch you" (Is. 43:2). This verse implies that your march through the flames will be quiet, calm, and safe. There is no need to increase your usual pace. If I had to go through literal fire, I would want to run and leap, but spiritually we are to walk through the fire.

There is a beautiful passage in the Psalter, "Yea, though I walk through the valley of the shadow of death, I will fear no evil" (Ps. 23:4). Walking is our pace; "whoever believes will not act hastily" (Is. 28:16) but will walk even through the fire.

What a blessing that "in all these things we are more than conquerors through Him who loved us. For I am persuaded that neither death nor life, nor angels nor principalities nor powers, nor things present nor things to come, nor height nor depth, nor any other created thing, shall be able to separate us from the love of God which is in Christ Jesus our Lord" (Rom. 8:37-39). Therefore, no trouble or trial can prevent our progress toward heaven. Through divine grace we will walk through the fire.

I WILL CARRY YOU. *Isaiah 46:4*

We are poor fools when we begin to deal with the future. It is a sea that we are not called to navigate. The present is the whole of life. When we enter the future, it is the present.

Still, some of you worry as you feel infirmities coming on. "What will I do when I come to extreme old age? My friends will be gone, and I will have no one to support me. When these fingers cannot work, when my brow is wrinkled and I can scarcely totter to my toil, what will I do?"

Ah! "His mercy endures forever" (Ps. 136:1). It does not stop at seventy or pause at eighty. It will carry you safely over ninety if your pilgrimage is prolonged.

The other day I visited a number of elderly people in a nursing home. Some had not been able to leave their bed in years, and I thought it far better to die than to live like that. But I was wrong. If Christ should make that bed as soft as downy pillows with His presence, there might be a glory in the nursing home and a heaven in the midst of poverty. They would learn that even in a nursing home, "His mercy endures."

"Even to your old age, I am He, and even to gray hairs I will carry you! I have made, and I will bear; even I will carry, and will deliver you" (Is. 46:4).

You whose days of weakness are coming, trust in the Lord and do not be afraid. He will not fail you. He will not forsake you.

In the Face of the Future. *Isaiah 46:10*

World events are not tangled, confused, or perplexing to God. "I am God, and there is none like Me, declaring the end from the beginning, and from ancient times things that are not yet done, saying, 'My counsel shall stand, and I will do all My pleasure'" (Is. 46:9-10).

Jehovah's power is apparent, from the least to the greatest, for God is in all and rules all. He guides the grain of dust in the March wind and the planets in their immeasurable pathways. He steers each drop of spray beaten back from the face of the rock. He leads the north star (Jer. 31:35). God is the dictator of destinies. He appoints both the ideas and the end. He is the King of kings (Rev. 19:16), ruling rulers and guiding counselors.

He is the same in the crash of battle or in the hush of peace. He is the same in famine or in the joy of an abundant harvest. He is Lord. He does according to His will, not only in heaven but among the inhabitants of this lower world.

The storm may rage, but all is well, for our Captain is the governor of storms. He who trod the waves of the Galilean lake is at the helm, and at His command winds and waves are quiet (Matt. 14:27).

Courage, dear friend. The Lord, the ever-merciful, has appointed every moment of sorrow and every pang of suffering. If He ordains the number ten, it can never rise to eleven, nor should you desire that it shrink to nine.

The Lord's time is best. The span of your life is measured to a hair's width. Restless soul, God ordains all, so let the Lord have His way.

THE FURNACE OF AFFLICTION. *Isaiah 48:10*

God's people are opposed by the current of the times, just as their Master was. It will cost sorrow and tears if you fully follow your Master. Do you want to be heavenly? I know some that, in a measure, already are. Their speech betrays that they have been with Jesus. Mark well this fact: they are a tested people and many of them are sick. We are little of what we should be until the Lord puts us on the anvil and uses the hammer. He is doing that now with some of you. Do not complain. Let the soft whisper of this promise sustain you, "I have tested you in the furnace of affliction" (Is. 48:10).

You have struggled hard, my brother, to rise out of your situation, but as often as you have striven you have fallen back to your hard lot. Do not be depressed. Live in your calling with contentment, because the Lord has said, "I have tested you in the furnace of affliction."

Young person, you have been to college, and you were completing your degree. You hoped to become a well-known scholar, but your health failed. Do not be depressed, for the Lord says, "I have tested you in the furnace of affliction."

Merchant, your firm is going to pieces, and you will be poor. But you have faith in God. It is the Lord's will that you should struggle. He says, "I have tested you in the furnace of affliction."

Mother, you have lost a little one, and another is sick, so you say, "I cannot bear it." But you will bear it, for the Lord says, "I have tested you in the furnace of affliction."

Are you alone? Weep no more. The Lord loves you when no one else does. He says, "I have tested you in the furnace of affliction."

I WILL NOT FORGET YOU. *Isaiah 49:15*

How long, O LORD? Will You forget me forever?" (Ps. 13:1). Can God forget you? Can Omnipotence forget you? Can unchanging love forget you? Can infinite faithfulness forget you? David seemed to think so, and some who are in deep trouble might agree.

You have been praying for mercy but cannot find it. You think that God forgets. You have been seeking peace but cannot find it. You think that God forgets. Perhaps you were the happiest of the happy as you bathed in the light of God's countenance, but now you are the unhappiest of the unhappy. You are at a distance from God, trying but unable to get back, and you think that God forgets. Wave upon wave of trouble rolls over you. You hardly have time to breathe between the surges of grief, and you are ready to perish with depression. You think God forgets.

That may be how it looks. But it is not possible for God to forget anything. "Can a woman forget her nursing child?" Mark that expression. The child still draws nourishment from her bosom and that is just what you are doing. You think God forgets, but you are living on what He daily gives. You would die if He did not give His grace and strength.

"Can a woman forget her nursing child, and not have compassion on the son of her womb? Surely they may forget, yet I will not forget you" (Is. 49:15-16). Hold on to this great truth, "I will not forget you."

God has not forgotten to be gracious. God has not forgotten you.

CONTINUALLY BEFORE ME. *Isaiah 49:16*

Can Jesus Christ, the Son of God (John 3:16), your brother (Matt. 12:50), ever forget His people? No! He has been made like us (Heb. 2:17). He can sympathize with our weakness and in all points He was tempted as we are (Heb. 2:18). He has inscribed us on the palms of His hand, and our walls are continually before Him (Is. 49:16).

Can we look into the face of the Crucified and believe that He is indifferent? It cannot be. Jesus is never indifferent to His people's trials. Do you think that Christ came from heaven to save you and that He is now indifferent? Do you think that He lived here for thirty years of work and weariness to redeem you and that He will now throw you away? Do you believe that He endured Gethsemane's terrible garden with its blood sweat and that He is not concerned about you? Do you think that He bore all of God's wrath on your behalf and that He now considers your salvation a trifling thing? Do you believe that He went to the grave (Matt. 27:59), rose again (Matt. 28:6), and is gone within the veil (Heb. 10:19-20) to plead your cause before God and that He has no real love for you? If what Christ has done for you cannot convince you, what can?

"Many waters cannot quench love, nor can the floods drown it" (Song 8:7).

TAUGHT BY THE LORD. *Isaiah 54:13*

All God's children go to school. The lesson is practical: we learn to obey. Our Lord took kindly to this lesson. He always did the things that pleased the Father. Now is our time of schooling and discipline, for we are learning the highest and best lesson of all: obedience. This brings our Lord close to us. We go to school to Christ and with Christ, thus we feel His qualifications to be our compassionate High Priest.

As swimming is learned only in the water, obedience is learned by doing and by suffering the divine will. Obedience cannot be learned at the university, unless it is at the College of Experience. You must allow the commandment to have its way with you. It will educate you. Who knows what it is to obey God to the fullest? Until you have laid aside your will in the most tender and painful respects, you will not know. To plead with God for the life of a beloved child, to see that dear child die, this is to learn obedience. To go alone and plead with God for the life of a husband or wife, to agonize with Him for the blessing, and then to be compelled to weep at a fresh grave and still be able to say, "The LORD gave, and the LORD has taken away; blessed be the name of the LORD" (Job 1:21), this is to learn obedience.

Our Lord as man was made to know by His suffering what full obedience meant. His was a practical, experimental, personal acquaintance with obedience, and in all this He comes near to us. A Son learning obedience, that is our Lord. May we not therefore walk joyfully with Him in all the rough paths of life? May we not safely lean on the arm of One who knows every inch of the way?

MY WAYS. *Isaiah 55:8*

God has not promised to rescue us according to our time schedule. If it appears that your prayers are unanswered, do not dishonor the Lord with unbelief. Waiting in faith is a high form of worship. In some respects, it excels the adoration of the shining ones above.

God delivers His servants in ways that exercise their faith. He would not have them lacking in faith, for faith is the wealth of the heavenly life. He desires that the trial of faith continues until faith grows strong and comes to full assurance. The sycamore fig never ripens into sweetness unless it is bruised; the same is true of faith. Tested believer, God will bring you through, but do not expect Him to bring you through in the way that human reason suggests, for that would not develop your faith:

God works in a mysterious way, His wonders to perform.
He plants His footsteps in the sea, and rides upon the storm.
You fearful saints, fresh courage take: the clouds you so much dread
Are big with mercy and shall break in blessings on your head.
Judge not the Lord by feeble sense, but trust Him for His grace;
Behind a frowning providence He hides a smiling face.
Blind unbelief is sure to err and scan His work in vain;
God is His own interpreter, and He will make it plain.

God has a way of His own. "My thoughts are not your thoughts, nor are my ways your ways, says the LORD" (Is. 55:8). "Stand still and consider the wondrous works of God" (Job 37:14). Obey Him, and that will be far more in accord with your position as a finite creature than the vain attempt to map out a course for your Creator.

In His love and pity. *Isaiah 63:9*

Jesus Christ is with you in your misery. Shadrach, Meshach, and Abednego never realized the presence of the Son of God so blessedly until they were thrown alive into Nebuchadnezzar's burning furnace (Dan. 3:20). There, His presence was so manifest that even the heathen king exclaimed, "I see four men loose, walking in the midst of the fire; and they are not hurt, and the form of the fourth is like the Son of God" (Dan. 3:25).

Many children do not receive special love while they are healthy, but when illness comes their mother's love concentrates on them. The Lord says to you who need comfort, "As one whom his mother comforts, so I will comfort you; and you shall be comforted" (Is. 66:13).

It was to His ancient people that God gave this gracious promise, "In all their affliction He was afflicted, and the Angel of His Presence saved them; in His love and in His pity He redeemed them; and He bore them and carried them all the days of old" (Is. 63:9). He still tenderly and lovingly deals with His tested and afflicted people. This thought should make you forget your poverty and misery.

Be of good courage weary pilgrim, for the years are flying fast and trials and troubles are flying just as fast. This world is, to the believer, like a country inn, where there are so many comings and goings that one cannot rest. Never mind. You are tarrying here only for one short night, and then you will be up and away to your eternal home.

WHAT WILL YOU DO? *Jeremiah 4:30*

When you meet with a sudden calamity, God is testing your love and faith. "When you are plundered, what will you do?" (Jer. 4:30). You thought you loved God; do you love Him now? You said that He was your Father, but that was when He blessed; is He your Father now that He chastens?

The ungodly kick against God; they only rejoice when He gives pleasant things. But His true children learn to kiss the rod. Can you believe in Jesus when you are in distress and needs assails you like an armed robber? You talk of faith in summer; do you have faith during the long winter nights? Can you trust the Lord when the fierce wilderness wind threatens to over-turn your tent?

Has the Holy Spirit given you the faith of God's elect to bear the strain? Faith that cannot endure trials is not faith. If the death of a child, or the loss of wealth, or depression, or disappointment, or sickness makes you doubt God, what will you do when you come to die? If these minor trials overwhelm you, what will you do in the last dread day when all things pass from your sight?

This is a trying time for your heart and a testing time for your graces. If all things are right, you will live closer to God in trials. If your bereavement brings you into the clear and ever-abiding sunlight of the Lord's face, be thankful that you lost what caused the eclipse.

RUN WITH THE FOOTMEN. *Jeremiah 12:5*

Just as the youths of Sparta were prepared for fighting by hard discipline, God's servants are trained for war with the affliction that He sends in the early days of their spiritual life. We must run with footmen or we will never be able to contend with horses. We must be thrown into the water or we will never learn to swim. We must hear the bullets whizzing or we will never become veteran soldiers.

The gardener knows that if the flowers are always kept in the hot house and raised in warm temperature they cannot live outdoors. Therefore, he does not give them too much heat; by degrees, he exposes them to the cold, that eventually they can survive in the open air. The only-wise God does not keep His servants in hothouses; He tenderly exposes them to trials, so that they know how to respond when trials come.

If you want to ruin children, never let them know hardship. If you want to prevent them from ever being useful, guard them from every kind of work and do not let them struggle. Pity them when they should be punished, supply all their wishes, avert all their disappointments, prevent all trouble, and you will surely train them to break your heart. If you put them where they must work, expose them to difficulties, purposely throw them into peril, then you will make them mature and ready for life.

My Master does not cradle His children when they ought to run alone. When they begin to run, He is not always putting out His hand; He lets them tumble and skin their knees. Thus they learn to walk carefully and to stand uprightly by the strength that faith confers on them.

Jordan's floodplain. *Jeremiah 12:5*

How will you do in the floodplain of the Jordan?" (Jer. 12:5). There, we will forget our wounds and think of "the crown of life which the Lord has promised to those who love Him" (James 1:12). We will bid adieu to loved ones; they will have the tears, but we will have the joy.

We will make the bed of death a throne. We will sit there and reign with Christ Jesus and recognize the Jordan as a tributary of the river of life. We will live in the land of Beulah (Is. 62:4) on the edge of the Jordan with our feet in the cold stream. We will sing of the better land and hear the songs of angels, as celestial breezes bring them across the narrow stream:

> My heart is with Him on His throne,
> And ill can brook delay,
> Each moment listening for His voice,
> "Make haste and come away."

This is how we will do in the floodplain of the Jordan. We will take off our clothes and put on the celestial robes. As one in exile longs to be delivered, as the galley slave longs to be separated from his oar, so we wait to be set free for glory and immortality:

> Since Jesus is mine, I will not fear undressing,
> But gladly put off these garments of clay;
> To die in the Lord is a comfort and blessing,
> Since Jesus to Glory through death led the way.

LOOKING TO THE LORD. *Jeremiah 17:7*

It is beautiful to see how the saints of old found comfort in God. When painful difficulties came, when troubles multiplied, when friends failed, and when earthly comforts were removed, they looked to the Lord, to the Lord alone. To them, God was a present reality. They looked to Him as their rock of refuge, their helper, their defense, and their very present help in time of trouble (Ps. 46:1). We can learn a valuable lesson from them. Lean on God and hold onto Him when heart and flesh are failing.

The apostle tells us, "Rejoice in the Lord always. Again I will say, rejoice!" (Phil. 4:4). Let us be thankful that the Lord lives, for "He is [our] rock" (Ps. 92:15). "Nor is there any rock like our God" (1 Sam. 2:2). He is ready to help those who serve Him. Believer, the fountain of your joy is never dried up. If, like Jonah, your plants are withered (Jon. 4:7), your God still lives. If, like Job, your goods have been plundered (Job 1:15), the highest good is still yours. Are the rivers dry? The ocean is full. Are the stars hidden? The heavenly sun shines on in eternal brightness. You have a possession that is unfading, a promise that is unfailing, and a Protector who is unchanging. Though you live in a faithless world, you dwell in a faithful God.

Do not go to friends, at best they are miserable comforters. "Cursed is the man who trusts in man and makes flesh his strength" (Jer. 17:5). Turn to the strong arm of God. "Blessed is the man who trusts in the LORD, and whose hope is in the LORD. For He shall be like a tree planted by the waters, which spreads out its roots by the river, and will not fear when heat comes; but its leaf will be green, and will not be anxious in the year of drought, nor will cease from yielding fruit" (Jer. 17:7-8).

153

EVERLASTING LOVE.   *Jeremiah 31:3*

Can our heavenly Father be unkind? "Oh give thanks to the LORD, for He is good! For His mercy endures for-ever" (Ps. 136:1). His name, His essence, is love, and "His mercy endures forever." He is the unchangeable God, the one "with whom there is no variation or shadow of turning" (James 1:17).

Heirs of heaven, can you believe that God is indifferent to His children? "If you then, being evil, know how to give good gifts to your children, how much more will your heavenly Father give the Holy Spirit to those who ask Him!" (Luke 11:13).

Have you ever felt that you would joyfully take your child's pain to relieve her suffering? Do you think that as a poor, fallen creature you have love and compassion, but that your heavenly Father has none? You may say with Jeremiah, "This I recall to mind, therefore I have hope. Through the LORD's mercies we are not consumed, because His compassions fail not. They are new every morning; great is Your faithfulness" (Lam. 3:21-23). Remember these verses, and know that the Lord cannot be careless about your welfare.

The eternal Jehovah loves you and chose you before the foundation of the world (Eph. 1:4). The snowcapped mountains are newborn babies compared with His love for you. He chose you! He might have passed you by, but He chose you to be His own. Jeremiah says, "The LORD has appeared of old to me saying, 'Yes, I have loved you with an everlasting love; therefore with lovingkindness I have drawn you'" (Jer. 31:3).

GOD'S FAITHFULNESS. *Lamentations 3:23*

Great is Your faithfulness," so great that there has never been an exception. Through the ages, our God has had billions of people to deal with. Yet there does not stand under heaven's cover, or above the stars, or in hell itself a single soul who can say that God is not absolutely faithful. No item in the list of our divine promises is unfulfilled. God remembers every promise that He ever made, and He honors each in the experience of those who believe in Him. They who trust in the Lord will find Him faithful, not only in great things, but also in little things. His faintest word will stand firm and steadfast. His least truth will never grow dim.

The glory of God's faithfulness is that no sin of ours has ever made Him unfaithful. Unbelief is a damning thing, yet even when we do not believe, God is faithful. His children might rebel. They might wander far from His statutes and be chastened with many stripes. Nevertheless, He says, "My lovingkindness I will not utterly take from him, nor allow My faithfulness to fail. My covenant I will not break, nor alter the word that has gone out of My lips" (Ps. 89:33-34). God's saints may fall under the cloud of His displeasure and provoke the Most High by their transgressions, still He will have compassion on them. He says, "I, even I, am He who blots out your transgressions for My own sake; and I will not remember your sins" (Is. 43:25). Thus, no sin of ours can make God unfaithful.

I HOPE IN HIM. *Lamentations 3:24*

What can threaten God's existence? Who can oppose His purpose? What can weaken His power? What can dim the clearness of His eye? What can diminish the tenderness of His heart? What can distract the wisdom of His judgment? "You are the same, and Your years will have no end" (Ps. 102:27).

Remember, child of God, you are a sheep that can never lose its Shepherd, a child that can never lose its Father. "I will never leave you nor forsake you" (Heb. 13:5), said Jesus as He revealed the Eternal Father's heart.

In dire straits, we still have a Father in heaven. A widow had been inconsolable at the loss of her husband, and her little child asked, "Mother, is God dead?" That question rebuked the woman and reminded her that she had a Guardian and Friend. "Your Maker is your husband, the LORD of hosts is His name" (Is. 54:5).

Listen, child of God, you can lose your possessions, but you cannot lose your God. Like Jonah, you can see your plant wither (Jon. 4:7), but your God remains. You may lose your land, but not your God. You may lose your savings, but not your Savior. Even if it came to the worst and you were left for a while as one forsaken by God, you still would not lose Him. Like the Lord Jesus on the cross, you may still call Him, "My God" (Matt. 27:46).

"'The LORD is my portion,' says my soul, 'therefore I hope in Him'" (Lam. 3:24). The Lord is a portion from which we can never be alienated. He lives! He reigns! He will be our guide even unto death.

HIS COMPASSION. *Lamentations 3:32*

Great sorrow can stun, and it can make you forget the best source of consolation. A little blow can cause great pain. Yet I have heard that in assaults serious blows do not cause pain because they have destroyed consciousness. Extreme distress can rob you of your wits and make you forget your source of relief. Under the chastening rod, the pain is remembered and the healing promise is forgotten.

The people of Israel, when they were under God's affliction, failed to remember His covenant because of the crushing effect of their sorrow and despair. Is that how it is with you? Has your ear grown dull through grief? Has your heart forgotten because of heaviness? Does your affliction seem more real than God? Does the black sorrow that covers you eclipse all the light of heaven and earth?

May I be my Master's messenger? Let me remind you that He is still in covenant with you. "Though He causes grief, yet He will show compassion according to the multitude of His mercies" (Lam. 3:32). It is written, "We know that all things work together for good to those who love God, to those who are the called according to His purpose" (Rom. 8:28). He will keep His Word!

He has also said, "When you pass through the waters, I will be with you; and through the rivers, they shall not overflow you. When you walk through the fire, you shall not be burned, nor shall the flame scorch you" (Is. 43:2).

Depend on it; He will sustain you. Brush those tears away, anoint your head, wash your face, and be of good courage (2 Sam. 12:20). The Lord will strengthen your heart.

I WAS LEFT ALONE. *Ezekiel 9:8*

I speak to believers who have been left behind when better saints were snatched from earthly ties, when brighter stars were clouded in night. I speak to believers who were preserved when so many perished, who were sustained on the rock of life when the waves of death dashed about.

Why am I left? In sparing me, my Lord, have you something more for me to do? Is there some purpose that You will suggest? Will You give me grace and strength? Will You spare me a little longer? Am I yet immortal, or at least shielded from death's sorrow, because my work is incomplete? What would You have me do? Since I have been left, help me to be especially consecrated, to be reserved for some purpose.

Christian, always ask this question, especially if you are preserved in times of more than ordinary sickness and mortality, "Why am I left alone? Why am I not taken home to heaven? Why do I not enter my rest?"

Great Lord and Master, show me what You would have me do. Then give me the grace and strength to do it. Amen.

DEATH'S SHALLOW VICTORY. *Ezekiel 18:32*

In a little while, I shall slumber in the tomb. Yet, "I know that my Redeemer lives, and He shall stand at last on the earth; and after my skin is destroyed, this I know, that in my flesh I shall see God" (Job 19:25-26). My eyes, which soon will be glazed in death, will not always be closed in darkness. Death will be forced to give back its prey. I see death, and it has the bodies of the just locked in its dungeons. It has sealed their tombs and marked them for its own. Oh death, foolish death, your caskets will be seized and your storehouses broken open.

The morning is come! Christ has descended! I hear the trumpet! "Awake! Awake!" From the tomb, the righteous spring and death sits in confusion and howls in vain, for its empire is deprived of its subjects. "Precious shall be their blood in His sight" (Ps. 72:14). Precious shall be their bones; their very dust is blessed. Christ will raise them.

Think of that, you who have lost loved ones. Weeping children of sorrow, your redeemed friends will live again. The hand that grasped yours with a death clutch will grasp you again in paradise. Those eyes that wept away in tears will wake in the noon-day of great happiness. The frame that you sorrowfully buried, yes that same body, will be raised incorruptible (1 Cor. 15:52).

If you are redeemed, you will see that loved one. Death will not keep one bone of the righteous, not a particle of their dust, not a hair of their heads. Christ has purchased every part of our bodies; the whole body will be complete and united forever in heaven with the glorified soul.

THE BANDS OF THEIR YOKE. *Ezekiel 34:27*

Wwe look cheerful and happy, but we do not know the burden of the person sitting in the pew with us. There is a merchant, here, who has been driven to his wit's end; he scarcely knows what to do. Tonight he said, "I will just run into the house of God and hear what the Lord may have to say." Often a sweet promise has come to God's bewildered children as the Master has sent a message through His servant.

There is a housewife in the same condition. One child is sick and another falling ill. Her husband is walking in a way that grieves her heart. Home affairs are not good. Yet while she sits before the Lord, a word of comfort comes.

Many of our brothers and sisters have a perpetual cross to carry. If we knew what they suffer in business, in body, or in their domestic circle, we would express words of comfort. We do not know, however, and so they are left without Christian sympathy.

You have been forced to carry a heavy yoke. Suddenly the Lord breaks the bands of your yoke (Ezek. 34:27). He delivers you, and you know that He is the Lord (Ezek. 34:30).

I can bear witness that trials are a great blessing. I would not have learned much except for trouble. When in painful difficulty and unable to see my way, I knew that the Lord was God when He appeared and broke the bands of my yoke. With a song I have magnified His surprising grace and blessed His delivering love.

NO SMELL OF FIRE. *Daniel 3:27*

When you cherish Christ, the things of the world are of little value, and their loss is not heavily felt. If you feel your losses and if your trials are so ponderous that Christ's love cannot lift you from the dust, then you have made too much of the world and too little of Him.

I see a pair of balances. I see on one scale the loss of a beloved relative, but I perceive on the other scale the great love of Christ. Now we will see which weighs the most. If Jesus lifts the light affliction, all is well. But if the trouble outweighs Jesus, then it is indeed ill for us.

If you are so depressed by your trials that you cannot rejoice, even though your name is written in heaven, then I think you do not love Jesus as you should. Get delightful thoughts of Him, and you will feel as if you lost a pebble but preserved a diamond. If you have a high sense of your Master's preciousness, you will rejoice in the deepest distress. The sweet love of Christ, when placed on the deepest wound the soul can ever know, heals at once.

Jesus, Jesus, Jesus. Be within us, and we will make no choice of situations. Put us in Nebuchadnezzar's furnace (Dan. 3:20); if Jesus walks the glowing coals as our companion, the fire will have no power, the hairs of our heads will not be singed, our garments will not be affected, and even the smell of fire will not be on them (Dan. 3:27).

LEFT ALONE. *Daniel 10:13*

Are you depressed because of some illness or great trial? Then you have forgotten that God has already provided. While you are asking, "Where can I find a friend?" or "Who will come to my rescue?", that friend is already there. While you are questioning, "How can I get out of this dilemma?", God has already solved the problem. The riddle has been answered, the question explained. You are complaining about a difficulty that has already been resolved by the divine hand.

Some believers are totally surprised when God delivers them. Their faith is small, and they are surprised that God would use something simple. They say, "How could it have happened? Why didn't I think of that? Why was the answer so close but I failed to see it? I was thirsty, and I cried to God for rain, while all the time there was this well bubbling up with water."

If you are troubled, ask God to help you trust when you cannot see Him. Ask God to help you yield to His will. Ask that His will throws a shadow over your soul, and let that shadow be your will. May we learn to be content in any state (Phil. 4:11), for this is the best foundation for true happiness.

Oh for grace to feel that if we do not know when God will deliver us, then it is none of our business! If God knows, that is enough. God has not made us the providers, and He does not intend us to hold the helm. We are to follow Him, not lead. We are to obey Him, not prescribe.

Your deliverance is near. But if it tarries it will be a richer blessing. Ships that are long at sea are more heavily loaded, but they carry a double cargo of blessing. Plants that grow quickly last only for a little while. Perhaps the blessing that is taking so long to spring out of the soil of your expectancy will last all your life.

A DOOR OF HOPE. *Hosea 2:15*

Believer, afflictions may alter your circumstances but not your acceptance with God. You were once a fine gentleman. You had a large house and grounds, but now you have to be satisfied with a small room and difficult circumstances. You were once a well-built young fellow, but now you are a gray old man. Everyone used to speak to you; now nobody knows you.

Forsaken by flatterers and forgotten by friends, you might sit down and weep were it not for the fact that the only Being worth caring for loves you as much as ever. He loved you before time began, for reasons known only to His sacred heart. He loves you now the same as ever. Dear friend, do not be discouraged because you are going downhill into deep adversities, for His love will go with you. The Lord's love does not rise and fall like the thermometer. His love stays the same whatever your condition. The furnace alters our friends. Before we go into the furnace, we are so fresh and fair that they are glad to know us, but when we come out of the furnace so wrinkled and scorched, they are ready to run away.

God does not change. "I am the LORD, I do not change" (Mal. 3:6). "Jesus Christ is the same yesterday, today, and forever" (Heb. 13:8). His friendship never turns to hate or to forgetfulness. Blessed be His name. He has known my soul in adversity and made "the Valley of Achor as a door of hope" (Hos. 2:15).

HE WILL HEAL. *Hosea 6:1*

I believe that God, who has appointed it, has also measured your trouble, set its bounds, and will bring it to an end. His gracious design is in all your difficulties. Do not think that God deals roughly with His children and gives them needless pain. "He does not afflict willingly, nor grieve the children of men" (Lam. 3:33). "He has torn, but He will heal."

Has not God helped you out of one trouble after another? Do you suppose that He will leave you in this trouble? "He shall deliver you in six troubles, yes, in seven no evil shall touch you" (Job 5:19).

This particular water, in which you are now struggling, is intended and included in this promise, "When you pass through the waters, I will be with you; and through the rivers, they shall not overflow you" (Is. 43:2).

It is, I must confess, sometimes difficult to apply the promises to a particular case. Sometimes unbelief fights hard. But remember, unless the promise is applied it is like medicine that is not taken. It may be powerful, but it is worthless unless applied.

Ask for grace, that you may believe while you are still under the cloud. Regardless of how dark the cloud, it contains blessings. "If the clouds are full of rain, they empty themselves upon the earth" (Eccl. 11:3).

I WILL CHASTEN THEM. *Hosea 10:10*

There are many of you who, like myself, understand what deep depression means. Yet we would not change our lot for the mirth of fools or the pomp of kings. No one takes our joy. We are singing pilgrims even if the way is rough. Amid the ashes of our pain live the sparks of our joy, ready to flame when the Holy Spirit's breath sweetly blows. Our latent happiness is a choicer heritage than the sinner's glee.

Once when suffering greatly and scarcely able to stand, I met someone who enjoys excellent health and prosperity. But his mind is coarse, his tongue cuts like a file, and he is fond of expressing his rational ideas as proof that he is superior. With sarcastic politeness, he said, "Dear, dear, what a sufferer you are. But it is expected, for whom the Lord loves He chastens" (Heb. 12:6). I barely had time to admit that the chastening had been severe before he added, "You are welcome to a love that shows itself in that fashion. For my part, I would rather be without it. I can do better without your God than with Him."

Hot tears scalded my eyelids and forced a passage. I could bear the pain, but I could not endure evil spoken of my God. I flamed up in indignation! I cried, "If instead of pain in my legs, I had a thousand agonies in every limb, I would not change places with you. I am content to take all that comes of God's love. God and His chastening are better than the world and its delights."

I know this to be so. My soul has a greater inner gladness in deep depression than the godless have in their high, foaming merriment. Every pain is a tutor to praise, for it teaches us how to play on all the keys of our humanity until a complete harmony, which perpetual health could never produce, is achieved.

Ransomed from death. *Hosea 13:14*

If Jesus tarries, it is certain that we believers will die and be put into the grave and then decay. I do not want my body wrapped in an expensive casket to prevent it from rapidly melting back to mother earth. It seems best and holiest to let the body speedily return to its native dust.

Now this is the issue: that dust will pass through many transitions. The roots of trees may drink up this form, or the dust may turn to grass or flowers to be eaten by animals. The wind may blow it thousands of miles, or it may be separated atom from atom and bone may be scattered from bone.

Be assured that no matter what becomes of the dust of our bodies, as surely as the Savior rose, we will rise again in a beauty and a glory that we know little about (1 Thess. 4:13-18). The body of that dear child of God you said good-bye to will rise again. Those eyes that closed, those very eyes, will see the King in His beauty. The ears that could not hear the last tender word you spoke— those ears—will hear the eternal melodies. The heart that grew cold will beat again with new life; it will leap with joy at the homecoming festivities.

Do not fear death. What is it? The grave is just a bath where our body, like Esther (Esth. 2:12), buries itself in spices to make it sweet and fresh for the embrace of the glorious King in immortality. Death is just the wardrobe where we lay aside the garment for a while and come out clean and pure.

EVERY ONE MARCHES. *Joel 2:8*

Child of God, do you sometimes ask, "Why this cross? Why this bereavement? Why am I perplexed by this dilemma? Why is this difficulty piled like a barricade across my path?" You do not have the answer now, but you will. Until then, settle firmly in your faith that "all things work together for good to those who love God, to those who are the called according to His purpose" (Rom. 8:28).

Your affliction does not jostle your prosperity; it promotes it. Your losses do not cause loss; they increase your true riches. Press on, for you are loaded with untold blessings. Every event is marching for the righteous and the humble spirit. God has His way in the whirlwind (Hos. 8:7), and the clouds are the dust of His feet. Be patient, and wait on Him with childlike confidence. The day will come when you will be astonished that there was order in your life when you thought it all confusion. You will be astonished that there was love and you thought it unkindness, that there was gentleness and you thought it severity, that there was wisdom when you were wicked enough to impugn God's rightness.

Believer, the events of history march as a victorious legion under a skillful leader. Do not think we can order our affairs in better style. Our good, ill, joy, and grief keep their place. "They do not push one another; every one marches in his own column" (Joel 2:8).

GOD'S RESTORATION. *Joel 2:25*

Lost years can never literally be restored. Time past is gone, and you cannot have it back. As you think about this, it will strike you that the locust did not eat the years; they ate the fruit of the years. There is a strange and wonderful way that God can give back wasted blessings, the unripened fruit of past years.

"If you can believe, all things are possible to him who believes" (Mark 9:23). There is a power beyond all things that can work great wonders. Who can make all the devouring locust restore their prey? God alone can do what seems impossible. This is the promise of His grace: "I will restore to you the years that the swarming locust has eaten" (Joel 2:25). God can give back all those years of sorrow, and you will be the better for them. God will grind sunlight out of your black nights. In the oven of affliction, grace will prepare the bread of delight. Someday you will thank God for all your sadness.

I said this to a devoted Christian woman, who for three years had defied all attempts of comfort. We prayed with her, and her godly, gracious husband, a minister of Christ, had laid out his heart in an attempt to cheer her. But she refused comfort. The other day, to my great joy, I received a letter saying, "The Lord has opened the gates of my dungeon, and my captivity is ended. Though sick in body, that does not matter, I am restored in spirit." Yes, the Lord can release the captives, and He does.

There are precious children of God who for ten or twenty years have been the victims of depression. This promise, in the fullness of time, has been sweetly fulfilled in their lives, "I will restore to you the years that the swarming locust has eaten."

Prepare to meet your God. *Amos 4:12*

A sudden death is an impressive warning. If old people die, we consider it the common course. But when a youth is snatched away, then we understand the thought that the old must die, the young may. No one among us may plan on a long day of life, for in a moment our sun may go down. In a moment, our strength is turned to weakness and our beauty to decay. Then, in accents as plain as they are terrible, the Lord says, "Because I will do this to you, prepare to meet your God, O Israel!" (Amos 4:12).

To us also in due time will come the message, "The Teacher has come and is calling for you" (John 11:28). My ear hears a loud voice crying, "Set your house in order, for you shall die, and not live" (2 Kin. 20:1). Death evidently pays no respect to character, age, or hopefulness. A man may be surrounded with a wall of affection, but this will not screen him. He may have all the comforts of life, yet his life may ooze out in front of the physician. He may be tenderly loved by an affectionate mother, and his name may be engraved on the heart of the fondest of wives, but death has no regard even for the love of women.

"It is appointed for men to die once, but after this the judgment" (Heb. 9:27). There is no discharge in this war! We all march into this fight, and unless the Lord Himself comes to end this present dispensation, we will all fall on this battlefield. I would to God that you would retain this truth. "LORD, make me to know my end, and what is the measure of my days, that I may know how frail I am" (Ps. 39:4). We have a clear conviction that others will die, but we do not care to dwell on this subject. We admit that we shall die, but not so soon as to make it a pressing matter. We are all in the same army, marching on the same field. How shall we escape where all others fall?

171

SIFTED IN A SIEVE. *Amos 9:9*

The trials of life are severe, and to some they are crushing. "Sufficient for the day is its own trouble" (Matt. 6:34). There are temptations in prosperity. Where adversity can ruin one, prosperity can destroy ten thousand. It is a sieve through which few can pass, for when they get into that sieve and become rich, they get too big for their former friends. They go to another religion that is more fashionable. They forsake God's simple truths. People who in prosperity ought to be pillars of God's church become her fiercest foes. Who is the most bitter against the truth? It is those who have grown rich and who have gone over to the adversary. Few can endure continued, undisturbed prosperity. Amid the luxuries of the valley, people degenerate.

The mountains, however, produce a brave and hardy race. The dangers of the crags and the cold brace of winter build nerve and muscle until each becomes vigorous, ready for acts of valor and deeds of heroism. It is in battle and service that veteran soldiers are bred. There is a sieve in prosperity, but adversity does the sifting.

Lord, deliver us from being filled with riches or stinted by poverty. From either extreme, save us. The prayer of Agur is most wise, "Give me neither poverty nor riches" (Prov. 30:8). Whether rich or poor, we must look on our present condition as a test in which God would make known to us whether we are solidly in Christ and in the work of the Holy Spirit or just superficial professors having a name to live, but who are dead.

Christ is ours, but who knows all that is ours in Christ? He is our jewelry vault, but we do not open its doors and take out all its treasures. We see the blessings of the covenant, but we do not feed on it as we might. We do not drink deep from it and satisfy our souls. I fear we do not fully enjoy our possessions.

It is your high privilege to have access to the mercy seat, but do you use that access? Do you come often and boldly to the throne of grace (Heb. 4:16)? Do you avail yourself of your opportunities? Do you make the most use of prayer (James 4:3)? Do you really stand where God would have you stand? Are you as rich as Christ has made you (Rom. 9:23)?

We may have great possessions and yet be practically poor because we are miserly with our expenditure. All things are ours (1 Cor. 3:21), yet we live as if nothing were ours. Like a horse shut out of the pasture, we nibble around the edges; far better to be like sheep that enter and lie down in green pastures (Ps. 23:2).

Oh for grace to appropriate those treasures of the covenant that make the soul "rejoice with joy inexpressible and full of glory" (1 Pet. 1:8)! I pray that we will not look in the windows of the banquet hall but that we will sit at the table and possess our possessions. Why should we hunger and thirst when Christ has given us His flesh to be meat and His blood to be drink (Matt. 26:26-28)? Why should we hang our heads when the Lord loves us? We should have His joy in us, "that our joy may be full" (2 John 1:12). Why are we so dispirited by infirmities? We know that Jehovah is our strength and our song, but we do not possess our possessions.

Let our prayer be that we may use and enjoy to the utmost all that the Lord has given in grace.

GOD'S TIMING. *Jonah 4:6*

Just when we need a mercy, and when the mercy is much more a mercy because it is so timely, that is when it comes. If it had come later, it might have been too late, or at any rate it would not have been so seasonable and thus not so sweet.

Who knows what is the right time? God, who sees all at a single glance, knows. He knows when to give and He knows when to take. In every godly life there is a set time for each event. There is no need to ask, "Why is the white here and the black there? Why this gleam of sunlight and that roar of tempest? Why here a marriage and there a funeral? Why sometimes a harp and at other times a trumpet?" God knows. And it is a great blessing when we can leave it all in His hands.

Let the plant come up in the night and it will be a good night. Let the plant wither in the morning and it will be a good morning (Jon. 4:6-7). All is well if it is in  God's hands. Let us distinctly recognize God in all our comforts: when they come when we are unworthy, when they come in a form in which we most require them, and when they come when we are most in need.

IS NOT THE LORD AMONG US? *Micah 3:11*

Sometimes great sweetness is found with intense bitterness. I have experienced immense joy in the depths of depression when I lean only on my God. I hardly know how to express this unrivalled pleasure of resting only on the Lord, for when I am hurled on God alone, my soul finds divine peace.

Dear friend, if both your circumstances and your spirit sink, all will be well if you lean on God alone. Never fear that you will become weary to Him, and never ask as little as possible. He says, "Open your mouth wide, and I will fill it" (Ps. 81:10). Never trust Him just a little. Never give Him only a part of your cares. Never rest just a portion of your trials on Him. Lean on Him with all your weight. Bring all the tons, pounds, and ounces and throw them all on God. Do not carry an extra ounce yourself. God loves His children to place their entire confidence in Him.

Do you know the Aesop's fable about the polite little gnat who when he flew off of the ox apologized for burdening him? The ox replied that he did not know he was there. God will never tell you that. He will tell you that your load is no burden. If you had fifty kingdoms burdening your brain, if you carried the politics of a hundred nations in your mind, and if you were loaded with all the cares of a thousand worlds, still you could safely leave them with the Wonderful Counsellor and go your way rejoicing. Lean hard brothers, lean hard sisters, for "is not the LORD among us?" "Cast all your care upon Him, for He cares for you" (1 Pet. 5:7). He counts the very hairs on your head (Matt. 10:30).

GOD WILL HEAR ME. *Micah 7:7*

Child of God, take this promise in your hand and into your heart: "My God will hear me" (Mic. 7:7). Use it like a wand; turn it whatever way you will, and it will clear your path. You are going to preach the gospel in a distant country, and your spirit sinks as you sigh, "Who is sufficient for this?" Lift up your heart to God, My grace is sufficient for you, for My strength is made perfect in weakness" (2 Cor. 12:9). God will hear you.

There is illness in your home, and you may lose one that is precious. But you will be sustained, for in your heart is this verse: "My God will hear me."

Perhaps you are terminally ill and will soon die. You ask, "What will I do in the floodplain of the Jordan" (Jer. 12:5)? Here is your happy answer: "My God will hear me." I will cry to Him, and He will answer, "Yea though I walk through the valley of the shadow of death, I will fear no evil; for You are with me" (Ps. 23:4). "My God will hear me."

When I lie in the grave, my God will remember me. He will call me with the sound of a trumpet, and I will live again (1 Thess. 4:16). My God will hear me sing His praises before His throne. My God will hear me, world without end, as my entire being lifts up joy notes of "Hallelujah, hallelujah, hallelujah" to Him who loved me out of the pit and lifted me to His own right hand.

GOD IS JEALOUS. *Nahum 1:2*

Believer, your Lord is jealous of your love. Did He choose you? Then He cannot bear that you would choose another. Did He buy you with His own blood? Then He cannot endure that you would think you are your own or that you belong to this world. He loved you with such a love that He would sooner die than you should perish. He cannot endure anything standing between Him and your heart's love.

He is jealous of your trust. He will not permit you to trust in an arm of flesh. He cannot bear that you should hew broken cisterns that can hold no water (Jer. 2:13).

When we lean on Him, He is glad. But when we transfer our dependence to another, when we rely on our own wisdom or that of a friend, or worst of all, when we trust in any works of our own, then He is displeased, and He will chasten us to bring us back to Him.

He is also jealous of our company. There should be no one with whom we converse so much as with Jesus. To abide in Him alone is true love. To fellowship with the world, to find sufficient solace in our carnal comforts, is grievous to our jealous Lord. He wants us to abide in Him and enjoy His constant fellowship. Many of the trials He sends are to wean our hearts from the creature and fix them more closely on Him.

Let this jealousy, which should keep us near Christ, also comfort us. If He loves so much as to care about our love, we may be sure that nothing will harm us, for He will protect us from all enemies.

May we have grace today to keep our hearts in a sacred purity for our Beloved alone. May we with sacred jealousy shut our eyes to all the fascinations of the world.

I WILL BLESS YOU. *Haggai 2:19*

The future is hidden from us, yet here is a glass in which we may see the unborn years, for the Lord says, "From this day I will bless you" (Hag. 2:19).

It is worth noting the day that is referred to in this promise. There had been failures of crops because of the people's sin, but now the Lord saw these chastened ones beginning to obey His Word and to build His temple. Therefore He says, "From the day that the foundation of the Lord's temple was laid, from that day forward, I will bless you."

If we have lived in any sin and the Spirit leads us to purge ourselves of it, we may count on the blessing of the Lord. His smile, His Spirit, His grace, and His fuller revelation of His truth will prove an enlarged blessing. We may fall into greater opposition from man because of our faithfulness, but we will rise to closer dealings with the Lord our God and a clearer sight of our acceptance in Him.

Lord, I am resolved to be more true to You, more exact in following Your doctrine and Your precept. I ask You, by Christ Jesus, to increase the blessedness of my daily life from this moment forward and forever. Amen.

A WALL OF FIRE. *Zechariah 2:5*

You that are children of God are not left in the power of the enemy. Being redeemed, "The LORD will be a wall of fire all around you" (Zech. 2:5). You are garrisoned by angelic strength. You are led by unfailing wisdom. The all-sufficiency of God is your treasure-house. "No good thing will He withhold from those who walk uprightly" (Ps. 84:11). This is a royal charter of boundless liberality. "For all things are yours: whether Paul or Apollos or Cephas, or the world or life or death, or things present or things to come—all are yours. And you are Christ's, and Christ is God's" (1 Cor. 3:21-23).

What royal provision is set apart for you! "All things work together for good to those who love God, to those who are the called according to His purpose" (Rom. 8:28). Everything is arranged for your benefit.

There were two brothers. One had been attentive to his worldly business but neglected true religion, and he succeeded in accumulating considerable wealth. The other brother was diligent in the service of the Master, and he had learned to distribute to the poor and, for con-science sake, to forego many opportunities of gain. When the devout brother lay sick and dying, in difficult circum-stances, his wealthy brother upbraided him, remarking that if it had not been for his religion he would not be dependent on others. With great calm the saintly man replied, "O Tom, I have a kingdom and an inheritance that I have not yet seen."

Speaking of laying up for a rainy day, there is infinite goodness laid up for them that fear the Lord, and no one can rob us of it. Every child of God is as David when Samuel anointed him to the throne (1 Sam. 16:1). We have a kingdom in reverse, and it is secured by an eter-nal covenant.

I WILL ANSWER THEM. *Zechariah 13:9*

I am addressing some child of God who is in deep trouble. Everything is wrong at home, in business, and even in church. At least you will never have to ask the question, "Why am I not chastened?" Remember, "as many as I love I rebuke and chasten" (Rev. 3:19).

Present chastening is not joyous; nevertheless, it will yield the peaceful fruit of righteousness. Therefore, gladly endure it. God's thoughts are toward you. He is refining you, and He desires your highest good. "I have tested you in the furnace of affliction. For My own sake, I will do it" (Is. 48:10-11). I "will refine them as silver is refined, and test them as gold is tested. They will call on My name, and I will answer them. I will say 'This is My people'; and each will say, 'The LORD is my God'" (Zech. 13:9).

IT WILL BE LIGHT. *Zechariah 14:7*

You can remember the time when you were greatly blessed. You can remember when the calf was in the stall, when the olive yielded fruit, and when the fig tree gave abundant harvest. Your barn was bursting with corn and your vats overflowed with oil. Your stream of life was so deep that your ship floated without one disturbing wave of trouble. You said, "I will see no sorrow, God has surrounded me, He has preserved me, He has kept me going, I can plainly see that all things work together for good" (Rom. 8:28).

Well, Christian, now you have had a sunset. The sun, which was so bright, began to cast long shadows. Clouds gathered, and it grew dark. Troubles came. Sickness entered your family, crops were meager, income diminished. You did not know what would become of you. You were brought low. There was not enough bounty to float your ship above the rocks of poverty. You did not know what to do, strive as you might, and your efforts only made it worse. You thought the night of your life had gathered with eternal blackness, and you were ready to die in despair.

Listen, believer, if God chooses to multiply your sorrow, He will prolong your patience. The time of your extreme distress is the moment of God's opportunity. When the tide runs to its lowest, it turns. Your ebb has its flow, your winter its summer, your sunset its sunrise. "At evening time it shall happen that it will be light" (Zech. 14:7). You will be completely delivered. Exclaim with old Habakkuk, "Though the fig tree may not blossom, nor fruit be on the vines; though the labor of the olive may fail, and the fields yield no food; though the flock may be cut off from the fold, and there be no herd in the stalls— yet I will rejoice in the LORD. I will joy in the God of my salvation" (Hab. 3:17-18).

A REFINER. *Malachi 3:3*

We cannot show courage unless we have difficulties and troubles. Therefore, rejoice in your trials, for they give you opportunities to exhibit a believing confidence, to glorify the name of the Most High.

This is the believer's view of affliction: it is "the LORD [who] has chastened me severely" (Ps. 118:18). The enemy struck to make me fall, but my gracious God used him to chasten me, that I might not fall. The enemy was moved by malice, but God worked through him to love my soul.

It is good to have grace enough to see that trials come from God. He fills the bitter cup as well as the sweet goblet. Trouble does not spring out of the dust, and affliction does not grow from the ground. The Lord Himself kindles the fiery furnace. He is like a refiner's fire. He will purify and He will purge you as gold and silver (Mal. 3:3).

Do not dwell on the part played by the devil, as though he were a power equal with God, for he is a creature, and fallen. The devil's existence depends on the will and permission of the Most High. His power is borrowed and can only be used as God's infinite omnipotence permits. The devil's wickedness is his own, but his existence is not self-derived. Blame the devil, and blame all his servants as much as you wish, but still believe that in the truest sense the Lord sends trials to His saints.

MY JEWELS. *Malachi 3:17*

There is a great depth of meaning in the word keep. A shepherd keeps sheep by feeding them, by supplying all their needs, and by guarding them from all their adversaries. He vigilantly keeps the flock, so that it is not diminished by the ravaging wolf or the straying sheep. Night and day, even an ordinary shepherd takes the utmost care to preserve his sheep.

Our Lord Jesus, that great Shepherd of the sheep who was brought up from the dead (Heb. 13:20), uses His omnipotence, His omniscience, and His divine attributes to keep His sheep. My dear believer, rest assured, He will preserve you! You are in good keeping. He is the Shepherd, the great Shepherd and the chief Shepherd (1 Pet. 5:4).

The Lord keeps His people, not only as a shepherd keeps sheep, but also as a king keeps his jewels. These rare and precious gems are his special treasure, and he will not lose them. He will put them in a secure vault, and his most faithful servants will guard the place where they are stored. He will charge those who have the custody of the crown jewels to see that none are lost.

The Lord Jesus keeps His people the same way. They are His jewels. He delights in them, and they are His honor and His glory. They cost Him a greater price than can ever be realized. He hides them in the vault of His power and protects them with all His wisdom and strength.

Concerning those who trust in Him, it is written, "'They shall be Mine,' says the LORD of hosts, 'on the day that I make them My jewels'" (Mal. 3:17).

God will never forget you, not for a single moment.

GOD WITH US. *Matthew 1:23*

Wonderfully true is this fact: when you and I come to the closing scene of life we will find that Emmanuel, "God with us" (Matt. 1:23), has been there. He felt the pangs and throes of death. He endured the bloody sweat of agony and parching thirst of fever. He knew the separation of the tortured spirit from the poor fainting flesh. He cried, as we shall cry, "Father, into Your hands I commit My spirit" (Luke 23:46).

He knew the grave—He slept there—and yet He left the tomb perfumed and furnished. He left it like a bed of rest and not as a house of decay. The garden's new tomb makes Him "God with us" until the resurrection calls us from our beds of clay. Then, in newness of life, we will find Him "God with us." We will be raised in His likeness, and the first sight our opening eyes will see is the incarnate God. "For I know that my Redeemer lives . . . and after my skin is destroyed this I know, that in my flesh I shall see God" (Job 19:25-26).

I will see Him as the Man, the God, and throughout all eternity He will maintain the most intimate relationship with me. As long as ages roll, He will be "God with us." He said, "You will see me. Because I live, you will live also" (John 14:19). Both His human and divine life will last forever, and so will our life. He will dwell in us and walk among us (2 Cor. 6:16) and lead us to the fountain of living waters (Jer. 17:13). The water He gives will become a fountain of water springing up into everlasting life (John 4:14). "Thus we shall always be with the Lord" (1 Thess. 4:17).

NOT BY BREAD ALONE. *Matthew 4:4*

When a true child of God is in trouble, the Bible becomes precious because in the text there are circumstances connected with God's dealings. I think you will find that tested saints are biblical saints. In summer weather, we delight in praise choruses. But in winter's storms, we fly to the Psalm. Lukewarm Christians quote Dickens or George Eliot. But God's afflicted quote David or Job. The Psalms are marvelous. David seems to have lived for us all; he was not so much one man as all men in one. Somewhere or other, the great circle of his experience touches you and me. Through the power of the Holy Spirit, David has furnished the best expressions we can articulate in prayer.

Give me a faith that loves the Scripture. "Faith comes by hearing, and hearing by the word of God" (Rom. 10:17). True faith always loves the Word from which it springs. True faith feeds and grows on the Word.

As people criticize the Scriptures, they begin to doubt the authenticity of this and that. They move out of the latitude of that which loves a warm climate and into a region of criticism that is as cold as the polar seas.

The faith of God's elect clings to God and has a reverence for His Word. "Man shall not live by bread alone, but by every word that proceeds from the mouth of God" (Matt. 4:4).

THE THINGS YOU NEED. *Matthew 6:8*

Being God's child has innumerable and joyous privileges. He said, "Bring out the best robe and put it on him" (Luke 15:22). I will be clothed in the robe of my Savior's righteousness. My shoes will be iron and brass (Deut. 33:25), and He will put a gold crown on my head (1 Pet. 5:4).

Because I am His child, He will feed me; bread will be given, and my water will be sure (Is. 33:16). He that feeds the birds will never let His children starve (Matt. 6:26). If a good farmer feeds the barnyard hens, the sheep, and the cattle, certainly God will not let His children starve.

If my Father clothes the lilies (Matt. 6:28), do you think that He will let me go naked? If He feeds the birds, who neither sow nor reap nor gather into barns (Matt. 6:26), do you think that He will let me go hungry? God forbid! My Father knows the things I have need of before I ask Him (Matt. 6:8), and He will give me all I need.

If I am His child, then I have a place in His heart today, and I will have a share in His house above. "The Spirit Himself bears witness with our spirit that we are children of God, and if children, then heirs—heirs of God and joint heirs with Christ, if indeed we suffer with Him, that we may also be glorified together" (Rom. 8:16-17). We are heirs of God and joint heirs with Christ! All things are ours—the gift of God, the purchase of a Savior's blood:

This world is ours, and worlds to come;
Earth is our lodge, and heaven our home.

TREASURES ON EARTH. *Matthew 6:19*

When you serve God, do not expect a reward. Be prepared instead to be misunderstood, suspected, and abused. An evil world cannot speak well of holy lives. The sweetest fruit is most pecked at by the birds. The tallest mountains are most battered by the storms. The loveliest character is the most assailed. If you succeed in bringing many to Christ, you will be charged with self-seeking, or popularity hunting, or some such crime. You will be misrepresented, belied, caricatured, and counted as a fool by the ungodly world.

If you serve God, the probabilities are that the crown you win in this world will contain more spikes than sapphires, more briers than emeralds. When it is put on your head, pray for grace to wear it, and count it all joy to be like your Lord. Say in your heart, "I feel no dishonor in this dishonor. The world may attribute shameful things to me, but I am not ashamed. People may degrade me, but I am not degraded. They may look on me with contempt, but I am not contemptible."

Yet, I have seen some who take much trouble to trouble themselves, such as those who work to increase their work. They hurry to be rich. They fret, toil, worry, and torment themselves to be loaded with the burdens that wealth brings. They wound themselves in order to wear the thorny crown of worldly greatness. There are many ways we can make rods for our own backs.

Believer, say this, "If my Lord wore my crown of thorns for me, then why should I wear it?" Jesus has borne your griefs and carried your sorrows (Is. 53:4), that you might be happy and able to obey His command: "Do not worry about tomorrow, for tomorrow will worry about its own things" (Matt. 6:34).

WHEN A SPARROW FALLS. *Matthew 10:29*

The providence of God is not only concerned with wars between mighty empires; it also comprehends everything else. The blooming of every daisy is arranged by eternal purpose. A frog croaking in the marsh or a leaf falling from an oak tree is part of eternal wisdom's plan. The migration of each swallow is as arranged as Columbus's voyage. The breaking of a fowler's net is as ordained as a nation's emancipation. God is in all things. Not one sparrow falls to the ground apart from His will. Even the hairs of your head are all numbered (Matt. 10:29-30). God surrounds these little things. He makes them part of His eternal purpose.

David thought, "When I consider Your heavens, the work of Your fingers, the moon and the stars, which You have ordained, what is man that You are mindful of him, and the son of man that You visit him?" (Ps. 8:3-4).

In all your grief, Jesus has deep sympathy. In the night, He sees your weakness and sleeplessness. When all leave, He is still with you, even making your bed in sickness.

Never say that God is so busy with heaven's glories and the world's management that He forgets you. Far from it! "As a father pities his children, so the LORD pities those who fear Him. For He knows our frame; He remembers that we are dust" (Ps. 103:13-14).

Depend on it. The great God is too mighty to forget one of His children (Is. 49:15).

NUMBERED HAIRS. *Matthew 10:30*

I beg you to believe that God is in the little things, even the little troubles that can annoy the most. At times, you can endure the loss of a dear friend better than a minor accident. The pebble in your shoe makes you limp but you can jump over great stones.

God arranges the smallest things. Take little troubles as they come, and remember them to your God because they come from Him. Nothing that concerns His people is small to God. Your little anxieties are not too small for His notice, for "the very hairs of your head are all numbered" (Matt. 10:30). You may pray to Him about your smallest grief. If not a sparrow falls to the ground apart from your Father's will (Matt. 10:29), then you have reason to see that He arranges the smallest events in your career. So accept them with joy. This is a truth on which you may implicitly rely. Think about it until you lull the sharpest pain, calm the most feverish excitement, and obtain the sweetest rest that a weary, restless spirit can indulge in.

This is the antidote of fear: God appoints everything in the future, so rejoice that everything is in the hand of the great King. The Lord is King! Rejoice:

> The Lord is King; who then shall dare
> Resist His will, distrust His care,
> Or murmur at His wise decrees,
> Or doubt His royal promises?
> Oh! When His wisdom can mistake
> His might decay, His love forsake
> Then may His children cease to sing,
> The Lord Omnipotent is King.

I WILL GIVE YOU REST. *Matthew 11:28*

You that are weary with the rounds of worldly pleasure, stuffed and nauseated with vain glories and delusions of life, come and find true joy. You that are worn with ambition, corroded with disappointment, or embittered by the faithlessness of those you trusted, come and confide in Jesus. He will be your rest.

Weary, weary, weary ones, here is the rest, here is the refreshment. Jesus expressly puts it, "Come to Me, all you who labor and are heavy laden, and I will give you rest. Take My yoke upon you and learn from Me, for I am gentle and lowly in heart, and you will find rest for your souls. For My yoke is easy and My burden is light" (Matt. 11:28-30).

If your back is breaking, if your eyes are failing through weary watching and waiting, come to the Savior just as you are. He will be your rest.

MY BARN. *Matthew 13:30*

Gather the wheat into my barn" (Matt. 13:30). Gathering wheat is a moment by moment process, as the saints are gathered into the heavenly barn. On a regular basis, I hear that the departed ones from my own dear church have great joy in being harvested. Glory be to God, for our people die well. Now the best thing is to live well, but we are delighted that our people die well, because a triumphant death is a witness for vital godliness.

Every hour saints are gathered into the barn and that is where they want to be. We feel no pain at the news of their harvest because we wish that one day our Lord would safely place us in His barn. If the wheat in the field could talk, every stalk would say, "The ultimate reason for living and growing is to be gathered into the barn." This is why we have frosty nights, sunny days, dew, and rain. Every process in raising wheat leads to the barn. The wheat is placed in the barn for security; there is no mildew, frost, heat, drought, or dampness there. Once in the barn, perils surrounding growth are past. The wheat has reached perfection and is safely housed.

I delight to think of heaven as the Father's barn because it is the place of security, the place of everlasting rest, and the homestead of Christ, the place to which we will be carried. The gathering into the barn involves having a harvest home, a time of ecstatic joy. I never hear of people sitting down to cry over an earthly harvest home; rather, they clap their hands, dance for joy, and shout energetically. Let us do something like that concerning those who are already housed. Let us sing sweet melodies around their graves and feel that the bitterness of death is surely passed.

BEGINNING TO SINK. *Matthew 14:30*

I like to think about the spontaneous character of Peter's prayer. As he begins to sink, as soon as he finds himself going down, he immediately prays, "Lord, save me" (Matt. 14:30). Peter's faith was a living thing. It might not always walk on water, but it could always pray. Prayer is better than walking on water.

Your faith may not always make you rejoice. But if your faith can always make you trust Jesus' precious blood, that is all you need. Your faith may not regularly take you to the mountaintop, to bathe in the sunlight of God's countenance, but if it enables you to keep on the straight road to eternal life, you may bless God for such a faith.

Walking on water is not an essential characteristic of faith, but it is essential to pray when you begin to sink. Doing great things for Christ is not indispensable to salvation, but to have the faculty of turning your heart to Him in distress is a mark of divine grace.

I am sure that Peter did not intone his prayer. I am quite certain that he did not search for a proper musical background to match to the words. The prayer came from his heart. Great prayer wells up from the soul and flows freely from the lips because the heart compels the tongue to speak.

It is a blessed plan to set aside a time for prayer, a time for secret devotions, a time to be alone with the Savior. A regular habit of prayer is a great help to holiness. Even better is the spirit of prayer, because it promotes habitual, constant, fellowship with God.

WALKING ON WATER. *Matthew 14:31*

The life of a Christian is described as walking by faith. To my mind, this is a most extraordinary miracle. Walking on water, as Peter did (Matt. 14:29), is more typical of every Christian life. It is like ascending an invisible staircase to the clouds; you cannot see a step, but you keep climbing toward the light. Looking down, all is dark, and before you lies nothing but clouds.

Yet for years, some of us have been climbing this perpetually ascending stairway without ever seeing an inch ahead. We have often paused and asked, "What next, and what next?" Yet what we thought was cloud has been solid rock. Darkness has been light, and slippery places have been safe. When the darkness was so dense that it could be felt, when the past had vanished, when nothing could be seen but the step we stood on, we said, "How did I get here? What a strange, mysterious life I have had." Then faith came to our aid and we believed, and believing, we see the invisible and grasp the Eternal. Now without stopping, we can run the shining way with joy.

Perhaps at this moment you feel that you are entering a gloomy valley. You have suffered a great loss, your spirit is sinking, and you are greatly depressed. Like Peter, your soul is sinking in the waves. A hand is reaching out to save you. You cannot sink while your heavenly Father's hand is near.

TAKE UP HIS CROSS. *Matthew 16:24*

Is the cross that you are carrying pressing heavy? You will be like your Master; someone will be found to help you. They found Simon to carry Jesus' cross (Matt. 27:32), and God has a Simon somewhere for you. Just cry to the Lord and He will find you a friend.

I believe that Simon found that carrying the cross was a blessed occupation. When the soldiers forced Simon to carry the cross, it brought him close to Jesus. Had he not been forced to carry the cross, Simon might have gone his own way or been lost in the crowd. But now he is near Jesus.

As they lifted the cross on Simon's shoulders, he looked at Jesus and saw the crown of thorns, the bloody sweat, the lacerations, the bruises. That face, that matchless face, was majesty blended with misery, innocence with agony, love with sorrow. Simon would never have seen that countenance or marked the form of the Son of man so clearly if he had not been called to take up that cross. It is amazing how much we see of Jesus when we suffer or work for Him.

The cross held Simon in Christ's steps. Do you get it? If Jesus carried the front part of the cross and Simon followed, then his feet had to follow the Master's. Dear friend, the cross is a wonderful implement for keeping us in the way of our Lord.

Believing child of God, I pray that today you will be compelled to carry the cross, that you will have closer and more precious fellowship with Him. "If anyone desires to come after Me, let him deny himself, and take up his cross, and follow Me" (Matt. 16:24).

NOTHING IMPOSSIBLE. *Matthew 17:20*

Your faith prospers when everything is against you. Your faith increases with every trial. No flowers wear so lovely a blue as those that grow at the edge of a glacier. No stars shine so bright as those that glisten in the polar sky. No water is sweeter than that which springs in a desert oasis. No faith is so precious as that which lives and triumphs in adversity.

Tested faith brings experience, and experience makes religion real. You will never know the bitterness of sin or the sweetness of pardon until you have felt both. You will never know your own weakness until you have been compelled to go through the rivers. You will never know God's strength until He has supported you in deep waters.

All the talk about religion that has not been personally experienced is just talk. If we have little experience, we cannot speak so positively as those whose experience has been deep and profound. Once in the early days of my ministry, I was preaching on God's faithfulness in trials, and my venerable grandfather was sitting in the pulpit behind me. He suddenly stood up, came to the pulpit, and said, "My grandson can preach this as a matter of theory. But I can tell it to you from experience because I have done business on great waters. I have seen the works of the Lord and His wonders in the deep" (Ps. 107:23-24). There is an accumulation of force in the testimony of one who has passed through great trials.

Faith increases in firmness, assurance, and intensity when it is exercised with trials. Praise Him for your trials, and you will have more and more of God's blessings until your faith will move mountains and nothing will be impossible (Matt. 17:20).

ALL THINGS ARE POSSIBLE. *Matthew 19:26*

I have known the day when perplexities pleased me, when dilemmas afforded delight, and when difficult tasks were thrilling. Even now I enjoy puzzling over a problem and attempting what others decline. Nothing good in this world can be accomplished without difficulty. The biggest diamonds lie under heavy stones, which the lazy cannot turn over. What is easy is hardly worth doing. In the face of difficulty the zealous persevere. They brace their nerves, sharpen their wits, and bring all their power into play to achieve an objective that will reward their effort.

Do you have great difficulties, dear friend? You are not the first. Look at Moses. He had to bring Israel out of Egypt, but his path was not clear. He had to go to Pharaoh and issue God's command, "Let My people go" (Ex. 5:1). The haughty monarch dismisses him, but Moses returns with, "Thus says the LORD God of the Hebrews: 'Let My people go, that they may serve Me'" (Ex. 9:13). And this was just the beginning of Moses' mission. His life was full of difficulty until he got to the top of Pisgah (Deut. 34:1).

My dear friend, when you meet with opposition, encounter it with prayer and exercise more faith. Antagonists should never hinder your progress in the cause of Christ. Diamond must cut diamond. There is nothing so hard that you cannot cut it with something harder. Ask God to steel your soul to the conquering point and to make your resolution like an unyielding stone. Then you can cut your way through a mountain of diamonds in the service of your Lord and Master. Therefore, be brave and fear not. Advance in God's strength.

If the Lord does not return and we are taken home by death, there is nothing to fear. Our Lord does not pick His fruit unwisely. Saints are prepared to go before they go. I have never visited a member of this church who expressed the slightest dismay or fear in dying. Grace is given, and they rise above the hour's weakness. The Lord Jesus gives them triumph over pain and death. They pass away as if going to a wedding rather than to a grave. Doubts are driven away when you see believers die.

What will the first five minutes in heaven be like? There is a larger question. What will thousands of years in heaven be like? What will myriads of ages in heaven be like?

My disembodied spirit will be perfectly happy in my Lord's embrace, and in due time the resurrection day will dawn. This body will rise again in full glory. There will be a remarriage of soul and body, and we will be like our risen Lord. Oh the glory of that expected end! We will be introduced to the society of angels, to the presence of cherubim and seraphim. We will see Him whom we have loved for so long. We will hear Him say, "Come, you blessed of My Father, inherit the kingdom prepared for you" (Matt. 25:34).

O My Father. *Matthew 26:42*

My dear friend, remember that you have a Father in heaven. When all is gone and spent, you can still say, "My Father." Relatives are dead, but your Father lives. Friends may leave, just as the birds fly south for the winter, but you are not alone because the Father is with you. Cling to this blessed text, "I will never leave you nor forsake you" (Heb. 13:5). In every moment of distress, anxiety, and perplexity, you have a Father on whose wisdom, truth, and power you can rely.

If your children have needs, they go to you. If they have questions, they ask you. If they are ill-treated, they appeal to you. If a thorn is in their finger, they run to you for relief. Little or great, your children's sorrows are your concern. This makes their life easy, and it would make our lives easier if we acted as God's children. Imitate Jesus. In your Gethsemane, pray as He did, "O My Father" (Matt. 26:42). This is a better defense than shield or sword. Jesus' resource was to approach His Father with prevailing prayer.

There are times when, moved by the Holy Spirit, we pray with a power of faith that can never fail at the mercy seat. Without this impulse, we must not push our will. There are many occasions when, if we had all the faith to move mountains, we would show wisely if only by saying, "Your will be done" (Matt. 26:42).

Prayer is always an open door. There is no predicament in which you cannot pray. If, like Jonah, you are at the bottom of the ocean and the weeds are wrapped around your head, you may still pray. If you are between the jaws of the lion, you may still pray. Prayer is a weapon that can be used in every position and every conflict. Do not look to the arm of flesh (2 Chr. 32:8), but look to the Lord your God.

WE ARE PERISHING. *Mark 4:38*

Often, the Lord permits our loved ones to suffer, and it seems that He ignores our prayers and pleas as their case grows worse and worse. We say, "Teacher, do you care that we are perishing?" (Mark 4:38). We readily forget that our complaint is based on error.

The laws of nature can do nothing of themselves. There is no such power as a law of nature acting by itself, for all power lies in God. A law of nature is nothing more or less than a description of the way the Lord works. Usually, God causes ships to obey their helms and rocks to retain their hardness. Thus it is the badly steered vessel that strikes the rocks and sinks. The one who dies of sickness does not die because of some ungovernable force in nature but because God gives energy to destructive agencies. The laws of nature are only powerless letters. I see them, and I know that God acts according to them. It is God working by the law, for He does it all.

This truth sets matters in another light. If the Lord brings the trial, we should yield to His will and not complain, for His ways of action are right. If His ways cause grief, we still believe that He does not afflict willingly or give us pain without design (Lam. 3:33). Instead of saying, "Teacher, do You not care that we are perishing," we ought to cry in submission, "It is the LORD. Let Him do what seems good to Him" (1 Sam. 3:18).

What happens occurs because God causes all thing to work together for good to those who love Him, to those who are the called according to His purpose (Rom. 8:28). God has His purpose and His way. His purposes are for His glory and for the good of His people.

THE POWER OF JESUS. *Mark 4:41*

Jesus' power has no limit. "Even the wind and the sea obey Him." The most fickle elements, and the most unruly forces are under the power of Jesus. Rejoice in this thought: the mighty Atlantic, which divides continents, and the little drops of water in a bowl are alike in Jesus' hands.

The power of God is seen in an earthquake destroying a village. Yet it is as indisputably present when the seeds are scattered from a flower's pod or when a rose leaf falls on a garden path. God is seen when an angel dashes from heaven to earth and when a bee flits from flower to flower.

Jesus is the master of the little and of the great. He is the King of all things. I rejoice when I think that even the wicked actions of ungodly people are overruled by our great Lord, "who works all things according to the counsel of His will" (Eph. 1:11).

In the front, I see Jesus leading His children, and behind, He guards the rear. On the heights, I see Jesus reigning as King of kings and Lord of lords. In the deep, I mark the terror of His justice as He binds the dragon with His chain (Rev. 20:1-3). Admire and adore His unlimited power; then fall on your knees and pay homage to our sovereign Master.

Take courage believer. Let waves dash and winds howl. "God is our refuge and strength, a very present help in trouble. Therefore we will not fear even though the earth be removed, and though the mountains be carried into the midst of the sea; though its waters roar and be troubled, though the mountains shake with its swelling" (Ps. 46:1-3). "The LORD of hosts is with us; the God of Jacob is our refuge" (Ps. 46:11).

The Lord bless you in storm and in calm for Christ's sake. Amen.

BE OF GOOD CHEER! *Mark 6:50*

After taking "arms against a sea of trouble," we find ourselves unable to stop the boisterous torrent. We are swept downstream, loss succeeds loss, and riches take flight. We see nothing but absolute want. It is then that we require abundant grace to sustain our spirits.

It is not easy to come down with perfect resignation from wealth to poverty and from abundance to shortages. That is a philosophy to be learned. Paul was taught it, for he said, "I have learned in whatever state I am, to be content" (Phil. 4:11).

Some would find it hard to be content in the widow's position, seven children and nothing to maintain them but the pittance that is wrung from her labor with the needle. Stitch, stitch, stitch, stitch. She sits far into the dead of night stitching her soul away.

You might not find it quite so easy to bear poverty if you were shunned by those who courted you in prosperity. Today they would not acknowledge you if they met you in the street. There is a business about being poor that is not easily rinsed from your cup. You need these promises, "Fear not for I am with you; be not dismayed for I am your God" (Is. 41:10). "Your Maker is your husband, the LORD of hosts is His name" (Is. 54:5).

May my Lord and Master say to you, "Be of good cheer! It is I; do not be afraid" (Mark 6:50).

Forsaken by God? *Mark 15:34*

Some of you are called to suffer in your minds, not because of any wrong but for the sake of others. Some years ago, I preached a sermon from the text, "My God, My God, why have You forsaken Me?" (Mark 15:34). I preached my own cry. I felt an agony of spirit. I was under an awful sense of being forsaken by God, and I could not understand why I was surrounded by such thick darkness. I wanted to clear myself if any sin remained in me, but I could not discover any evil that I was tolerating.

When I went back into the vestry, I learned the secret of my personal distress. There was an elderly man in a horror of great darkness. He said, "I have never met any person who has been where I am. I trust there is hope." I asked him to sit down, and we talked. I hope I conducted him from the verge of insanity to the open healthy place of peace through believing. I could never have helped if I had not been in the miry clay myself. Then I understood why I felt like one forsaken. The Lord was leading me to where I would be taught to know this man, to where I would be willing to sit with him in the dark prison-house and lend him a hand to escape.

In presenting myself to my Lord for service since then, I have said to Him, "Make me useful to the doubting and depressed. I do not bargain for comfort, peace, or joy if I can be more helpful to Your poor, weary children without them. Place me where I can best answer Your purpose by being made to sympathize with Your troubled people. I only want to bring them to heaven, to the praise of the glory of Your grace. As for me, let me rejoice or suffer as best suits their case."

For this you must have faith in God and be sure that your trials will have great compensation.

TENDER MERCY. *Luke 1:78*

The tender mercy of our God" (Luke 1:78) gleams with kindly light. I see in His mercy a soft radiance like the matchless pearls that form heaven's gates (Rev. 21:21). Mercy is a melody to my ear as well as to my heart. Mercy is music, and to the brokenhearted, "tender mercy" is its most exquisite form.

If you are desperate and depressed, "tender mercy" is life from the dead. Think of this in connection with God, and you will be struck with wonder that One so great is so tender. We often think of God as a crushing energy that scarcely can take into account our little, feeble, and suffering things. Think again. And with a new wonder of admiration, know that it is so.

We read of His gentleness and His tenderness toward the children of men (2 Cor. 10:1). The "tender mercy" of God's heart is seen in the Dayspring from on high, who has visited us to give light to those who sit in darkness and in the shadow of death, to guide our feet into the way of peace (Luke 1:78-79).

Mercy is divine essence, and mercy lies in the heart of God. He has bound up His mercy with His existence. The mercy of God's heart means His mercy proceeds from His heart and is therefore sincere, tender, intense, warm, and affectionate. If you desire to read the character of God's mercy written in capital letters, study the visitation of His dear Son and all the wonderful works of infinite grace that proceed from Jesus.

God is love (1 John 4:8). Not only is He loving, He is love itself.

CAUGHT NOTHING. *Luke 5:5*

If you are out of work, if you are searching for employment, if you have walked until your feet are blistered and still cannot find a job, do not give up. Listen, and apply Peter's words to your painful trial. "Master, we have toiled all night and caught nothing; nevertheless at Your word I will let down the net" (Luke 5:5). Show the world that a believer is not readily driven to despair. Let people see that when the yoke is made heavy then the Lord strengthens His children's backs. Through the Holy Spirit's power, you will be calmly resolute and able to honor God with a happy persistence.

The affairs of common life are the place to prove God's truth and to bring Him glory. It is not by extraordinary works but by the holiness of ordinary life that Christians are known and that their God is honored. "Trust in the LORD and do good; dwell in the land and feed on His faithfulness. Delight yourself also in the LORD, and He shall give you the desires of your heart" (Ps. 37:3-4).

It may be that you are endeavoring to acquire business skills and have not succeeded. Do not give up. Our Lord Jesus would never have it said that His disciples are cowards who, if they do not succeed the first time, will never try again. We are to be patterns of moral virtue and spiritual grace. When the Lord calls, obey Him. Let down the nets one more time. Work with both mind and hand, and look to Him for the blessing.

AFTER THE STORM. *Luke 8:25*

When God has done great things for you, when He has brought you through your present difficulty, repay Him with your loudest and most triumphant music. Praise Him in the courts of His house (Ps. 100:4). Bless again and again in the name of the Lord.

After a severe storm, there is generally a long rest. You will get through this trouble, and afterward it will be smooth sailing. I have known children of God who have been in the center of the hurricane, and it seemed as if they would be totally destroyed. But when it was over, there was not a ripple on the calm of their lives. People envied them and wondered at their quietness. They had all their storms at one time, and when it was over they came into smooth waters.

Perhaps you will have the same experience. Ask the great Pilot of the Galilean lake to steer you safely through your tempest (Luke 8:24). When the storm ceases at His command, you will be glad that you were quiet. He will bring you to your desired haven. May these words comfort you. I know how tried and tested you are. I pray the Lord, the Comforter, to apply these words to your troubled heart.

I have a sad thought. Some of you are not believers. You have never trusted in Christ. If this is so, you have to fight your own battles, bear your own trials, and carry your own burdens. When you come at the last great day before the judgment seat (Rom. 14:10), you will have to answer for your sins and bear the punishment. God have mercy on you and deliver you from this condition. May you be brought to receive Christ as your substitute and security. May you glorify His name forever.

WHEN YOU PRAY. *Luke 11:2*

When you pray, try to fully understand your trouble. It is a good idea to write it down and then come to the Lord. There is frequently too much indistinctness in our prayers. We really do not know what we are aiming at, and consequently we miss the mark. We have no clear idea what it is that we are seeking from the Lord. Therefore we do not get it.

If we really know our grief, our pain, our sin, and the plague of our hearts, we can go before the Lord and say, "This is my trouble. Lord, I confess it to You with a broken heart and a contrite spirit." Then it will not be long until the Lord in mercy will give us peace.

Dear troubled friend, there is no relief like prayer. If you are in despair, let me gently tell you that there is One who is ready to give you a full hearing, whatever your trouble. The Lord Jesus Christ already knows all about your trouble. I do not know about it. I cannot tell all that you need. But I do know that all you want between here and heaven is stored up in Christ Jesus.

You need Jesus. And if you get Jesus, you never will have a want that is outside of Christ. You will never have a need that is not within the matchless circle of His unspeakable all-sufficiency.

Take Christ to your heart, and your fortune is made! When the Lord Jesus Christ is yours, you will have all that you need for time and eternity. May the Lord bless you for Jesus' sake.

ASK AND IT WILL BE GIVEN. *Luke 11:9*

I am constantly witnessing the most unmistakable examples of answers to prayer. My entire life is made up of them. They are so common that they no longer surprise me. I could no more doubt the power of prayer than I could disbelieve the law of gravity. For more than forty years, I have tested my Master's promises at the mercy seat, and I have never been repulsed. In the name of Jesus, I have asked and received. It is true that I have had to wait because my time was ill-judged and God's time was far better. But delays are not denials.

If you need evidence, try this. The Lord has said, "Call upon Me in the day of trouble; I will deliver you, and you shall glorify Me" (Ps. 50:15). God answers the supplications of His believing people.

I remind you of the words of the Lord Jesus. "So I say to you, ask, and it will be given you; seek, and you will find; knock, and it will be opened to you. For everyone who asks receives, and he who seeks finds, and to him who knocks it will be opened. If a son asks for bread from any father among you, will he give him a stone? Or if he asks for a fish will he give him a serpent instead of a fish? Or if he asks for an egg, will he offer him a scorpion? If you then, being evil, know how to give good gifts to your children, how much more will your heavenly Father give the Holy Spirit to those who ask Him!" (Luke 11:9-13).

IF HE ASKS FOR AN EGG. *Luke 11:12*

If a son asks for bread from any father among you, will he give him a stone? Or if he asks for a fish will he give him a serpent instead of a fish? Or if he asks for an egg, will he offer him a scorpion? If you then, being evil, know how to give good gifts to your children, how much more will your heavenly Father give the Holy Spirit to those who ask Him!" (Luke 11:11-13).

If we ask God for our daily bread, He will not give us useless, teeth-breaking, unsatisfying stones. When we pray for needful things, He will supply them. As our faith grows stronger, we may ask for a fish that is not a necessity but a tasty relish. Then, if we are bold enough to ask for spiritual comforts, consoling gifts, and sufficient graces, our heavenly Father will give as much as we can carry.

Only once in Scripture did anyone eat an egg (Job 6:6). We don't find poultry until our Savior's day. Chickens were so valuable that eggs were an uncommon luxury. Yet if a child was bold enough to ask for something this valuable, the father did not put a scorpion in the child's hand. If I can summon enough faith to ask for Christ's highest blessings and the most rapt and intense fellowship with Him, I will not receive an intoxicating excitement, a delirious fanaticism, or some other deadly or injurious thing.

Your present condition is from the Lord. He has not given you a stone, a serpent, or a scorpion. What He has given you may seem hard, but it is for your lasting good. Trials may surround you, but God will bring good out of the apparent evil (Gen. 50:20). Even now, infinite wisdom is fulfilling your wish. Amid fiery trials your faith is honoring God. Every circumstance of your affliction is made subservient to the perfection of your soul.

NOT ONE IS FORGOTTEN. *Luke 12:6*

God cares for all the work of His hands. Not even a sparrow falls to the ground apart from your Father's will (Matt. 10:29). "Not one of them is forgotten before God" (Luke 12:6). God cares for every fish in the sea. Even fish that dwell in black pools deep in the earth's caverns, fish that never see light, are not forgotten by Him (Ps. 8:8).

There is a special fatherly consideration and pity that the Lord has for His children. What great care He gives them. No farmer cares as much for barn chickens as God does for His own little chicks. "He shall cover you with His feathers, and under His wings you shall take refuge" (Ps. 91:4). "As a father pities his children, so the Lord pities those who fear Him. For He knows our frame; He remembers that we are dust" (Ps. 103:13-14).

God gives liberally and without reproach (James 1:5). You who are God's saints are first in the Almighty's care. "I am poor and needy; yet the LORD thinks upon me" (Ps. 40:17), said David. It is worthwhile to be poor and needy if we have more of God's thoughts set on us.

Oh sanctified one, see what a special position you occupy—not only in creation and in the covenant, but also in God's tender care!

GOD FEEDS THEM. *Luke 12:24*

The Lord has laid many burdens on me, and I sometimes grow weary. Then the Holy Spirit leads me to understand that I can do nothing by myself. All I have to be is God's obedient servant, His ready instrument, and then I can leave every care with Him. Then peace returns and my thoughts become free and vigorous. My soul throws its burdens aside; runs without weariness and walks without fainting.

I am sure, my dear fellow servant, that life will break you unless you learn the habit of leaning on Jesus. Do not be afraid to lean too much. There has never been a saint blamed for possessing too much faith. There has never been a child of God scolded by the Divine Father for having placed too implicit a reliance on His promise.

The Lord has said, "As your days, so shall your strength be" (Deut. 33:25). He has promised, "I will never leave you nor forsake you" (Heb. 13:5). He has told you, "Consider the ravens, . . . which have neither storehouse nor barn; and God feeds them" (Luke 12:24). He has asked, "Why do you worry about clothing? Consider the lilies of the field, how they grow; they neither toil nor spin; and yet I say to you that even Solomon in all his glory was not arrayed like one of these. Now if God so clothes the grass of the field, which today is, and tomorrow is thrown into the oven, will He not much more clothe you, O you of little faith?" (Matt. 6:28-30).

Give your cares to Him who cares for the ravens and for flowers of the field. Rest assured that He will also care for you.

WHY DO YOU WORRY?   *Luke 12:25*

Christians are forbidden to be anxious (Matt. 6:31-34). "Look at the birds of the air," said Christ, "they neither sow nor reap nor gather into barns; yet your heavenly Father feeds them. Are you not more valuable than they?" (Matt. 6:26). If you have a Father in heaven who cares for you, every little bird that sits on a branch and sings, even though it doesn't have a grain of barley in all the world, should put you to shame if you are anxious. The birds live exempt from care, why not you?

Our Lord taught that anxiety is useless and needless. Care and worry cannot add one cubit to our stature (Luke 12:25). If the farmer worries about lack of rain, will this open the clouds of heaven? If the merchant is concerned because an unfavorable wind delays his loaded ship, can this turn the gale to another quarter? We do not improve our lot by fretting and fuming. If we were infinitely wiser we would throw our cares on God. Prudence is wisdom, for it adapts a means to an end. Anxiety is folly, for it groans and worries and accomplishes nothing.

According to our Savior, anxiety about worldly things is heathenish, "For all these things the Gentiles seek" (Matt. 6:32). Heathens have no God, and so they try to be their own providence. The believer who can say, "God's providence is my inheritance," will not worry. Let the heirs of heaven live on a higher plane than sinners who live without God and without hope. If we are in Christ, let us believe in our God and leave the governing of both the outside world and the little world within to our heavenly Father.

"Trust in the LORD with all your heart, and lean not on your own understanding; in all your ways acknowledge Him, and He shall direct your paths" (Prov. 3:5-6).

DO NOT FEAR. *Luke 12:32*

Do you believe anything is left to chance? Is there any event outside the circle of divine predestination? No, my friend, with God there are no contingencies. The mighty Charioteer of Providence has gathered the reins of all the horses, and He guides them according to His infallible wisdom. Foreknowledge and predestination are in everything, from the motion of a grain of dust to a flaming comet blazing across the sky. Nothing can happen unless God ordains it; nothing happens without divine power. The Lord said, "Behold, I have created the blacksmith who blows the coals in the fire . . . and I have created the spoiler to destroy" (Is. 54:16). The most violent people could not move a finger if strength were not lent them by the Lord.

As for nature's catastrophes, the Lord is distinctly in them. "He shakes the earth out of its place" (Job 9:6). "He removes the mountains" (Job 9:5). Our Father works all things! Why then should His children be afraid? Regardless of how tremendous events may be, we know that nothing can happen to shake the kingdom of God, even the gates of Hades shall not prevail against that kingdom (Matt. 16:18). Our chief possession lies there, and if that is secure then all is safe. Our highest, best, and most vital interests are beyond even the shadow of harm. "Do not fear."

Suppose an accident should take our lives? I smile as I think that the worst thing that could happen would be the best thing that could happen. If we should die, we shall be with the Lord (1 Thess. 4:17). So, if the worst that can befall is the best that can come, why should we fear?

This is good reasoning. If you are a believer, and if God is your refuge, there is no logical reason to fear.

To give you the kingdom. *Luke 12:32*

Christ addresses anxiety with these words, "Do not seek what you should eat or what you should drink, nor have an anxious mind" (Luke 12:29). Never question whether God's bounty can provide food, drink, and clothing, for He has promised you a crown and a mansion. "Do not fear, little flock, for it is your Father's good pleasure to give you the kingdom" (Luke 12:32). Surely He who takes the trouble to give you a kingdom will not let you starve on the road to it.

Affairs of heaven draw my mind from the paltry things of earth. Heir of heaven, you cannot afford to worry about the little annoyances of this fleeting life. Anxiety dishonors God.

I heard about a street sweeper who worked with great diligence. He had a valuable broom that he highly prized, and the few pennies that he spent to purchase it were of great importance. One day a lawyer tapped him on the shoulder and said, "My good friend, is your name so and so?"

"Yes it is."

"Did your father live in such a place?"

"He did."

"Then I have the pleasure of informing you that you have inherited an estate worth over a million pounds a year." The street sweeper walked away without his broom. Neither would I have pushed that broom another moment had I been in his position.

Christian, let me tug your sleeve and tell you about a possession that may well turn you away from your present paltry pickings. Jesus Christ informs you, "It is your Father's good pleasure to give you the kingdom," and this kingdom is worth infinitely more than all the gold of this world.

GO TO MY FATHER. *Luke 15:18*

When you are suffering from severe pain, when you are surrounded by bitter grief, when you are depressed, pray. Do not cry for the sake of crying, and do not moan to the physician or the nurse. Cry, "Father." For isn't this how a lost child cries?

Have you ever cried to God? Have you ever said, "Father"? Oh may my Father put His love in your heart! May He make you say, "I will arise and go to my Father" (Luke 15:18). If that cry is in your heart and on your lips, then you will truly be a child of God.

Give yourself to God. Trust in Him. Every morning when you arise, put yourself in God's divine protection. Every night before you fall asleep, give yourself to Him who is able to keep you when the image of death is on your face. Before you fall asleep, commit yourself to God. Do it when there is nothing to frighten you, when everything is going smoothly, when the south wind blows softly and your ship is speeding toward its desired haven.

Realize God's personal and continuous presence. "Father, into Your hands I commit My Spirit" (Luke 23:46). Say to Him, "You are here, Father. I know that You are here. I realize that You are here in my pain, sorrow, and danger. I put myself in Your hand. If anyone or anything attacks me, I commit myself to You, the unseen Guardian of the night and the unwearied Keeper of the day. You are my God. You have covered my head in the day of battle (Ps. 140:7), and under Your wings I will trust."

I HAVE PRAYED FOR YOU. *Luke 22:32*

If you are deeply depressed and your heart is aching, this verse should bless you. "He shall give His angels charge over you, to keep you in all your ways. In their hands they shall bear you up, lest you dash your foot against a stone" (Ps. 91:11-12).

There are times when your faith walks on a slender thread, high above the ways of the world, poising the balancing pole of experience. Faith tries to keep on her feet, but if she slips there is this gracious safety net of Jesus. "I have prayed for you, that your faith should not fail" (Luke 22:32). God's people will be safe. Satan may try to knock you down, but God will hold you up.

Watch your walk as if your perseverance depended entirely on you. Look to Jesus, however, knowing that He alone keeps the feet of His saints. Holiness, strength of faith, and ultimate perfection are our goals. Yet it is a blessed consolation that if we fail we are not thrown away. "The steps of a good man are ordered by the LORD, and He delights in his way. Though he fall, he shall not be utterly cast down; for the LORD upholds him with His hand" (Ps. 37:23-24).

FAITH THAT DOES NOT FAIL. *Luke 22:32*

Believe in a universal providence. The Lord cares for ants and angels, for worms and for worlds, for cherubim and for sparrows, for seraphim and for insects. Throw your cares on Him. "He counts the number of the stars; He calls them all by name" (Ps. 147:4). Let His universal providence cheer you.

Think of His special providence over all the saints. "He will redeem their life from oppression and violence; and precious shall be their blood in His sight" (Ps. 72:14). "Precious in the sight of the LORD is the death of His saints" (Ps. 116:15). "And we know that all things work together for good to those who love God, to those who are the called according to His purpose" (Rom. 8:28). While He is the Savior of all men, He is especially the Savior of those that believe. Let this cheer and comfort you; special providence watches over the chosen. "The angel of the LORD encamps all around those who fear Him, and delivers them" (Ps. 34:7).

Let the thought of His special love to you be the essence of your comfort. "I will never leave you nor forsake you" (Heb. 13:5). God says that as much to you as He said it to any saint of old. Do not be afraid, for I am your shield and your exceedingly great reward (Gen. 15:1). Oh that the Holy Spirit would make you feel the promise as being spoken to you! For the promises are to you and meant for you. Grasp them! Hear the Master say, "Let not your heart be troubled; you believe in God, believe also in Me" (John 14:1). Think that you heard Him say, "I have prayed for you that your faith should not fail" (Luke 22:32).

Oh those sweet words of Christ! Lord, speak them to me. Speak them to Your poor, sorrowing child, and speak them to each one of us. May we hear Your voice and say, "Jesus whispers consolation, I cannot refuse it. I will sit under His shadow with great delight."

NOT MY WILL. *Luke 22:42*

If God does it all, if nothing happens apart from God, if even the wickedness and cruelty of this world is permitted by Him, then you can graciously kiss the hand that strikes.

Is your husband gone to heaven? God took him. Is your property melted away? God permitted it. Were you robbed? Do not think of the second cause, look to the great First Cause. You strike a dog and he bites the stick. If that dog were wise, he would look at you who used the stick.

Do not look at the second cause of the affliction; look to the great First Cause. It is your God who is in it all, your Father, God the infinitely good. What do you want to have done on earth, your will or God's will? If you are wise, you will say, "Not my will, but Yours be done." Accept the ways of providence, for God appoints them. Accept them with grateful praise.

It is true sacrifice when we can say, "Though He slay me, yet will I trust Him" (Job 13:15). If we receive good from His hand and bless Him, even sinners might do that. But if we receive what seems to be evil and bless Him, this is grace; this is the work of the Holy Spirit.

Give us grace enough, Oh Lord, never to fail in our loyalty but to be faithful servants, even to sufferings' bitterest end. Amen.

Never see death. *John 8:51*

Some of you are comforted by the belief that you will live until the Lord returns, and so you will not sleep in the grave but be changed, in a moment, in the twinkling of an eye (1 Cor. 15:51-52). The hope of our Lord's appearing is a blessed one.

I do not, however, believe that to be alive at His coming is anything to desire. Is there any great preference in being changed rather than in dying? "We who are alive and remain until the coming of the Lord will by no means precede those who are asleep" (1 Thess. 4:15). This is a great truth. If I die rather than being changed, throughout eternity I will be able to say that I had fellowship with Christ in death. This is an experience that those saints who survive will never know. How precious will Christ be when, in the ages to come, we shall think of His death and be able to say, "We too have died and risen again."

You that are alive and remain will certainly not have a preference over us, who, like our Lord, will taste death. We do not grieve for those that have fallen asleep before the Lord's gracious appearing, because our Lord has said, "If anyone keeps My word, he shall never see death" (John 8:51). This is not only for the few who will remain at His second coming, but also for the entire company of those who have kept His Word. Even though they pass into the grave, they will never see death.

I KNOW MY SHEEP. *John 10:14*

God has not left us. He has not left us as the ostrich leaves her eggs on the ground to be crushed by a foot (Job 39:13-15). God is watching over us every moment. He exercises an unceasing care and a watchful providence; therefore, we should praise Him.

Some think of God as having taken the universe like a watch, wound it, and placed it under His pillow and gone to sleep. This is not true. God's finger is on every wheel of the world's machinery. God's power is the force in the laws of the universe, laws that would be dead if He were not powerfully active.

Child of Adam, you are not rocked in your cradle by wild winds but by the hand of love. Daughter of affliction, you are not bedridden to be the victim of heartless laws. There is One who, with His own kind and tender hand, makes your bed in sickness.

Day by day God gives us our daily bread and clothes us. He gives breath for our heaving lungs and blood for our beating hearts. He keeps us alive. If His power was withdrawn we would immediately sink into death.

"I am the good shepherd; and I know My sheep" (John 10:14). You are the sheep of His hand. The hourly provision, the constant protection, the wise and judicious governing, the royal leadership through the desert to the pastures on the other side of Jordan, the power to chase away the wolf, and the skills to find pasture in the wilderness, all flow from the fact that He is your Shepherd.

Praise Him! Adore the God who keeps you living and feeds you from the storehouse of divine grace. Serve your God. Serve Him with all your heart, soul, and strength. "You are His people and the sheep of His pasture" (Ps. 100:3).

They shall never perish. *John 10:28*

If you are depressed by present difficulties, if your outlook is exceedingly dark, take courage. Your Lord has done great things. His death and resurrection are prophetic of good things to come. "Your kingdom come, Your will be done on earth as it is in heaven" (Luke 11:2). His will shall be done as surely as He came from heaven to earth and has returned from earth to heaven. His purpose will be carried out as surely as He died and lives again.

This is why the Lord appeared and said to His sorrowing servant John, "I am He who lives, and was dead, and behold I am alive forevermore. Amen. And I have the keys of Hades and of Death" (Rev. 1:18). The dying and then living Shepherd is the safety and the glory of the flock.

Comfort one another with your Lord's words, "I am the good shepherd: and I know My sheep and am known by My own. As the Father knows Me, even so I know the Father; and I lay down My life for the sheep" (John 10:14-15). "My sheep hear My voice, and I know them, and they follow Me. And I give them eternal life, and they shall never perish; neither shall anyone snatch them out of My hand. My Father, who has given them to Me, is greater than all; and no one is able to snatch them out of My Father's hand. I and My Father are one" (John 10:27-30).

My Father's Hand. *John 10:29*

Our position is guaranteed, and it is a place of honor, for we are in Christ's hands (John 10:28). It is a place of property, for Christ holds His people, and all the saints are in His hand. It is a place of love: "See, I have inscribed you on the palms of My hands, your walls are continually before Me" (Is. 49:16). It is a place of discretion, for we present our members as slaves of righteousness for holiness (Rom. 6:19). It is a place of guidance (Ps. 32:8) and protection (Ps. 59:16). We will never perish. No one will snatch us out of His hand (John 10:28). As arrows are to be used by a mighty warrior, as jewels are to be used by a bride, so are we in the hand of Christ, for we are the ring on His finger.

John 10:28 reminds us that there are some who want to snatch us out of our Savior's hand. Some will rise and show great signs and wonders to deceive, if possible, even the elect (Matt. 24:24). Roaring persecutors want to frighten God's saints and make them turn back. Scheming tempters—pimps of hell, jackals of the lion of the pit—desire to drag us to destruction. Even our own heart tries to snatch us from His hand. But Jesus says, "Neither shall anyone snatch them out of My hand."

"Neither death nor life, nor angels nor principalities nor powers, nor things present nor things to come, nor height nor depth, nor any other created thing, shall be able to separate us from the love of God which is in Christ Jesus our Lord" (Rom. 8:38-39). No person, devil, or conceivable thing is able to snatch us from His hand. Under no circumstances can anyone, by any scheme, remove us from being His favorites, His property, and His protected children. What a blessed promise!

FOR YOUR SAKES. *John 11:15*

Then Jesus said to them plainly, 'Lazarus is dead, and I am glad for your sakes that I was not there'" (John 11:14-15). You see, dear friend, Jesus Christ was glad, glad that His disciples were blessed with trouble. Think about this, you who are so troubled: Jesus Christ sympathizes with you. But He does it wisely, for He says, "I am glad for your sakes that I was not there."

You would never possess a precious, supporting faith were it not for your fiery trials. You are a tree that would never have rooted so well if the wind had not rocked and made you take firm hold on the precious truths of the covenant of grace. Special trials bring special visits. It may be that Christ would never have come to Bethany if Lazarus had not died. Christian, it will comfort and strengthen your faith if Christ comes to you in your troubles.

In prosperity, you do not see the smiles in His face. But you will see them in adversity because the Lord Jesus will go out of His way to visit you. You may be healthy and strong and have little fellowship with Christ, but when you are sick He will make your bed. Though you might walk on green grass without the Savior, when you come into the midst of the fire He will be with you (Dan. 3:25). Christ will reveal Himself when trials surround you, and then you will have deliverance.

JESUS WEPT. *John 11:35*

Lazarus was dead, but Jesus was going to raise Him (John 11:11). Lazarus' resurrection was at hand, yet Jesus wept (John 11:35). We are sometimes told that if we really believe our friends will rise again, and if we really believe they are safe and happy, then we should not weep. Why not? Jesus did. And there cannot be any error in following Jesus' example. Jesus knew that Lazarus' death was for God's glory. He said, "This sickness is not unto death, but for the glory of God, that the Son of God may be glorified through it" (John 11:4). Still He wept.

Have you ever thought it wicked to weep at a loss that will glorify God? It is not wicked. If it were, Jesus would not have wept under similar circumstances. Tears, which might have been regarded as contraband, now have free admission into the realm of holiness because "Jesus wept."

Dear friend, you may weep because "Jesus wept." He wept with the full knowledge of Lazarus' happiness, with the full knowledge of his resurrection, with the firm assurance that God was glorified through this death. We may not condemn what Christ allows. If you can weep and thank God, if you can weep and know that you are in His presence, then your weeping is not sinful. Let your tears roll in floods. This is good instruction.

May the Holy Spirit teach us. May the Lord write it on every weeper's heart. You may weep because "Jesus wept."

DO NOT BE TROUBLED. *John 14:1*

All too often, we believers watch the gathering clouds and forecast storms and anticipate troubles. Some of us confess that times of depression are coming. We see our business slipping away, and we worry about the future. We worry about our children, for we see the various tendencies in young people, and we worry about the way they will go. Our health declines, and we wonder what to do when the disease gets worse. Yet our Lord Jesus Christ counsels us, "Let not your heart be troubled" (John 14:1).

Do not fear! Has not God helped you in every plight already? When we cast our cares on the Lord, to do as He wills, at no time will He be unkind. He will never put us in the furnace unless He intends to purge our dross, and the furnace will not be one degree warmer than is absolutely necessary. Mercy will always balance misery; strength will always support burden. The Lord is our friend; He will never be our foe.

Cheer up! "Do not fear little flock," shake off your fears and rejoice, "for it is your Father's good pleasure to give you the kingdom" (Luke 12:32). The road may be rough, but the end is sure. We are going to the kingdom, to a land where all the believers will be princes and kings. Take heart. What difference does it make if our accommodations are sparse, if the passage is rough, if the winds boisterous? There is a kingdom ahead! Make the best of this voyage. Do not be fainthearted, but sing:

> With a bag on my back and a staff in my hand,
> I march on in haste through an enemy's land;
> The way may be rough, but it cannot be long,
> So I'll smooth it with hope, and I'll cheer it with song.

ANOTHER HELPER. *John 14:16*

Do you think that the Holy Spirit, the dear, precious, and ever-blessed Holy Spirit, does not have pity on us? The Holy Spirit condescends to dwell in us as the Helper (John 15:26). This is matchless condescension.

Do you think that the Comforter cannot sympathize with us? A Comforter without sympathy, who mocks our human woes, would indeed be a strange being. No, my friend, He is full of tender pity.

Ponder the Holy Spirit's love. Never think even for a moment that He is mindless or careless about whether you will perish. The Triune God is love (1 John 4:16). "For as the heavens are high above the earth, so great is His mercy toward those who fear Him; as far as the east is from the west, so far has He removed our transgression from us. As a father pities his children, so the LORD pities those who fear Him. For He knows our frame; He remembers that we are dust" (Ps. 103:11-14).

I WILL NOT LEAVE YOU. *John 14:18*

Let us rejoice that God's people, whose lives are recorded in Scripture, were like us. I have known many a poor sinner who found hope in observing the sins and struggles of those who were saved by grace. I have known many heirs of heaven who have found comfort as they observed how imperfect people have prevailed with God in prayer and been delivered in times of difficulty.

I am glad that the apostles were not perfect. Had they been perfect, they would have immediately understood all that Jesus said, and we would have lost our Lord's instructive explanations. If they had been perfect, they would have lived above all trouble, and the Master would not have said these golden words, "Let not your heart be troubled" (John 14:1).

Jesus promised, "I will pray the Father, and He will give you another Comforter, that He may abide with you forever. . . . I will not leave you orphans; I will come to you" (John 14:16-18). When trials depress our hearts, and when the most tender ministry fails to give consolation, it is an encouragement for those failing to be comforted to remember the unfailing Comforter and to commit the trial and depression into divine hands.

Since one Person of the blessed Trinity has undertaken to be the Comforter, we see how important it is that our hearts should be filled with consolation. Happy religion, in which it is our duty to be glad! Blessed gospel, by which we are forbidden to be troubled.

I WILL COME TO YOU. *John 14:18*

It is a blessing to have precious relationships associated with the word home: husband, wife, children, father, mother, brother, sister. Many are blessed with good relationships, but do not be content to comfort yourself with ties that must be broken. Ask that you may be blessed over and above these.

I thank God for earthly fathers. But if You, God, will be my Father, then I am indeed blessed. I thank God for a mother's love. But if You, God, comfort my soul as one whom a mother comforts, then I am indeed blessed. Lord, I treasure and thank You for the home You have given me, but "I would dwell in the house of the LORD forever" (Ps. 23:6) and be a child that never wanders from my Father's house.

Are you separated from home and family? I know some of you have left behind, in the bivouac of life, graves that are a part of your heart, and the remainder of your heart is bleeding with many wounds. May the Lord bless you. Widow, "Your Maker is your husband" (Is. 54:5). Orphans, He has said, "I will not leave you orphans; I will come to you" (John 14:18). "The LORD watches over the strangers; He relieves the fatherless and widow" (Ps. 146:9).

You will be blessed indeed to find all of your relationships in Him. May you have human and temporary blessings to fill your heart with gladness. But may these blessings not foul your heart with worldliness or distract your attention from the things that belong to your everlasting welfare.

Have you any food? *John 21:5*

The Lord is concerned about our needs. During His earthly days, He fed multitudes on two grand occasions (Matt. 14:13-21; 15:32-38). Now that He has died, is risen, and is in His glorified body, He still thinks of His people's hunger. He still calls, "Children, have you any food?" (John 21:5). Finding they have nothing, He says, "Come and eat breakfast" (John 21:12). These words fall graciously from His lips and prove His care for our earthly needs.

Our Lord and Savior is particularly mindful of the needs of His people. If you are needy and in difficult circumstances, be encouraged. He that said to His disciples, "Come and eat breakfast," will not forget you in your time of need. On your part, this is the time to exercise faith. On His part, now is the time for the display of His power.

If you look to friends, they may fail to help. So-called friends are far too ready to give the cold shoulder to those who are not well-to-do. But if you look to Him, your prayers will be answered, in some way or other, the Lord will provide. I cannot tell how, any more than I can tell how the Lord lighted that fire of coals or procured the fish that lay broiling on the fire, but there was the fire and there was the fish (John 21:9). The Lord provided. "Trust in the LORD, and do good; dwell in the land, and feed on His faithfulness. Delight yourself also in the LORD, and He shall give you the desires of your heart" (Ps. 37:3-4).

He that taught you to say, "Give us this day our daily bread" (Matt. 6:11), did not teach an empty phrase. If your needs are so pressing as to make you hunger, Jesus loves and pities you. Look to Him for help. He is the same today as He was by the lake of Galilee.

I speak to some whom I know are under a severe trial. You seem to have given up, but I beg you to call on the name of the Lord. You cannot perish praying; no one ever has. If you perished praying, you would be a new wonder in the universe. A praying soul in hell is an utter impossibility.

A person calling on God and being rejected, impossible! The supposition is not to be entertained. "Whoever calls on the name of the Lord shall be saved" (Acts 2:21). God cannot lie. He must quit His nature, forfeit His claim to mercy, and destroy His character of love if He refuses to hear a sinner who calls on His name. There will come a day when He will say, "When I called, you did not answer" (Is. 65:12), but that is not today. Where there is life, there is hope. "Today, if you will hear His voice, do not harden your hearts" (Heb. 3:15). Call on God at once.

This warrant of grace runs through all the regions of life: "Whoever calls on the name of the Lord shall be saved."

GREAT GRACE. *Acts 4:33*

God gives a deeper and stronger grace to those who endure exceedingly great trials. There is a glorious aurora in the frigid zone, where stars glisten in the northern skies with unusual splendor. Old Rutherford had a saying that when he was cast into the cellars of affliction he remembered that the great King always kept His wine there. So he looked to drink "of the well-refined wines on the lees" (Is. 25:6).

Those who dive in the sea of affliction bring up rare pearls. My companions in affliction, you know that this is true. You whose bones are ready to come through the skin from lying long on a weary bed. You who have seen your earthly goods carried away and been reduced to poverty. You who have gone to gravesites so often that you feared your last earthly friend would be carried away by unpitying death. You have proved that He is a faithful God. As your trials increase, "He gives more grace" (James 4:6).

My prayer is that some prisoner of the Lord will have a joyous promise. You who are burdened with present heaviness will hear Him say in a soft whisper, "Call to Me, and I will answer you, and show you great and mighty things which you do not know" (Jer. 33:3).

I BELIEVE GOD. *Acts 27:25*

I believe God." This is a grand thing, to believe God when the winds are wild, to believe God when the waves howl like wild beasts seeking to devour you.

"I believe God." Faith that can stand a storm is faith's genuine breed. The common run of faith is fair-weather faith, which loves to see its beautiful image mirrored in a calm sea. But fair-weather faith is far away when the storm clouds are marshaling for battle. The faith of God's elect is a faith that can see in the dark, a faith that is calm in the chaos, and a faith that is brightest when everything is dark as midnight. Paul said, "I believe in God," when he had nothing else to believe in.

"My soul, wait silently for God alone, for my expectation is from Him. He only is my rock and my salvation; He is my defense; I shall not be moved" (Ps. 62:5-6). "God is our refuge and strength, a very present help in trouble. Therefore we will not fear, even though the earth be removed, and though the mountains be carried into the midst of the sea; though its waters roar and be troubled, though the mountains shake with its swelling" (Ps. 46:1-3):

God liveth still!
Trust, my soul, and fear no ill:
Heaven's huge vault may cleave asunder,
Earth's round globe in ruins burst;
Devil's fullest rage may hinder,
Death and hell may spend their worst;
Then will God keep safe and surely;
Wherefore then, my soul despair?
Mid the shipwreck, God is there.

STANDING IN GRACE. *Romans 5:2*

Our trials are appointed (1 Thess. 3:3), and there is an appointed portion of grace that will sustain us (2 Cor. 12:9), grace exactly according to the measure of our needs. Our tests are appointed, and there is appointed an extraordinary help to deliver our souls from going into the pit.

Do you fear sickness? It might be appointed, but it is also appointed that the Lord will strengthen you on your bed of illness and sustain you on your sickbed (Ps. 41:3).

It is perhaps appointed that you will be in need. "Better is a little with the fear of the LORD, than great treasure with trouble" (Prov. 15:16).

Unless the Lord in His glory should suddenly come, "it is appointed for men to die" (Heb. 9:27), but it is also appointed that the dead in Christ shall rise (1 Thess. 4:16). Our appointed death is not the death of common humanity; it is sleeping in Jesus, and the trumpet of God will awaken us (1 Thess. 4:16). It is appointed that believers will rise from the grave in the image of the Lord Jesus. "It has not yet been revealed what we shall be, but we know that when He is revealed, we shall be like Him, for we shall see Him as He is" (1 John 3:2). What difference does it make if your body lies in the clods of the valley? It is appointed that these very hands will play the celestial strings of the golden harp. These very eyes will see the King in His beauty. You will be a partaker of His everlasting blessedness.

Rejoice! God's appointments concerning His children are sure and effective. "God has not cast away His people whom He foreknew" (Rom. 11:2).

CHRIST DIED FOR US. *Romans 5:8*

If you do not know Jesus Christ, troubles may force you to face a stern reality. Have you ever been on the edge of death? Have you ever had your body racked with pain and the chance of recovery only one in ninety-nine? Have you ever felt that death was near? Have you ever peered into eternity with anxious eyes? Have you ever pictured hell and thought you were there? Have you ever thought of being shut out of heaven?

It is in these times that God's Holy Spirit works great things. Christ is pleased when you are brought low and forced to cry to God. He is pleased because this is the stepping stone to genuine trust in Him. It is much better to lose an eye or a hand than to lose your soul (Mark 9:47). It is better to go to heaven poor and ragged than to enter hell rich. It is better to melt into heaven with cancer than go down to hell with your bones full of marrow and your muscles full of strength. To God be the glory when trials and troubles bring us to Christ.

Once you prevail with God and believe in Him you will have deliverance. Remember this: the one thing necessary for eternal life is to trust in the Lord Jesus Christ (John 3:16). You know the story. Christ came down from heaven and took your sins on His shoulders (Heb. 9:26). He died as your substitute (Rom. 5:8), and if Christ suffered for you, you cannot suffer that way. Jesus paid your debts, and you are free (Heb. 9:28). If you believe this, then you are as pure as the angels in heaven.

May God bring you to faith for Jesus' sake. Amen.

INTERCESSION. *Romans 8:26*

Never give up praying, even when Satan suggests that prayer is in vain. Pray in his teeth. "Pray without ceasing" (1 Thess. 5:17). If the heavens are brass and your prayer only echoes above your head, pray on! If month after month your prayer appears to have miscarried, if you have had no answer, continue to draw close to the Lord. Do not abandon the mercy seat for any reason. If it is a good thing that you have been asking for, and if you are sure that it is according to the divine will, wait, tarry, pray, weep, plead, wrestle, and agonize until you get what you are praying for.

If your heart is cold, do not wait until your heart warms. Pray your soul into heat with the help of the ever-blessed Holy Spirit, who helps in our weakness, who makes intercession for us with groanings that cannot be uttered (Rom. 8:26).

Never cease prayer for any reason. If the philosopher tells you that every event is fixed and that prayer cannot possibly change anything, go on praying. If you cannot reply to every difficulty that man suggests, resolve to be obedient to the divine will. "Pray without ceasing." Never, never, never renounce the habit of prayer or your confidence in its power.

ALL THINGS. *Romans 8:28*

W e know that all things work together for good to those who love God, to those who are the called according to His purpose. For whom He foreknew, He also predestined to be conformed to the image of His Son" (Rom. 8:28-29). Everything that happens to you is for your own good. If the waves roll against you, it only speeds your ship toward the port. If lightning and thunder comes, it clears the atmosphere and promotes your soul's health. You gain by loss, you grow healthy in sickness, you live by dying, and you are made rich in losses.

Could you ask for a better promise? It is better that all things should work for my good than all things should be as I would wish to have them. All things might work for my pleasure and yet might all work my ruin. If all things do not always please me, they will always benefit me. This is the best promise of this life.

ACCORDING TO HIS PURPOSE. *Romans 8:28*

When God has a plan for an individual, He often begins with discipline in the form of affliction and sorrow. Just as a good farmer cuts down the trees and clears the land before planting, God cuts down our trees of pleasure and pride, that our hearts may be plowed, broken, raked, and prepared to receive the good seed of the word.

Sometimes a storm brings people to their senses and arouses their consciences until they cry to the Lord. At other times, serious business losses bring such distress that people are driven to seek riches that are more enduring than gold, a competence that is more reliable than profits, and a comfort that is more genuine and lasting than wealth. Yes, and without these the Holy Spirit has frequently been pleased to convict of sin and reduce individuals to total despondency and abject self-abhorrence.

Submit cheerfully. There is no affliction that comes by chance. We are not left to the misery of believing that things happen independent of a divinely controlling power. Not a drop of bitter ever falls into our cup unless the heavenly Father's wisdom places it there. We dwell where everything is ordered by God. Whenever adversity must come, it is always with a purpose. And if it is God's purpose, should I wish to escape it?

We have this blessed assurance. "All things work together for good to those who love God, to those who are the called according to His purpose" (Rom. 8:28). Adversity is a healing medicine and not a deadly poison. Thus without a murmur, drink it all and say with your Savior, "O My Father, if it is possible, let this cup pass from Me; nevertheless, not as I will, but as You will" (Matt. 26:39).

IF GOD IS FOR US. *Romans 8:31*

You may assume that those of us who are always before the public speaking of the blessed promises of God are never downcast or heartbroken. You are mistaken. We have been there, and perhaps we know how to say a word in season to any who are now going through similar experiences. With many enterprises on my hands, far too great for my own unaided strength, I am often driven to fall flat on this promise of my God, "I will never leave you nor forsake you" (Heb. 13:5).

If I feel that any plan has been of my devising, or that I sought my own honor, then I know that the plan must rightly fail. But when I can prove that God has thrust it on me, that I am moved by a divine impulse and not my own feelings and wishes, then how can my God forsake me? How can He lie, however weak I may be? How is it possible for Him to send His servant to battle and not comfort him with reinforcements when the battle goes hard? God is not David when he put Uriah in the front lines and left him to die (2 Sam. 11:15). God will never desert any of His servants.

Dear brothers and sisters, if the Lord calls you to things you cannot do, He will give you the strength to do them. If He should push you still further, until your difficulties increase and your burdens become heavy, "as your days, so shall your strength be" (Deut. 33:25). You shall march with the indomitable spirit of those who have tried and trusted the naked arm of the Eternal God.

"I will never leave you nor forsake you." Then what is the trouble? Though all the world were against you, you could shake all the world as Samson shook the lion (Judg. 14:6). "If God is for us, who can be against us?" Roll this promise under your tongue. It is a sweet food.

THE WAY OF ESCAPE. *1 Corinthians 10:13*

God is true to His promises. "God is faithful, who will not allow you to be tempted beyond what you are able" (1 Cor. 10:13). "I will never leave you nor forsake you" (Heb. 13:5). "God is faithful," and He will fulfill that promise. This is one of Christ's promises, and Christ is God. "My sheep hear My voice, and I know them, and they follow Me. And I give them eternal life, and they shall never perish; neither shall anyone snatch them out of My hand" (John 10:27-28). "God is faithful," and God will fulfill these promises.

You have often heard this promise, "As your days, so shall your strength be" (Deut. 33:25). Do you believe it? Or will you make God a liar? If you believe it, then banish all dark depression with this blessed little sentence, "God is faithful."

God sends our trials at the right time. If He puts an extra burden on us in one way, He takes something off in another. John Bradford, the famous martyr, suffered with rheumatism and depression, in which I can greatly sympathize. Yet when they imprisoned him in a foul damp dungeon, and he knew that he would never come out except to die, Bradford wrote, "It is a singular thing that ever since I have been in this prison and have had other trials to bear, I have had no touch of my rheumatism or depression."

How blessed, and you will find that this is true, "God is faithful, who will not allow you to be tempted beyond what you are able, but with the temptation will also make the way of escape, that you may be able to bear it" (1 Cor. 10:13).

THE LAST ENEMY. *1 Corinthians 15:26*

Those who have stood by a fresh grave and buried half their hearts in it can tell you what an enemy death is. Death takes the friend from our side, the child from our arms, the pillar of our homes, and the brightness of our hearth. Death has no pity for the young and no mercy for the old. Death has no regard for the good or the beautiful. The scythe of death cuts both sweet flowers and noxious weeds with equal readiness. Death comes into our garden, tramples our lilies, and scatters our roses. Death finds even the most modest flowers that are hiding under the leaves, and it withers them with its burning breath. Death is our enemy. "The last enemy that will be destroyed is death" (1 Cor. 15:26). Why do saints die? Because "flesh and blood cannot inherit the kingdom of God; nor does corruption inherit incorruption" (1 Cor. 15:50). A divine change must take place in our bodies before we can enter heaven. Death and the grave are the refining pot, the furnace that makes the body ready for its future bliss. Death cuts the ropes, that the boat may freely sail to the fair haven. Death is the fiery chariot that ascends to God. Death is the gentle voice of our Great King.

We fly on eagles' wings, far from this land of mist and cloud, into the eternal serenity and brilliance of God's house above. It is not death to die.

I DIE DAILY. *1 Corinthians 15:31*

I thank God that I do not fear death. Over the years, I never rose from my bed and planned on living until night. Those who die daily will die easily. Those who make themselves familiar with the tomb will find it transformed into a bed. Those who rejoice in the covenant of grace are encouraged that even death is comprehended by the believer. Let us live as dying among a dying people, for then we will truly live.

It would be a sad sentence if we were forced to dwell in this poor world forever. But to grow ripe and to be carried home like corn shocks at harvest is proper and pleasing. To labor through a blessed day and go home at night to receive the wages of grace is not dark and dismal. If you are the Lord's child, I invite you to look this home-going in the face until you no longer see it as a grave of gloom and dread but as a heaven of hope and glory.

In the midst of malaria and plagues we are safe with God. "Because you made the LORD, who is my refuge, even the Most High your dwelling place, no evil shall befall you, nor shall any plague come near your dwelling" (Ps. 91:9). Under Jehovah's wings you shall take refuge. You shall not be afraid of the terror by night, nor of the arrow that flies by day, nor of the pestilence that walks in darkness (Ps. 91:4-6).

We are immortal until our work is done. Rest peacefully. All things are ordered by His wisdom, and "precious in the sight of the LORD is the death of His saints" (Ps. 116:15). No forces are outside of His control. God does not permit any foe to trespass on the domain of Providence. All things are ordained of God. Our deaths are under the special oversight of our exalted Lord and Savior. He Himself will guide us through the iron gate of death. Let us rejoice that in life and in death we are in the Lord's hands.

GOD OF ALL COMFORT. *2 Corinthians 1:3*

The Lord can take away all present sorrow and grief by providentially removing its cause. Providence is full of sweet surprises and unexpected turns. When the sea has ebbed, it turns again and covers the sand. When we think the dungeon door is rusted shut, He can make the door fly open. When the river rolls deep and black, He can divide it with a word or bridge it with His hand.

How often have you found this to be so? As a pilgrim to Canaan, you have passed through the Red Sea, where you once feared you would drown, and the bitter waters were made sweet with God's presence. You fought the Amalekite. You made it through the terrible wilderness, passing by the fiery serpents, and you have been kept alive. As the clear shining comes after rain, so shall peace succeed your trials. As the black clouds fly before that compelling power of the wind, the eternal God will make your grief fly before the energy of His grace. The smoking furnace of trouble will be followed by the bright lamp of consolation.

To say, "My Father, God," to put myself into His hand and feel that I am safe, to look up to Him, though it be with tears in my eyes, and feel that He loves me, and then to put my head on His bosom as the prodigal did and sob my griefs into my Father's heart, this is the death of grief and the life of all consolation. Jehovah is called the "God of all comfort" (2 Cor. 1:3), and you will find Him so! He has been "our help in ages past, and He is our hope for years to come."

I bear testimony that you cannot go to Him and pour out your heart without finding a delightful comfort. When your friends cannot wipe away the tears, when your heart bursts with grief, pour out your heart before Him. Go to Him, and you will find that even here on earth God will wipe away all tears from your eyes (Rev. 7:17).

WHO IS SUFFICIENT? *2 Corinthians 2:16*

Believing in grace for past and future trials is easy,
but resting in grace for the immediate need is true
faith. Believer, grace is sufficient right now. Do not
say that this is a new trouble, but if you do, remember
that the grace of God is always new. Do not complain
that some strange thing has happened, but if you do,
remember that blessings are provided to meet your
strange difficulties. Do not tremble because the thorn in
the flesh is so mysterious (2 Cor. 12:7), but if you do,
remember that grace is mysterious too, and so mystery
will meet mystery.

Right now and at all moments that will occur between
now and glory, God's grace will be sufficient. This sufficiency is declared without any limiting words. Thus the
Lord Jesus is sufficient to uphold, sufficient to strength-
en, sufficient to comfort, sufficient to make trouble useful, sufficient to enable you to triumph, sufficient to bring
you out of ten thousand trials, and sufficient to bring you
home to heaven.

Whatever is good, Christ's grace is sufficient to
bestow. Whatever would harm, His grace is sufficient to
avert. Whatever you need, His grace is sufficient to give,
if it is for your good. Whatever you would avoid, His
grace can shield, if His wisdom dictates.

I am glad that they cannot put all sufficiency into
words. If so, it would be finite. Since we can never
express it, glory be to God, for it is inexhaustible. Our
demands can never be too great.

GOD'S SUFFICIENCY. *2 Corinthians 3:5*

As long as we have a grain of self-sufficiency, we will never trust in the All-Sufficient. While there is anything of self left, we prefer to feed on it. Only when our stale bread becomes too sour and too moldy for eating do we humbly ask for the bread of heaven to satisfy.

My soul, learn to hate every thought of self-sufficiency. "And we have such trust through Christ toward God. Not that we are sufficient of ourselves to think of anything as being from ourselves, but our sufficiency is from God, who also made us sufficient as ministers of the new covenant, not of the letter but of the Spirit; for the letter kills, but the Spirit gives life" (2 Cor. 3:4-6).

NOT DESTROYED. *2 Corinthians 4:9*

We will deliver the needy" (Ps. 72:12). You are brought into great trouble, but you will be delivered. You may have many fears, but you will be delivered. It seems as if the enemy would jump on you, put his foot on your neck, and drive you into the ground. But you will be delivered.

You are like a bird taken in the fowler's net. Your neck is ready to be wrung, but you will be delivered from the hand of the fowler. You will be brought safely through the perils that threaten. Oh that we could exercise faith when in deep waters! It is good to talk about faith on land, but we want faith to swim with when we are thrown into the flood. May you get such a grip on this precious Word that you can take it before the Lord and say, "I am poor and needy. I have no helper. Oh God, deliver me now."

"He will spare the poor and needy" (Ps. 72:13). You will be afflicted, but it will be in measure. He will spare you as a parent spares its child. The rod may sting, but it will not make you bleed. You may suffer, but you will not die. "We are hard-pressed on every side, yet not crushed; we are perplexed, but not in despair; persecuted, but not forsaken; struck down, but not destroyed" (2 Cor. 4:8-9). There is a gracious limit on the blows that come from Jehovah's hand.

Oh the mercy to be among His poor ones and to know that He will spare us!

Perishing, yet Renewed. *2 Corinthians 4:16*

I watched a close friend go home this week. He laid on the bed, pain afflicting him, pulse growing fainter, eyes beginning to glaze. Then a brighter light dawned, and while the outer man was decaying, the inner man was being renewed in youth. His pain grew worse. He wanted to go, and he said, "I cannot endure living." But checking himself, he said, "Not my will but Your will be done."

He sat patiently on the river's bank, expecting his Master to open the passage. He prayed, "Speak Lord, and the sooner You speak the more I will rejoice. Call me home. Speak, Lord, for Your servant now hears more distinctly because I am nearer to You. My ear is almost closed to the din and bustle of the world, but in silence I wait for Your still, small voice. Speak, Lord, for if you will come and meet me I will cheerfully plunge into the river. My journey is over. I am almost home. It is victory, glory, triumph!"

The physician says that he can see the death-change, and the nurse agrees. But to the believer it is a life-change, a prognosis of coming glory. Now come the shouts of victory over death and defiance over the grave, for the soul has left all care, all doubt, and all fear behind. His foot is not only on the Rock of Ages, but also on that part of the rock which is on the other side of the Jordan. He cries with delight, "I am with Him. Another moment and I will be in His arms! I see Him. Victory, victory, victory, through the blood of the Lamb!"

I hope something like that departure will be yours and mine. And it will if we are resting in Christ. Let us trust Jesus, and trust Him alone, for then we will find eternal happiness.

OUR LIGHT AFFLICTION. *2 Corinthians 4:17*

Have you been misunderstood, misrepresented, or slandered? Have you been accused of being deranged and fanatical, and I know not what else, because you are determined to follow in your Master's steps, to believe the truth, and to do right? Do not worry. Do not vindicate your cause. Refer it to the King's bench above.

Are you poor, sick, or sad? Are you also Christ's own? Do you trust Him? Do you live in fellowship with Him? Then your hope is found in Matthew 26:64, "Hereafter you will see the Son of Man sitting at the right hand of the Power, and coming on the clouds of heaven." This will take the sting out of your present trials.

You will not suffer long, for the glory will soon be revealed. The streets of gold are symbolic of your future wealth (Rev. 21:21). The celestial harps are emblematic of your eternal joy (Rev. 14:2). Soon you will have a white robe (Rev. 6:11), and the dusty garments of troubles and trials will be laid aside forever. Your light affliction, which is but for a moment, is working for you a far more exceeding and eternal weight of glory (2 Cor. 4:17).

Has your work seemed futile? Have you tried to bring souls to Christ without results? Do not worry. To many labors that appear unsuccessful to the human eye, it will be said by our Master, "Well done, good and faithful servant" (Matt. 25:21).

Set very little store by anything you own. Wish only lightly for anything you do not have. Let the present be what it really is, temporal life, an empty show. Project your soul into "Hereafter you will see the Son of Man." This is solid and enduring. What music! What delight to a true child of God!

WORKING FOR US. *2 Corinthians 4:17*

There are times when through acute physical pain or deep depression, the soul utterly falls in sheer helplessness on Jesus. It gives up struggling, and resigns to His will. Then into the soul comes a great calm and a quiet joy, deeper and purer than we have ever experienced.

I speak what I know. I testify to what I have felt. I have looked back on nights of pain, pain so excruciating that it forced tears from my eyes. I have almost asked to have this suffering repeated if it might give a repetition of the deep, intense, and indescribable bliss that I felt when I glorified God in the furnace of affliction.

You will not merely acquiesce to the Lord's dealings. You will also devoutly thank Him for using affliction's sharp knife:

Let me but hear my Savior say,
Strength shall be equal to thy day!
Then I rejoice in deep distress,
Leaning on all-sufficient rest.

"Our light affliction, which is but for a moment, is working for us a far more exceeding and eternal weight of glory" (2 Cor. 4:17).

But for a Moment. *2 Corinthians 4:17*

You cannot place too high a value on health. If you are healthy, you are infinitely more blessed, regardless of possessions, than one who is sick. If I have health, if my bones are strong, if my muscles are well-toned, if I scarcely know an ache or pain, then let me not glory in my strength, which could fail in a moment. A few short weeks may reduce the strongest to a skeleton. If today you are strong, do not glory in your strength. The Lord "does not delight in the strength of the horse; He takes no pleasure in the legs of a man. The LORD takes pleasure in those who fear Him, in those who hope in His mercy" (Ps. 147:10-11).

If you are healthy, say, "'Oh, that You would bless me indeed' (1 Chr. 4:10). Give me a healthy soul, and heal my spiritual diseases. Jehovah Rophi, come and purge the leprosy that nature has placed in my heart and make me healthy in the heavenly sense. Bless my health, that I may properly use it in Your service and for Your glory. Otherwise, though blessed with health, I may not be blessed at all."

Some of you are poor, and weary days and long nights are yours. There is much about you to be pitied. I pray that you will be blessed. I can sympathize with a sister who said, "I had such nearness to God when I was sick, such full assurance and joy, that I regret I have now lost it. I could almost wish to be ill again, if I might have a renewal of God's fellowship."

Often I gratefully look back to my sick bed. I am certain that I grew greatly in grace on my bed of pain. Frequently, pain is more healthy than joy.

Whenever we suffer weakness, pain, or anguish, may His divine presence be so real that "our light affliction, which is but for a moment, is working for us a far more exceeding and eternal weight of glory" (2 Cor. 4:17).

ETERNAL GLORY. *2 Corinthians 4:17*

Within a short time, you and I shall face death. The Lord Himself will come, and thus we shall be with the Lord.

Anticipate the triumphant hour when your head, which often aches with weariness, "will receive the crown of glory that does not fade away" (1 Pet. 5:4). Think of the time when your hands, worn with toil, will grasp the palm branch (Rev. 7:9) and your weary feet will stand on the sea of glass (Rev. 15:2). Then, our only occupation will be to glorify Him who has brought us up out of a horrible pit, out of the miry clay, and set our feet upon a rock and established our steps (Ps. 40:2). All of this is prepared for us, for we are the specified heirs. We are ordained to it by a decree that neither death or hell can change.

Then the trials of this life will be known as a "light affliction, which is but for a moment" and as having worked "for us a far more exceeding and eternal weight of glory" (2 Cor. 4:17). God has prepared an inconceivable heritage that the mind cannot imagine. Thus, it cannot be expressed.

OUR EARTHLY HOUSE. *2 Corinthians 5:1*

This poor body of ours, which at times is so full of aches and pains, will one day be taken away to make room for a more glorious one. This one is getting worn-out; some parts of it have already fallen away. It is like a very old lath and plaster building, which cannot last much longer and seldom stands to the end of the ninety-nine year lease. It soon crumbles and, by-and-by with all of us, the old house will fall to pieces and be done with.

Shall we then worry? Shall our soul cry concerning the body, "Alas my sister! Alas my brother"? No! "He takes away the first that He may establish the second" (Heb. 10:9). As we have carried the image of the earthly in this body of humiliation, we will, in the second condition of this body, carry the image of the heavenly. "The body is sown in corruption, it is raised in incorruption. It is sown in dishonor, it is raised in glory. It is sown in weakness, it is raised in power. It is sown a natural body, it is raised a spiritual body" (1 Cor. 15:42-44).

"He takes away the first that He may establish the second." And what a glorious second that will be! Our resurrection body will know no pain, no weariness, no weakness, no sign of disease, no sin, and no possibility of corruption or death.

Well may we sing:

O glorious hour! O blessed abode!

Since this poor body will be made like the glorious body of Christ Jesus our Savior, let the first body go, without a murmur or a sigh.

SWALLOWED UP. *2 Corinthians 5:4*

While some of us rejoice in the prospect of heaven, the thought of death is sometimes surrounded with gloom. It cannot be an easy thing to go down to the chill darkness of the river, to have the soul separated from the body, to leave this earthly tabernacle behind. Death sometimes has a hideous appearance. Even the apostle Paul shuddered at it when he said, "For we who are in this tent groan, being burdened, not because we want to be unclothed, but further clothed, that mortality may be swallowed up by life" (2 Cor. 5:4). Death seems a bitter pill, and unless it is swallowed up in a victory that takes away the sting of death (1 Cor. 15:54), the hour of death will be too bitter.

Would you agree that our thoughts of gloom about death arise from forgetting that Jesus will be there with us? If our faith could see Jesus making our bed in sickness and then standing by our side in the last solemn article, to conduct us safely through the iron gates, would we not look on death in a different light? You know how Isaac Watts put it:

> Oh! If my Lord would come and meet,
> My soul should stretch her wings in haste,
> Fly fearless through death's iron gate,
> Nor feel the terrors as she passed.
>
> Jesus can make a dying bed
> Feel soft as downy pillows are,
> While on His breast I lean my head,
> And breathe my life out sweetly there.

INEXPRESSIBLE WORDS. *2 Corinthians 12:4*

Many times believers give precious testimonies in their last moments. If ever I have mistaken human comment for inspiration, it has been during these dying speeches. Have you ever heard the saying of a dying saint and thought it was borrowed from Scripture? Yet sometimes if you search for it later you cannot find it anywhere in the Bible. The voice was so close to inspiration that, if it had been permitted, you would have written it in your Bible.

Brave things do dying believers tell of the heavenly world! What glorious speeches! The veil is thrown back, and they speak of things unseen by us. They almost declare "inexpressible words, which it is not lawful for a man to utter" (2 Cor. 12:4). Their speech is broken and mysterious, like dark sayings on a harp. We can hardly understand them. They are overwhelmed with glory. They are confounded with unutterable bliss, asking, "Did you see the glory?"

We reply, "The sun is shining on you from the window." But they shake their heads, for they see a brightness not generated by the sun. They cry, "Do you not hear it?", and we suppose that a sound in the street attracted them. But all was silent except to their ear, which was ravished with heavenly harpers. I shall never forget hearing a friend say:

> And when ye hear my eye strings break,
> How sweet my minutes roll;
> A mortal paleness on my cheek;
> But glory in my soul.

SUFFICIENT GRACE. *2 Corinthians 12:9*

I have attempted some things that were far beyond my capacity, but because I rely on the Lord I have never failed. As a church, we have never hesitated to attempt great things for God, and we have accomplished all that we proposed. I have sought God's aid, assistance, and help in many undertakings, and He has heard my prayers! Not now and then, not once or twice, but so often that it has become a habit to spread my case before God with the absolute certainty that whatever I ask He will give.

It is not a perhaps or a possibility. I know that my Lord answers me. I dare not doubt; it would be folly if I did. Just as a certain amount of leverage will lift a weight, so too a certain amount of prayer will get anything from God. As rain clouds bring showers, prayer brings blessings. As spring scatters flowers about, earnest prayer ensures mercies. There is profit in all labor, but most of all in the work of intercession. I am sure of this and have reaped it.

I put my trust in the Queen's money, because when I produce the cash I have never failed to buy what I want. In the same way, I put my trust in God's promises, and I will continue to do so, for God hears prayer. Remember, however, that it must be offered in submission to God's will. Never pray without inserting this clause, "Nevertheless, not as I will, but as You will" (Matt. 26:39). He does not always literally give what we ask for, but He does give what is best. If He does not give the mercy we ask for in silver, He provides it in gold. If He does not take away the thorn in the flesh, He says, "My grace is sufficient for you, for My strength is made perfect in weakness" (2 Cor. 12:9).

PERFECT IN WEAKNESS. *2 Corinthians 12:9*

Your faith will never be weak when you are weak, but when you are strong your faith cannot be strong. To the apostle Paul, Jesus said, "My strength is made perfect in weakness" (2 Cor. 12:9). The only way to increase our faith is through great trouble. We do not grow strong in faith on sunny days; only in stormy weather do we obtain it. Strong faith does not drop from heaven in a gentle dew; generally, it comes in the whirlwind and the storm.

Look at the old oaks. How did they become so deeply rooted? The March winds will tell you. It was not the April showers or the sweet May sunshine that caused the roots to wrap around the rock. It was the rough, bluster-ing, north winds of March shaking the trees.

Life in the barracks does not produce great soldiers. Great soldiers are made amid flying shot and thundering can-nons. Nor are good sailors made on calm seas. Good sailors are made

on the deep, where the wild wind howls and the thunder rolls like drums. Storms and tempests make tough and hardy sailors. "They see the works of the LORD and His wonders in the deep" (Ps. 107:24).

It is that way with the Christians, great faith must have great trials. Bunyan's character would never have been Mr. Great-heart if he had not once been Mr. Great-trouble. Valiant-for-truth would never have defeated the foes if they had not attacked him.

So it is with us. We must expect great troubles before we attain great faith.

FOR CHRIST'S SAKE.   *2 Corinthians 12:10*

Do not ask to be rid of your trouble. Do not ask for ease, comfort, or any other form of happiness. It is enough if you remember this delightful expression, "'My grace is sufficient for you, for My strength is made perfect in weakness.' Therefore most gladly I will rather boast in my infirmities, that the power of Christ may rest upon me. Therefore I take pleasure in infirmities, in reproaches, in needs, in persecutions, in distresses, for Christ's sake. For when I am weak, then I am strong" (2 Cor. 12:9-10). Repeat these words. Believe that the Well-beloved looks on you and whispers, "My love is enough." If you have asked Him three times to deliver you from your present affliction (2 Cor. 12:8), hear Him reply, "Why ask any more? My love is enough."

"Yes, Lord, indeed it is." If I am poor, if You willed me to be poor, then I am content because Your love is enough. If I am sick, Your love is enough if You visit and reveal Your heart. If they persecute and forsake me, I will bear it cheerfully if a sense of Your love sustains me. If I am left alone with no one to care for me, if my father and my mother forsake me, and if every friend proves a Judas, Your love is enough.

Can you see how these words comforted Paul as he understood them in this primary and most natural sense? "Oh Paul, it is sufficient that I have made you a chosen vessel to witness My name among the Gentiles. It is enough that I have loved you from before the foundation of the world. I have redeemed you with My precious blood. I called when you were a blasphemer. I changed your heart and made you love Me. I have kept you to this day, and I will keep you by My boundless love to the end. My love is enough. Do not ask to be set free from this buffeting. Do not ask to be delivered from weakness and trial. These will enable you to better enjoy My favor, and that is enough."

THE POWER OF GOD. *2 Corinthians 13:4*

Much of life's happiness depends on little things going well. If God ordained only the great events but left the little things to chance, we would be most unhappy. When God's lovingkindness gilds the full landscape with sunshine, it also has a sunbeam for the tiniest insect and a sun ray for the eye of the smallest bird.

Let our love to God go into the minutest details. Let us be earnest in all essentials but never indifferent to the non-essentials. God's lovingkindness goes into detail, and so should my obedience. May gratitude to God permeate my entire life; may it flood all my faculties, and may it saturate me through and through.

Great God, Your love surrounds me. I breathe it. I live on it. I shall die in it. I shall live forever in it. It will make my bliss eternal. I give my soul to You in obedience. I give up my thoughts, work, desires, judgments, tastes, and everything else to Your sweet love, which so wonderfully embraces and surrounds me. Amen.

There is a logical consistency between thinking on the love of God and seeing its details, on marking its attributes and ordering our lives accordingly, in the way of truth. One is the natural cause from which the other is sure to spring. "We shall live with Him by the power of God toward you" (2 Cor. 13:4).

LIVING BY FAITH. *Galatians 3:11*

Faith is the great sustaining energy when you are under trials, difficulties, suffering, or hard labor. The Holy Spirit implants an active, operative faith in the Christian. It is sent to sustain you during trials, and it is a riddle that we cannot explain. Divine purpose eternally fixes everything; nevertheless, the prayer of faith moves the arm of God. And though the mystery cannot be explained, the facts cannot be denied.

My brothers and sisters may think me fanatical, but it is my firm belief that in ordinary matters, such as obtaining your living, educating your children, and running your household, you are to depend on God as much as in the grand matter of salvation. "The very hairs of your head are all numbered" (Matt. 10:30), so go to God with your trifles. Not a sparrow falls to the ground apart from your Father's will (Matt. 10:29), so throw your minor trials on the Lord. Never think that anything is too little for your heavenly Father's love. He who rides the whirlwind (Is. 66:15) also walks in the garden in the cool of the day (Gen. 3:8). He who shakes the avalanche from its mountain (Ps. 46:3) also makes the autumn leaf twinkle as it falls from the aspen. "He has stretched out the heavens by His understanding" (Jer. 51:15). He guides each grain of dust that is blown from the summer's threshing floor.

Confide in Him for the little as well as for the great. You will find that He does not fail. He is the God of the hills as well as the God of the valleys.

HE CHOSE US. *Ephesians 1:4*

Blessed be God, all the shame and spitting that people put on us can never put our God away. He has said, "I will never leave you nor forsake you" (Heb. 13:5). Some people are thrown aside like household goods that are worn out. Depend on it, people will not forsake us while they can get anything from us. But when there is nothing left, we are like the soldiers in Napoleon's march; we drop out of line to die and thousands either march over us or, if they are a little more merciful, march around us. Few will stop and help.

But He has said, "I will never leave you nor forsake you." If we should get so old that we cannot serve the church of God, if we should become so sick that we are only a burden to those of our house, if we should grow so feeble that we could not lift our hand to our lip, still the eternal love of Jehovah would not have diminished. It will not diminish so much as by a single jot toward the souls "whom He chose . . . before the foundations of the world" (Eph. 1:4). However low your condition, you will find God's love is ever underneath. However weak you are, His strength shall be revealed in the everlasting arms, which will not permit you to sink into disaster.

People may forsake us for reasons too numerous to be mentioned. But He has said, "I will never leave you nor forsake you." Let the rest go. If the Lord Jehovah stands at our right hand, we can well afford to see the backs of all our friends, for we shall find friends enough in the Triune God, whom we delight to serve.

ALL THINGS IN CHRIST. *Ephesians 1:10*

Y ou do not have an income. You do not have wealth. You do not have friends. You do not have a comfortable house. You do not have health. Do not tell me what you do not have! Remember, you have a Christ and you have a Savior, and therefore you have all things. "He who did not spare His own Son, but delivered Him up for us all, how shall He not with Him also freely give us all things?" (Rom. 8:32).

The person who has Christ has everything. "Together in one [are] all things in Christ, both which are in heaven and which are on the earth—in Him" (Eph. 1:10). If you have Him, you are rich and blessed. If you have Christ, you have God the Father to be your protector and God the Spirit to be your comforter. You have all things working together for your good (Rom. 8:28). Angels are your attendants, for "He shall give His angels charge over you, to keep you in all your ways. In their hands they shall bear you up, lest you dash your foot against a stone" (Ps. 91:11-12).

The wheels of Providence are revolving for your benefit (Ezek. 1:15-21); they sanctify your daily trials to your advantage. Your gains and losses, your additions and reductions, are all profitable. You have more than any other creature can boast. You have more to delight your pure taste and to please your happy spirits than all the world could yield.

Now be glad. Christ is yours. Rejoice!

EXCEEDING RICHES. *Ephesians 2:7*

When David wrote Psalm 17, he was evidently in great distress. He says, "I have called upon You, for You will hear me, O God; incline Your ear to me, and hear my speech" (Ps. 17:6).

Believers can draw comfort both from God's ordinary and extraordinary dealings with them. God's lovingkindness is both ordinary and extraordinary. The wonder of extraordinary love is that God makes it ordinary. He gives "marvelous lovingkindness" (Ps. 17:7) so frequently that it becomes a marvelous daily blessing.

After the world's wonders have been seen a few times, they cease to generate excitement. Sooner or later, you will have seen enough of every building, regardless of its cost and rare architecture. Yet God's wonderful works are always new. You could look at the Alps or watch Niagara Falls and never feel that you have exhausted its wonders. The ocean is never the same. Those who live near it and continually look on it see God's wonders in the sea.

God blessing us daily is a comforting theme. Appeal to Him for His "marvelous lovingkindness," for His miracles of mercy, for His extravagances of love, for His overabundance of kindness. Ask Him to "show the exceeding riches of His grace in His kindness toward us in Christ Jesus" (Eph. 2:7).

I have called on You, for You will hear me, O God. I know that You will. The blessing I am about to ask for is something that I have been accustomed to receiving from You. I know You will hear me, for You have heard me in the past. It is Your habit to listen to my supplications and grant my requests. Amen.

No longer strangers. *Ephesians 2:19*

I want a few direct and personal words with you, my friend. Those of you who are the children of God, do not wonder if you have discomfort and trials here. If you are what you profess to be, then you are strangers and foreigners here. Do not expect the people of this world to treat you as a member of their community. If they do, be afraid. Dogs bark at strangers, not those well known to them.

When people persecute and slander you, do not wonder. If you are a stranger, they naturally bark at you. In this world, do not expect to find the comforts that you crave, the comforts that your flesh longs for. This world is only our inn, not our home. We just stay for a night; we leave in the morning. We tolerate the annoyances of evening and night, for the morning will soon break. Remember that your greatest joy while you are a pilgrim is your God. Do you want a richer source of consolation than you have? Here is one that can never be diminished, much less exhausted. When the created streams are dry, go to this eternal fountain and find it ever springing up. Your joy is your God. Make your God your joy.

MEMBERS OF HIS BODY. *Ephesians 5:30*

The children of God, favored by divine grace, are permitted interviews with Jesus Christ. Like Enoch, we walk with God (Gen. 5:22), we walk as children, and we put our hand into our Father's hand. We look up with loving eyes and walk in love, confidence, and familiarity. We talk to Him. We tell Him our anguish, and we hear His gracious words of love.

We are members of His body, of His flesh, and of His bones (Eph. 5:30). We shall never perish, neither shall anyone snatch us from His hand (John 10:28). Fellowship with Jesus is richer than any gem that ever glittered in an imperial crown.

In addition to receiving complete justification, full assurance, and fellowship with Christ, God's elect are favored with the Holy Spirit's sanctification. No matter how humble our situation, God the Holy Spirit dwells in us and we in Him. The Spirit sanctifies the believer's daily actions, so that everything we do is for God. If we live it is to Christ, if we die it is gain (Phil. 1:21). Beloved, when you feel the sanctifying influence of the Holy Spirit, it is to sit with princes.

My God, if I could always feel Your Spirit overcoming my corruption and constraining my soul to holiness, I would not even think of being a prince in comparison with my joy.

My dear brothers and sisters in Jesus Christ, I am sure you can testify that when you fall in sin it brings you low and that you again smell the vile ash heap and are ready to die in its dust. But when the Holy Spirit enables you to overcome sin and to live as Christ lived, you feel that you have a royal standing (Ps. 113:7-8), and you feel more than an imperial privilege in being sanctified in Christ Jesus.

STRONG IN THE LORD. *Ephesians 6:10*

Abraham's faith was so severely tested by God (Gen. 22:1) that the great Angel of the Lord could say to him, "Now I know that you fear God" (Gen. 22:12). Through His omniscience, God already knew this, but He would know it practically by testing Abraham. Thus, we have trials.

There are no fair-weather soldiers in God's army. All must endure difficulty. Our courage must be tried and proven. God's ships never go to sea without being tested, and only when their seaworthiness is proven do they go on longer voyages. Unless you have been through a great trial, you cannot help those who are in great difficulty.

If we were placed in a glass case, we would not grow. If we were never injured, there would be no forgiving grace. Without suffering, we would not have patience. We grow in grace only when the stormy winds of trials blow. It is through harsh experiences that believers grow "strong in the Lord and in the power of His might" (Eph. 6:10). Christian, when Satan tests and tries you, hold the world loose but firmly grip the invisible things of God.

It is possible that God might use you to scatter His seed with a hand that was never wounded, but He will not use you to minister to the brokenhearted until trials have made you tender and sensitive. Your present, painful experience is a necessary preparation for something that will give you tenfold joy. If we are not tested, we cannot be victorious. The rule of the kingdom is: no battle, no crowns; no conflict, no conquest.

"In this you greatly rejoice, though now for a little while, if need be, you have been grieved by various trials, that the genuineness of your faith, being much more precious than gold that perishes, though it is tested by fire, may be found to praise, honor, and glory at the revelation of Jesus Christ" (1 Pet. 1:6-8).

ABLE TO WITHSTAND. *Ephesians 6:13*

In this world you will have trials (John 16:33). I believe that Jesus' reference to the rain, the flood, and the wind that beat on the wise man's house (Matt. 7:24-25) refers to three types of trials.

The rain depicts affliction from heaven. God will send adversities like showers, trials as numerous as rain drops, and between now and heaven you will feel the pelting storm. You will be sick, or you will have trouble in your home, or your children and friends will die, or your riches will take wings and fly like an eagle. If you rely on Jesus, you will be able to stand the trials. If you are not one with Jesus Christ, then even God's rain will be too much for you.

The flood represents the earth's trials. In the past the floods of persecution were more terrible. But persecution still exists, for the world has never loved the true church. If you are a believer, you will have your share. You can handle slander and reproach for Jesus' sake only if you are firmly rooted and grounded in the faith. In both persecution and trials, the rootless plant soon withers.

Then there are the mysterious trials that are portrayed by the winds. The prince of the power of the air (Eph. 2:2) will assail you with blasphemous suggestions, horrible temptations, and artful insinuations. Satan can attack the four corners of our house, tempt us cleverly, and drive us to our wit's end. "We do not wrestle against flesh and blood, but against principalities, against powers, against the rulers of the darkness of this age, against spiritual hosts of wickedness in the heavenly places" (Eph. 6:12). "Therefore take up the whole armor of God, that you may be able to withstand in the evil day" (Eph. 6:13).

Where there is a good biblical foundation, trials will not harm us. Where there is no foundation, we will be ruined.

PRAYING ALWAYS. *Ephesians 6:18*

Believer, you are surrounded by enemies and in your own strength you are helpless. If you are not clothed with heavenly armor (Eph. 6:11), you are naked and every enemy dart will penetrate you. If the shield of faith (Eph. 6:16) does not cover you, the spears of the tempter will soon reach your heart. Without the whole armor of God, you are crushed by a moth and trampled like a worm. You are as weak as water and as frail as dust. Your strength, your imagined strength, is perfect weakness. Your highest natural wisdom is folly.

You need God's eternal arm to carry you. Cease from self-confidence and how know how feeble you are. Look above to a worthier and surer source of strength. "Stand therefore, having girded your waist with truth, having put on the breastplate of righteousness, and having shod your feet with the preparation of the gospel of peace; above all, taking the shield of faith with which you will be able to quench all the fiery darts of the wicked one. And take the helmet of salvation, and the sword of the Spirit, which is the word of God; praying always with all prayer and supplication in the Spirit, being watchful to this end with all perseverance and supplication" (Eph. 6:14-18).

GOD SHALL SUPPLY. *Philippians 4:19*

When I have been in need of money for the orphanage and the college (these times have occurred often), I have felt a wonderful joy in my spirit. I have watched the funds ebb until nearly everything is gone. Then I have joyfully said, "Now go for it, the vessels are empty, I will see the miracle of filling them."

What wonders the Lord has worked. Many of my faithful helpers know that in our deep needs hundreds and even thousands of pounds have poured in from our great Lord. It will always be the same, for Jesus Christ is always the same yesterday, today, and forever (Heb. 13:8). Until the funds run low, we cannot expect to see them replenished. Yet when they get low, God comes and deals graciously.

Money, however, is our smallest need. We need grace, wisdom, light, and comfort, and these we will have. All of our needs are occasions for blessing. The more needs, the more blessings. God has promised to fill all your needs. God will fill all your empty vessels (2 Kin. 4:3). The more in need the better. I would have your faith believe that strange statement. Your poverty will be riches, your weakness strength, your humbling exaltation. Your extreme distress is God's opportunity to show the riches of His grace. God will fill your exhaustion with the fullness of His inexhaustible grace. He will replenish your need until your cup overflows.

Do not weep over empty jars. Place them in rows with the full expectation that God will fill them. "God shall supply all your need" (Phil. 4:19).

THE HOPE WHICH IS LAID UP. *Colossians 1:5*

When you and I have been in heaven ten thousand years, we will look back on our time here as nothing. Our pain will seem like a pin's prick, our gain a speck, and our duration the twinkling of an eye. Even if you tarry eighty or ninety years in this exile, when you have been in heaven for a million years, the longest life will seem no greater than a thought. You will wonder why you said that the days were weary and the long nights dreary. You will wonder why the years of sickness dragged at such a weary length. Eternal bliss will overflow our present sea of sorrow!

We make too much of this poor life, and the fondness costs us dearly. Oh for a higher estimate of the home country with its eternal delights! Then the trials of a day would vanish like the morning dew. We are only here long enough to feel an April shower of pain. Then we are gone among the unfading flowers of the endless May. Therefore, make the most of the least and the least of the most. Put things in order. Allot to this brief life its brief consideration and to everlasting glory its weight of happy meditations.

We are to dwell throughout eternity with God. Is not that our home? We are pilgrims because we are here for so short a space when compared with the length of time we will spend in the dear country beyond.

THINGS ABOVE. *Colossians 3:2*

If hard times should come, if industry should crash, and the banks are broke, take care to watch and be sober (1 Thess. 5:6). Nothing will get us over a panic so well as everyone trying to keep our spirits up. When you rise, say, "Times are hard and today I may lose all. Fretting will not help. Let me set a bold heart against sorrow and go about my business. The wheels of commerce may stop, but I bless God that my treasure is in heaven, for I cannot go bankrupt. My mind is set on things above, not on things of the earth (Col. 3:2), and I cannot lose those things.

Hard times are here, and many who are respectable will soon be beggars. Your business is to put your trust in Jehovah so that you can say, "God is our refuge and strength, a very present help in time of trouble. Therefore we will not fear, even though the earth be removed, and though the mountains be carried into the midst of the sea; though its waters roar and be troubled, though the mountains shake with its swelling" (Ps. 46:1-3). If you can say that, you will create more probabilities by which to avoid destruction than any method dictated by earthly wisdom.

Be prudent in business. Do not sleep as others. Watch and be sober. Do not be carried away by the sleepwalking of the world. Precious Holy Spirit, help us to watch and to be sober.

LEST YOU SORROW. *1 Thessalonians 4:13*

Suppose that you are a professional gardener, responsible for a garden that is not yours. You take great care of several prize rose bushes. You fertilize, water, prune, and train them. Now that they are blooming in great beauty, you take considerable pride in them.

One morning you come into the garden and find that the best rose has been taken. You are angry and accuse your fellow workers of taking it. They declare their innocence, saying that they had nothing to do with it. But one says, "I saw the master walking here this morning. I think he took it."

Is the gardener still angry? No, he immediately says, "I am pleased that my rose's beauty attracted the master's attention. That rose was his, and he has taken it. Let him do what seems good."

It is the same with your loved ones. They did not die by chance. The grave is not filled by accident. People die according to God's will. Your child is gone, but the Master took her. Your husband is gone, but the Master took him. Your wife is buried, but the Master took her. Thank God that He let you have the pleasure of caring and tending for them while they were here. Thank Him that as He gave, He Himself has taken.

If you believe in providence, you may grieve, "but I do not want you to be ignorant, brethren, concerning those who have fallen asleep, lest you sorrow as others who have no hope. For if we believe that Jesus died and rose again, even so God will bring with Him those who sleep in Jesus" (1 Thess. 4:13-14).

Thee at all times I will bless;
Having Thee I all possess;
How can I bereaved be,
Since I cannot part with Thee.

285

WITH A SHOUT. *1 Thessalonians 4:16*

The glorious doctrine of Jesus' resurrection is intended to take away the sorrow of death. Faith being exercised upon immortality relieves us of all concern over the spirits of the saved. The destroyed body will live again; it has not been annihilated. The frame that we lay in the dust will only sleep there until "the Lord Himself will descend from heaven with a shout, with the trumpet of God. And the dead in Christ will rise first" (1 Thess. 4:16). Our bodies will be reunited with our spirits and clothed in superior beauty, clothed with attributes unknown here.

The Lord's love to His people is not a love of disembodied spirits, but of men and women dressed in flesh and blood. The love of Jesus Christ toward His chosen is not an affection for just their souls. He keeps all our parts. He guards all our bones (Ps. 34:20). The very hairs of our head are all numbered (Matt. 10:30). He took into union with His Deity not only a human soul, but also a human body. Moreover, our Redeemer has perfectly ransomed both soul and body. It was not a partial redemption that our Kinsman effected for us. "I know that my Redeemer lives, and He shall stand at last on the earth; and after my skin is destroyed, this I know, that in my flesh I shall see God, whom I shall see for myself, and my eyes shall behold, and not another. How my heart yearns within me!" (Job 19:25-27).

I know that He has redeemed us, not only with respect to our spirit, but also with regard to our body. He has redeemed it from the power of death and ransomed it from the prison of the grave.

WITH THE LORD. *1 Thessalonians 4:17*

God will be with us even in death. "For I know that You will bring me to death" (Job 30:23). He leads me beside the still waters that so many fear (Ps. 23:2). "Yea, though I walk through the valley of the shadow of death, I will fear no evil; for You are with me; Your rod and Your staff, they comfort me" (Ps. 23:4). Dear friend, we live with God. Shall we not die with Him?

Our life is one long holiday when the Lord Jesus keeps us company. We go out with joy and are led out with peace. The mountains and the hills break forth into singing, and all the trees of the field clap their hands (Is. 55:12). Will they not be equally glad when we rise to our eternal reward? It is not living that is happiness, but living with God. It is not dying that will be wretched, but dying without God.

The child has to go to bed, but she does not cry if mother goes with her. It is dark, but the mother's eyes are the child's lights. It is lonely, but the mother's arms are the child's company. It is quiet, but the mother's voice is the child's music. Lord, when the hour comes for me to go to bed, I know that You will take me there and speak lovingly in my ear.

Dismiss all fear of death. Even though the shadows deepen, the Lord is your light and salvation (Ps. 27:1). Though our bodies will sleep for a little while in their lowly resting places, our souls shall be forever with the Lord. "The Lord Himself will descend from heaven with a shout, with the voice of an archangel, and with the trumpet of God. And the dead in Christ will rise first. . . . And thus we shall always be with the Lord. Therefore comfort one another with these words" (1 Thess. 4:16-18).

PRAY WITHOUT CEASING. *1 Thessalonians 5:17*

Observe what the above verse follows. It comes immediately after "rejoice always" (1 Thess. 5:16). Has that command ever staggered you and made you ask, "How can I rejoice always?"

The apostle gives the answer, "Pray without ceasing" (1 Thess. 5:17). The more praying, the more rejoicing. Prayer gives a channel to pent up sorrow, and it flows away in a steady stream of scared delight. The more rejoicing, the more praying. When the heart is quiet and full of joy, it will draw near to the Lord in worship. A holy joy and prayer act and react on each other.

Now look at the verse that follows, "In everything give thanks" (1 Thess. 5:18). When joy and prayer are married, the firstborn child is gratitude. When we joy in God for what we have and in faith pray for more, then our souls thank Him for the enjoyment of what we have and for the prospect of what is to come.

These three verses are companion-pictures representing the life of a true Christian. The middle verse is the link. These three precepts are an ornament of grace to every believer. Wear them for glory and beauty.

"Rejoice always."
"Pray without ceasing."
"In everything give thanks."

GRACE FOR THE TESTS. *2 Thessalonians 1:4*

It is true that God's people are tested, but it is also true that God's grace is equal to their trials. It is true that through many tribulations we enter the kingdom of God (Acts 14:22). We wade through waters of woe, but the billows will not overflow us (Is. 43:2). Listen to Jeremiah, "Through the LORD's mercies we are not consumed, because His compassions fail not. They are new every morning; great is Your faithfulness" (Lam. 3:22-23). Compassions, what a blessed word!

The thought that God's mercy is always new is pleasing, that it is new every morning is wonderful—new every morning, not just some mornings but every morning, from the first of January to the last of December.

Every morning brings new mercy. Every morning ushers in another day. Every morning brings a reason to praise God, because we have no right to an hour or to even a minute, much less to a day. We have another day to walk with God as Enoch did. We have another day to trust God as Abraham did. We have another day to reap the golden harvest. We have another day to be ripened for glory. We have another day to fellowship with the Lord.

God gives us our days. May He teach us their value, for they are pearls of great price. Then, as each new morning breaks, we may say to Him, "This I recall to my mind, therefore I have hope. Through the LORD's mercies we are not consumed, because His compassions fail not. They are new every morning; great is Your faithfulness."

PEACE ALWAYS. *2 Thessalonians 3:16*

These words are inexpressibly sweet. If you think for a moment, you will see that we never obtain peace except from the Lord. In your trials, what will bring peace? Let me tell you, the Lord of peace Himself. I find great peace thinking about His mysterious person. He is a Man, "tempted as we are, yet without sin" (Heb. 4:15). A Man who knows every grief of the soul and every pain of the body—thus His tender sympathy and power to deliver. His person is a source of peace.

Rest in your soul by meditating on His death. View Him wounded, bleeding, and dying on the tree. A wonderful calm will steal over your heart. Jesus is that bundle of myrrh and spice (Song 5:1) from which peace flows like a sweet perfume. When He comes near your heart and shows you His wounds and speaks His love, you feel the divine fervency of His peace. When He assures you that you are one with Him, united in an everlasting embrace that knows no divorce, your soul is steeped in peace.

This is an experiential business, and words cannot express it fully. "The Lord of peace Himself gives you peace always in every way. The Lord be with you" (2 Thess. 3:16). He does not merely offer peace, or argue that you ought to have it, or merely show the grounds for it. He gives it. He can give you peace. He will give you peace.

A PEACEABLE LIFE. *1 Timothy 2:2*

The LORD is my strength and my shield; my heart trusted in Him, and I am helped; therefore my heart greatly rejoices" (Ps. 28:7). This passage has great charm. It is charged with softness and sweetness, like a gentle strain of tender music.

I think of a battle furiously raging. And after fighting valiantly, the one whom it most concerns steps aside. He goes to a quiet, bomb-proof place almost out of the cannon's roar. There he talks with his heart and forgets the raging strife. He knows his weakness, yet he has caught a glimpse of the guaranteed divine strength and thus expects a joyful victory. He is trembling, certainly, perhaps from the toil of the battle, but he also rests as one insensibly subdued to calm and composure. He rests in God.

In the same way, I want you to get out of the crowd and take shelter in a quiet place. Forget the various troubles of business, or the domestic cares that often harass, or the inner conflict that plagues your soul. Whatever may disturb, distress, or distract, let it alone. Now for a while, revel in the sweet peace that God alone can give. "The peace of God which surpasses all understanding will guard your hearts and minds through Christ Jesus" (Phil. 4:7).

Say to your soul, "The LORD is my strength and my shield; my heart trusted in Him, and I am helped; therefore my heart greatly rejoices, and with my song I will praise Him."

ONE MEDIATOR. *1 Timothy 2:5*

We all want sympathy, so we readily tell friends our troubles, but faith teaches that there is no sympathy equal to that of the man Christ Jesus and no power the equal of our heavenly Father. Therefore, tell your troubles to your best Friend. Take your burdens to your Mediator, Jesus Christ, and unload them at the foot of the cross. With childlike reliance on His power, go to Jesus for help. Go without hesitation, and go without delay.

This is a rule of God's providence, "Call upon Me in the day of trouble; I will deliver you, and you shall glorify Me" (Ps. 50:15). Rest assured that the Lord, who daily provides for the millions of fish in the sea and the myriads of birds in the air (Matt. 6:26), will not allow His children to perish. He who cares for the glowworm on a damp bank and for a bug in the woods will never forsake His own (Ps. 94:14).

Whether your troubles are tangible or spiritual, leave them with God. Cry to Him in prayer. Walk in His fear and trust in His name, and sooner or later, in one way or another, He will make a way of escape. Friends may fail, but the Lord God never can. Other promises may turn out to be mere wind, but faithful is He that has promised. "He shall deliver you in six troubles, yes, in seven no evil shall touch you" (Job 5:19). You shall "dwell in the land, and feed on His faithfulness. Delight yourself also in the LORD, and He shall give you the desires of your heart" (Ps. 37:3-4). "No good thing will He withhold from those who walk uprightly. O LORD of hosts, blessed is the man who trusts in You" (Ps. 84:11-12).

We will be happy if we believe and act on this.

THAT WHICH IS TO COME. *Timothy 4:8*

At the moment of death the Christian will begin to enjoy a glorious and pleasure-filled eternal life in the company of Christ, the presence of God, the society of disembodied spirits, and holy angels. How does Paul put it? "Absent from the body." Yet you have hardly said that word when he adds "present with the Lord" (2 Cor. 5:8). The eyes close on earth and open in heaven.

How long that state of disembodied happiness will last is not for us to know. But in the fullness of time, the "Lord Himself will descend from heaven with a shout with the voice of the archangel, and with the trumpet of God. And the dead in Christ will rise first" (1 Thess. 4:16). Raised by divine power, our bodies will be reunited with our souls to live with Christ. Our bodies, planted as dull unattractive bulbs, will develop into the glory of a lovely lily with snowy cup and gold petals. Our bodies, sown like shriveled wheat, will rise as a golden ear.

"It has not yet been revealed what we shall be, but we know that when He is revealed, we shall be like Him, for we shall see Him as He is" (1 John 3:2). What a promise! These aches and pains will be repaid. This weariness and sickness will be compensated. The body will be remarried to the soul from which it departed with so much grief. Then in perfect body and soul, the fullness of our bliss will have arrived.

FIGHT THE GOOD FIGHT. *1 Timothy 6:12*

Our trophies are never won without a battle. When we live by faith our earthly careers are a constant conflict. We may never doubt Christ, but we may wonder if God has forgotten to be gracious. One day you are on Tabor's summit witnessing your Master's transfiguration (Matt. 17:2), and another day you are in the Valley of Humiliation, brought low through oppression, affliction, and sorrow. One day you are as strong as a giant and all things seem possible; another day you are as weak as a baby, weeping for joys that have fled. Sometimes full of hope, you leap forward with joyful steps, but then the sun ceases to shine and large raindrops fall. The fog rises, and you sit with folded arms and tearful eyes and become depressed.

If you have just begun your journey with Christ, you may think that you will never have to fight sin. Remember, you have just left the shore. You will not reach port until your vessel has been buffeted, tossed, and heaved by contrary winds. You may not understand this now, because it appears to you as if God's saints live in perpetual sunshine. Not so! Those that God highly honors will tell you quite another tale. God has a way of taking His children behind the door and showing them some of their abominations. Yet at the same time, He is showing them the beauties of Christ and enabling them to feed on Him.

If you are well into your journey with Christ, do not think your case is extreme because your spiritual life is much contested with sin. Far from it! I believe that this is typical of the way in which the Lord deals with all His own beloved ones.

WHOM I HAVE BELIEVED. *2 Timothy 1:12*

Some years ago, I was deeply depressed. I knew whom I had believed, but I could not get comfort from the truth I preached. I even began to wonder if I was really saved.

While on vacation, I went to a Wesleyan chapel. The sermon was full of the gospel and tears flowed from my eyes. I was in a perfect delirium of joy. I said, "Oh yes, there is spiritual life within me; the gospel can still touch my heart and stir my soul."

When I thanked the good man for his sermon, he looked at me and could hardly believe his eyes. He said, "Are you not Mr. Spurgeon?"

I replied, "Yes."

"Dear, dear," said he, "that was your sermon I preached this morning."

I knew it was, and that was one reason why I was so comforted. I realized that I could take my own medicine. I asked the preacher to my inn for dinner. We rejoiced that he was led to give the people one of my sermons that day, that I could be fed from my own kitchen.

I do know this. Whatever I may be, there is nothing that moves me like the gospel of Christ. "For this reason I also suffer these things; nevertheless I am not ashamed, for I know whom I have believed and am persuaded that He is able to keep what I have committed to Him until that Day" (2 Tim. 1:12).

Do you feel the same way?

IF WE ENDURE. *2 Timothy 2:12*

If you cannot work, if you are forced to lie still and suffer, remember this: acquiescence is a silver pipe through which the joy of the Lord comes. It is a pleasure to feel that if God would have us suffer, we are happy to do so. It is a joy when we are crushed like an olive between the millstones to yield nothing but the oil of thankfulness. It is a joy when we are bruised beneath affliction to yield the precious grain of entire submission to God. To glory in trials is to climb toward our Lord's likeness. It is a little heaven on earth.

The usual fellowship we have with our Beloved, though exceedingly precious, never equals the fellowship we enjoy when we have to break through thorns and briars to be with Him. It is joyous in the midst of sorrow to feel that we cannot mourn because the Bridegroom is with us (Matt. 9:15). Blessed is the person who, in the most terrible storm, rides the crest of the lofty waves toward heaven. Blessed is the person whom the storm drives toward God. This is true happiness.

There is a safe highway to heaven, and in the middle of that road there is a special place, an inner path where all who walk are both happy and safe. Many believers are just inside the hedge. They walk in the ditch by the road, and because they are safe they put up with all the inconveniences. Those who walk in the center of the road find no lion or ravenous beast there, for the Lord is their companion.

You cannot be with a strong God without receiving strength. God is always a transforming God. Fellowship with Him changes our likeness until we become more like Him.

THE LORD KNOWS. *2 Timothy 2:19*

Jesus' power can only be perfectly revealed in His people by holding, keeping, and sustaining them in trouble. Who can know the perfection of God's strength until he sees God making poor, puny creatures strong?

There is a timid, sick woman who lives in agony. Almost every breath is a spasm, every pulse a bang. Each member of her body is subject to great pain. Yet you hear no complaint. She is cheerful, and as much as possible she conceals her pain. Frequently, she utters words as joyful as those who are in robust health. When she must tell of her afflictions, you feel that she has accepted them with complete resignation. She is willing to bear them for as many years as the Lord may appoint. I do not wonder when strong people say strong things, but I do marvel when I hear heroic sentences from the weak or when the sorrowing comfort others. For you would think that they need the comfort themselves. Mark their cheerfulness! If you and I had suffered half as much, we would have sunk.

These trials perfectly reveal God's strength. When you see a child of God brought into poverty, suffering, distress, and infirmities, and when you see their character assailed, yet when they also stand like a rock in the waves, you see the power of God.

Great trials bring out God's great strength.

301

I HAVE FINISHED THE RACE. *2 Timothy 4:7*

It is my desire that death will perfect my entire career, that death will be the capstone on the building, so that nothing is needed to complete my life's work. Is it this way with you? Suppose you were to die at this moment, would your life be complete? Or would it be a broken column snapped off in the center?

May our death not be one that needs flurry and hot haste to make us ready. Some die in that fashion, but they have so little grace as to be only "saved, yet so as through fire" (1 Cor. 3:15). True Christians stand ready for death; they know the Bridegroom is coming soon and they keep their lamps well trimmed (Matt. 25:4). This is the way to live, and this is the way to die. Our home-going will be a simple matter if the Holy Spirit puts us in such a condition that the death angel may not catch us by surprise.

It must be sad to be taken unwillingly, plucked like an unripe fruit from the tree. The unripe apple holds fast to its place, and many hold hard to their riches. They cling so fondly to earthly things that it takes a sharp pull to separate them from the world. Ripe fruit, however, adheres only lightly. When a gentle hand comes to take it, it yields freely, as if willing to be gathered.

God made you unworldly. May He forbid you to cling so resolutely to things below, that your departure be not violent and full of terror.

FINALLY. *2 Timothy 4:8*

Our Master taught us how to die as well as how to live. He could say, "I have finished the work which You gave Me" (John 17:4). Triple blessed is the believer who, in permanently laying down the shepherd's staff or the carpenter's plane, or in putting aside the ledger or the schoolbook, can exclaim, "I have fought the good fight, I have finished the race, I have kept the faith. Finally, there is laid up for me the crown of righteousness which the Lord, the righteous Judge, will give to me" (2 Tim. 4:7-8).

They asked good old Mede, the Puritan, how he was doing. He answered, "Going home as fast as I can, and bless God I have a good home to go to." Dear aged saint, so near home, faith will transform death from an enemy to a friend as it brings the glory near. You will soon be in the Father's house and leave me behind. But I am not sure. I remember that the other disciple outran Peter and came first to the tomb (John 20:4), and so may I. You have the start on me in years, but I may be called home first.

Let death come. We will not be afraid. Jesus, who loved us and gave His life for us, is the resurrection and the life (John 11:25). Why should we not want to go? What is here that we should want to wait? What is there on this poor earth to detain a heaven born and heaven bound spirit? Let us go. He, our treasure, is gone. He whose beauties have enthralled our love is not here. Why should we linger? He has risen (Matt. 28:7). Let us rise.

THE SAVIOR'S FELLOWSHIP. *Titus 3:4*

It is sweet to see the Savior fellowship with His beloved people. There is nothing more delightful than being led by the divine Spirit to this fertile field of happiness.

Consider the history of the Redeemer's love to you. A thousand enthralling acts of affection come to mind, and each act weaves your heart to Christ. Thoughts and emotions intertwine to secure your renewed soul to Jesus.

When we meditate on this amazing love and see our all-glorious Savior endowing His church with all His ancient wealth, our souls may well faint with joy. Who can endure this weight of love? Even a partial sense that the Holy Spirit gives is sometimes more than the soul can contain. How rapturous it would be to see it completely.

When our soul understands how to discern all the Savior's gifts and has the wisdom to estimate them and the time to meditate on them, we will commune with Jesus in a far sweeter fellowship.

Who can imagine the pleasantness of this fellowship? It must be that "eye has not seen, nor ear heard, nor [has it] entered into the heart of man the things which God has prepared for those who love Him" (1 Cor. 2:9). Oh to burst open the door of our Joseph's granaries (Gen. 41:49) and see the bounty He has stored for us! This will overwhelm us with love.

By faith, we see as "in a mirror dimly" (1 Cor. 13:12) the reflected image of His boundless treasures. But when we actually see the heavenly things with our own eyes, how deep will be the stream of fellowship where our souls will bathe. Until then, our loudest sonnets will be reserved for our loving benefactor, Jesus Christ our Lord.

WE SEE JESUS. *Hebrews 2:9*

Are you poor, my dear brother? Do you see Jesus? He was poorer than you. You have somewhere to sleep tonight, but He could say, "Foxes have holes, and birds of the air have nests, but the Son of Man has nowhere to lay His head" (Luke 9:58).

Are you racked with pain? Let it help you to see Jesus. You are not "exceedingly sorrowful, even to death" (Matt. 26:38), nor is your grief to be compared with His.

Have you been betrayed and deserted? See Jesus as He is kissed by Judas (Matt. 26:49). Have you been denied by some friend who promised to be faithful? Look into the face of Jesus as He turns to Peter (Luke 22:61).

Is death staring you in the face? Remember Him who "being found in appearance as a man, humbled Himself and became obedient to the point of death, even the death of the cross" (Phil. 2:8).

We would never be alone if we could see Jesus; or if we were alone it would be a blessed solitude. We would never feel deserted if we could see Jesus; or if we were deserted we would have the best of helpers. If we could always see Jesus we would not feel weak for He would be our strength and our song.

Oh to see Jesus! You have seen Him as your Savior, and you desire to see Him as your Master. Oh to see Him as a friend on whom you can still lean your aching head, someone into whose ear you can pour your tale of sorrow! Through this wilderness, you may continually lean on Him and have perpetual sweet enjoyment. Then this earth, desert as it is, will seem to blossom like a garden of roses, and your spirit will enjoy heaven below.

IN THE DAY OF TRIAL. *Hebrews 3:8*

When you wonder why you are being severely tested, remember that the reason does not lie so much with you but with those to whom God will make you useful. You are being led along a rough road. You are being tested and instructed in order to help those whom you will find in some of the earth's dark regions.

You are being trained as a hardy mountaineer to climb after the Lord's sheep who are lost in the wild, craggy places. You are being taught to find your way through the country of depression and despair in order to help lost pilgrims find their way to the celestial city. They frequently fall into the marshy places of fear and doubt, and you will know how to bring them out, set their feet on the rock, and once again establish their goings.

The effect of one life on another can hardly be fully known. Even when we are able to look back on the completed life, we rarely know how much it has been twisted by other lives. Certainly, until this life is complete, we will never know how much our present suffering has to do with our usefulness to others. We will never understand how being prepared here, there, and in a thousand other places has helped a fellow pilgrim.

THE THRONE OF GRACE. *Hebrews 4:16*

True prayer is not a mere mental exercise or a vocal performance; it is far deeper than that. It is spiritual business with the Creator of heaven and earth. Its aim and object is to reach God Himself. Here the work of the Holy Spirit is necessary. If prayer were of the lips alone, we would only need breath in our nostrils to pray. Prayer will not be true prayer without the Spirit of God, and it will not be prevailing prayer without the Son of God.

We may be familiar, but we must be sacred. We may be bold, but not impertinent. We do not pray to God to instruct Him on what to do. Neither for a moment must we presume to dictate the line of divine procedure. We are permitted to say to God, "Thus and thus would we have it," but we must always add, "since we are ignorant and may be mistaken—seeing that we are still in the flesh and activated by carnal motives—not as we will, but as You will."

We do not come in prayer only to a place where God dispenses His favors to the poor. Nor do we come to the back door of the house of mercy to receive scraps, though that is more than we deserve. When we pray, we are standing in the palace before God's throne. We are on the glittering floor of the great King's reception room, and thus we are placed on advantaged ground.

Shall we come with stunted requests and a narrow, contracted faith? No, for it does not become a King to be giving away pennies. Our God distributes pieces of broad gold. Oh that we always felt this way when we came before the throne of grace! Then He would do "exceedingly abundantly above all that we ask or think" (Eph. 3:20).

GRACE TO HELP. *Hebrews 4:16*

Here are four comforts when you face a severe trial.

1. There is no curse in your cross. It may be as heavy as a ton of sorrow, but there is not a single ounce of curse. "'Whom the LORD loves, He chastens, and scourges every son whom He receives.' If you endure chastening, God deals with you as with sons; for what son is there whom a father does not chasten?" (Heb. 12:6-7). The God of love, who inflicts our sorrows, is as good when He chastens as when He caresses.

2. Your trials are assigned by divine wisdom and love. He who weighs the mountains in the scales (Is. 40:12) measures your troubles, and you will not have a grain more than His infinite wisdom determines. The devil may be turned loose on you, but remember, he is a defeated enemy. Everything that you suffer is the appointment of wisdom, ruled by love.

3. When you bear the cross, God gives special comforts that He never gives to the healthy. Dark caverns do not keep miners from searching for diamonds. You need never fear suffering if you remember it will richly bless your soul. The nightingale only sings at night, and there are promises that only sing when we are in trouble. It is in the cellar of affliction that the fine wine of the kingdom is stored. You will never see Christ's face so clearly as when all others turn their back on you.

4. Trials bring you nearer to God. Yet there are times when our faith staggers and we fail to leave our worldly cares with Him. Like Martha, we worry about many things (Luke 10:41). But Jesus says, "Come My child and trust Me. 'Come boldly to the throne of grace, that we may obtain mercy and find grace to help in time of need'" (Heb. 4:16).

BLESSING I WILL BLESS YOU. *Hebrews 6:14*

The God with whom you and I have to deal is a God who may do as He wills. He is an absolute sovereign, but He never can do anything unless it is right. He has promised to speak with reverence and with bonds and pledges in the person of Jesus Christ, saying, "Surely blessing I will bless you" (Heb. 6:14).

There is a covenant entered into on our behalf between the Lord Jesus and the Father. This covenant, assuredly and certainly, brings unnumbered blessings because God cannot lie. He has given two unalterable pledges so that we may have strong comfort and will never doubt His faithfulness. Beloved, the God of the promises has appointed your future and your inheritance, so you shall stand in it at the end of the days. The God of the promises has appeared to you in Jesus Christ, and He has sworn an oath; therefore, you may rest in the blood of Jesus, which makes the covenant sure.

He has promised never to leave His people. He told Jacob, "I will not leave you" (Gen. 28:15), and He says the same to you. He will never forget to give what He has promised. "I will not leave you until I have done what I have spoken to you." What blessed words! This divine statement is so rich, so full of the best, that to talk about it is gilding gold or adding whiteness to the lily's beauty.

Remember this promise, and let the Holy Spirit apply it. The God who does not change has made all the promises in Christ Jesus to the glory of God. Every one of His promises made to believers will stand fast and firm. "For assuredly, I say to you, till heaven and earth pass away, one jot or one tittle will by no means pass from the law till all is fulfilled" (Matt. 5:18).

SURE AND STEADFAST. *Hebrews 6:19*

Believers may be as poor as poverty but still wealthy. We do not worry about tomorrow, for tomorrow will worry about its own things (Matt. 6:34). We throw ourselves on God's providence. We believe that He who clothes the grass of the field will much more clothe us (Matt. 6:30). He who clothes the lilies and feeds the birds of the air (Matt. 6:26, 29) will not allow His children to go starving or barefoot.

Believers have little concern about their worldly estates. We fold our arms and sing as we float down the stream of providence. Whether we float by dark, dreary, and destructive mud banks or by estates fair and valleys pleasant, it does not change our position. We neither move nor struggle. Our only desire is to lie passively in God's hand and know no will but His.

When the storm comes, we find Christ to be "a hiding place from the wind, and a cover from the tempest" (Is. 32:2). When the heat is hot, we find Christ to be "the shadow of a great rock in a weary land" (Is. 32:2). We put our anchor deep in the sea and we sleep. Hurricanes may blow, the masts may creak, the timbers may strain, and every nail may pull from its place, but still we sleep because Christ is at the helm. We have an anchor of the soul that is both sure and steadfast (Heb. 6:19).

The earth shakes, but we say, "God is our refuge and strength, a very present help in trouble. Therefore we will not fear, even though the earth be removed, and though the mountains be carried into the midst of the sea" (Ps. 46:1-2).

LOVED ONES TAKEN AWAY. *Hebrews 10:9*

From some of you, the Lord has been taking away considerable portions of your family. Dear children are now with Him in glory. Father and mother have also gone, so too husband or wife, brother or sister. Some dear ones are now home, and you may be left alone. You begin to count the friends of your youth on your fingers. God is evidently taking away "the first" (Heb. 10:9), but do not forget how blessedly He is establishing "the second." When you enter heaven, you will be no stranger inside those pearly gates. There will be many there whom you knew and loved on earth, whom you will know and love above. They will meet you at the gates, and they will rejoice with you before the great Father's throne.

"Alas," says one, "I have lost all my family, and I am alone and desolate." If you are a child of God, remember what the apostle wrote, "I bow my knees to the Father of our Lord Jesus Christ, from whom the whole family in heaven and earth is named" (Eph. 3:14-15). Though God has taken away that first family, He has established the second, and it is a far more numerous and glorious one.

"God sets the solitary in families" (Ps. 68:6). This is what He has done for you. He has taken your first family connections, your first bonds of brotherhood and sisterhood, to establish the second, higher, relationships. He has dissolved the ties of blood, that you may find better spiritual relationships. Jesus spoke of this when He said, "Whoever does the will of My Father in heaven is My brother and sister and mother" (Matt. 12:50). Today, we say of the saints on earth and the saints before the throne of God in heaven, "These are sister, and brother, and father, and mother to us."

"He takes away the first that He may establish the second" (Heb. 10:9).

SEEING HIM. *Hebrews 11:27*

Many are called to suffer much in daily life. What a world of misery there is in this great city, even among good and gracious people. You might study London until it turned your brain. The suffering and poverty even of godly people would be a subject too harrowing for those who have tender hearts.

Let us not forget those members of Christ's mystical body that are in the fire. "His feet were like fine brass, as if refined in a furnace" (Rev. 1:15). Few, if any, are without sorrow, and many saints have a double portion of grief in their pilgrimage. Sitting here with your brothers and sisters in Christ, you look cheerful, but I may be addressing one whose life is a protracted struggle for existence. Assuredly, you will not hold out without a great deal of true faith. You must endure as "seeing Him who is invisible" (Heb. 11:27). You must rejoice in God, or you will not rejoice at all. Earthly comforts are not yours. But if you grasp the spiritual and the eternal, you will not worry.

If only in this life you have hope, you would be most pitiable (1 Cor. 15:19). But having that hope, you are among the most happy. The wilderness and the wasteland shall be glad for you, and the desert shall rejoice and blossom as the rose (Is. 35:1). Commend me to firm faith for power to bear the daily cross. He that believes has everlasting life and the joys that come of it (John 5:24).

Trust in your God, in His love and care of you, and you will be like the lilies of the field, which neither toil or spin and yet are clothed. Therefore, do not worry about tomorrow (Matt. 6:28-34). Know by faith that heaven is prepared for you. Know for certain that you will soon be there among the angels, and you will defy cold, hunger, nakedness, shame, and everything else.

OUT OF WEAKNESS. *Hebrews 11:34*

Dear friend, would you like to do something great for God? Have you heard the motto of our early missionaries, "Attempt great things for God"? Does that thought burn within your heart? Do you long to be of some great use?

"Oh, yes," says one, "I would attempt great things for God, but I am terribly weak." Make the attempt by faith in God, for it is written about people "who through faith subdued kingdoms, worked righteousness, obtained promises, stopped the mouths of lions, quenched the violence of fire, escaped the edge of the sword, out of weakness were made strong, became valiant in battle, turned to flight the armies of the aliens" (Heb. 11:33-34).

If you feel incapable, throw yourself on the infinite capacity of God. As long as you are willing to be used, as long as God has given you a concern and a labor of spirit for the souls of others, you need not fear. You may by faith get to work in all your feebleness, for "as your days so shall your strength be" (Deut. 33:25). Has not the Lord said to you, "My grace is sufficient for you, for My strength is made perfect in weakness" (2 Cor. 12:9)? Is not this word true?

TRIAL OF MOCKINGS.   *Hebrews 11:36*

Possibly I speak to some who are suffering from the evils of persecution. Trials of cruel mockings are still common. There are many ways in which the devil's whip can reach the back of the child of God. Persecution is still abundant. Many a man's foes are in his own household. I will not tell stories of Christian women with jeering husbands or godly youths who endure mockings far worse. But many a house is still a place of martyrdom.

Gracious sufferers, may the Lord keep you from anger and unkindness. By faith alone can you bear persecution and turn it for the good of others. Do not attempt to escape by yielding what is right and true. Ask the Lord to help you to stand firm for Him. If it is true that the Lord still has martyrs, let it be seen that they are as brave as ever. They no longer gather in the great amphitheatre, where the emperor sits in state, with all the proud citizens of Rome gazing at them with cruel eyes. Not now do I see them lift the great iron door and let loose the monsters that come out roaring, hungry for their prey. Not now do I hear the shout of the mob, cheering as Christians are given to the lions. This is all over. Christ, in His suffering members, has conquered Caesar and pagan Rome.

Though a softer spirit comes over the human mind, still there is as much enmity against God as ever, but now it finds a less public arena. Today, the tested one suffers alone and misses the encouragement of Christian eyes. At times, he has to feel that it were better to fight with the beasts at Ephesus than to hear the taunts, threats, and slander of ungodly relatives. My sister and my brother, have faith in God in your hidden sorrow! Cry to Him in the secret of your soul, and you will carry your burden. Yes, you will bear it calmly, and you will win those who hate you. Do not fear.

THEY ... WERE TEMPTED. *Hebrews 11:37*

It seems to me that the trials and temptations of this life are preparing us for the life to come, building character for eternity. Have you ever been in a piano factory? Did you go there to hear music? Go into the tuning room and you will say, "This is a dreadful place, I cannot stand it, I thought you made music here."

"No, we do not produce music here. We make instruments and tune them, and in the process much discord is produced."

Such is the church of God on earth. The Lord makes the instruments and tunes them down here. A great deal of discord is easily perceptible, but it is all necessary to prepare us for the everlasting harmonies up yonder.

I am to stand one day so near to God that between Him and me there will be but one person, and that person is the Lord Jesus Christ, my Lord and Mediator. In Christ, I am to have dominion over all the works of God's hands and to be crowned with glory and honor. Angels are to be my servants and heaven my inheritance.

Will I ever grow proud? Will self-exaltation creep in? No! The character will be fixed for holiness as though etched in eternal brass. It may be that all the afflictions and temptations that God permits to pass over us here below are forming us for eternal bliss.

Thus the corn is ripening for the harvester and the fruit is mellowing for the basket. Here, the engraving tool and hammer bring out the beauties that will shine in the courts of the Lord forever, when on us also the record will be written, "They were tempted" (Heb. 11:37).

315

HEAVEN'S FAVORITES. *Hebrews 12:5*

Jesus loved Martha, Mary, and Lazarus (John 11:5). They were three of His special favorites, and thus He sent them an extraordinary trial (John 11:1). When a dealer in precious gems finds a stone of minimum value, little time is spent cutting it. But when a rare diamond is found, that stone will be cut, and cut, and cut again. When the Lord finds a saint whom He loves much, He may spare others trial and trouble but not this one, His well-beloved. The more Jesus loves you, the more of the rod you will feel (Heb. 12:5-6). It is painful to be a favorite of heaven, but seek it and rejoice in it.

Being in the King's council-chamber involves such work for faith that flesh and blood might cringe from the painful blessing. If a gardener gets an inferior tree, he lets it grow wild and takes whatever fruit it produces. But if the tree is exceptional, he will want every branch in its proper place, and he will cut here and cut there because this produces more fruit. The gardener leaves nothing on the tree that would be detrimental.

You who are God's favorites must not be astonished when trials appear. Rather keep your door wide open, and when trials come say, "Welcome messenger of the King! The sound of your Master's feet is behind you. You are welcome, for my Master has sent you."

ILLEGITIMATE AND NOT SONS. *Hebrews 12:8*

I know an old friend who used to tell me that for sixty years he had never known a day's illness. A splendid, healthy old man he was. Then, about three months ago, he contracted typhoid fever. I went to see him, and when he got better he came to see me. Sitting down, he said, "Well, sir, you see I am not the man I was, but I have made a great advance through this sickness. I have never known any weakness before, but now I have been brought very low. The Bible says, 'If you are without chastening, of which all have become partakers, then you are illegitimate and not sons' (Heb. 12:8). I am not illegitimate after all. I have had my chastening, and I hope I will take up my sonship more than I ever did."

God grant that every chastened child may gather assurance from the covenant rod! You, dear child of God, will not be long without a touch of the rod. May you have as little of it as the Lord judges to be proper. As for myself, I owe everything to the furnace, hammer, and file. I have made no progress in heavenly learning except when I have been whipped by the great Schoolmaster. The best piece of furniture in my house has been the cross. My greatest enricher has been personal pain, and for that I thank God.

"If you endure chastening, God deals with you as with sons" (Heb. 12:7). It is wondrous love that we should be called the children of God, and we are. Illegitimate children kick against the Father's stroke, but the wise child kisses the rod and blesses the hand that uses it. "Though He slay me, yet will I trust Him" (Job 13:15). This is a sure seal that we are true sons.

LET US HAVE GRACE. *Hebrews 12:28*

If you are called to endure great affliction, sharp pain, and frequent sickness, if business goes amiss, if riches take wings and fly away, if friends forsake you, if foes surround you, be of good courage, for God will never forsake you. Accept your Father's will. Rejoice that you have such a Father's will to bear.

If grace cannot enable you to endure all that nature can heap on you, what is grace worth? "Let us have grace, by which we may serve God acceptably with reverence and godly fear" (Heb. 12:28). Dear believer, the time to see if your faith is real is in the floods of adversity; mere sunshine faith is not worth having. We want a faith that will outlive the most terrible storm that ever clouded heaven.

Even though heart and flesh fail, even though eyes grow dim and the light of day is shut out, even though hearing fails and the music is silent, even though the doors of the senses close, even though the body totters and the keeper of the house trembles, trust in the Lord (Eccl. 12:2-7). Yes, even though death itself removes this feeble body, there is no cause to fear. Be of good courage.

"Peace I leave with you, My peace I give to you; not as the world gives do I give to you. Let not your heart be troubled, neither let it be afraid" (John 14:27). Wait on the Lord and your courage will be revived.

318

BE CONTENT. *Hebrews 13:5*

How does this promise apply to temporal things? At first glance it does not appear to have anything to do with ordinary expenses. According to this verse, we are not to be covetous but content with such things as we have. Thus, the text applies to ordinary working-people, to the merchant and to every Christian in both money and soul matters. He that does not let a sparrow fall to the ground without His permission will not let His children want (Matt. 10:29). If they should for a little time be in need, that will work to their lasting good, for they will dwell in the land and eat their fill (Lev. 25:19).

The fullness that lies in this promise is perfectly boundless. When God says that He will be with His servants, He means this, "My wisdom shall be with them to guide them. My love shall be with them to cheer them. My Spirit shall be with them to sanctify them. My power shall be with them to defend them. My everlasting might shall be put forth on their behalf so that they may not fail or be discouraged."

To have God with you is better than to have an army of ten thousand. A host of friends is not equal to that one name, Jehovah, for He is a host in Himself. When God is with you, He is not there asleep, negligent, or indifferent. He is there intensely sympathizing, bearing the trouble, helping and sustaining the sufferer. And in due time, His good time, He will deliver you in triumph. Precious word! Heartening promise! Plunge into it, for it is a sea without a bottom. "I will never leave you nor forsake you." Thus, be content with such things as you have. For among them is Christ.

I WILL NEVER LEAVE YOU. *Hebrews 13:5*

In life and death we prove the attributes of God's righteousness. We find that He does not lie but is faithful to His Word. We learn the attributes of mercy, for He is gentle in the time of our weakness. We prove the attributes of His immutability, for we find Him "the same yesterday, today, and forever" (Heb. 13:8).

God's characteristics are delightfully seen when the saint is departing. Precious promises are illustrated on death beds. "I will never leave you nor forsake you" (Heb. 13:5). Who could have known the certainty of this promise without having once been with a dying saint for whom all else was gone? "When you pass through the waters, I will be with you" (Is. 43:2). Who could have known the fullness of that promise without having once seen a believer triumphant on the day of death?

"Yea, though I walk through the valley of the shadow of death, I will fear no evil, for You are with me; Your rod and Your staff, they comfort me" (Ps. 23:4). You may read commentaries on that psalm, but you will never fully value it until you are in that valley.

My dear departed friend said on one of my last visits, "Read me a psalm, dear pastor."

"Which one?"

"There are many precious ones," said he, "but as I get nearer my departure, I love the twenty-third best. Let us have that again."

"Why?" I said. "You know that by heart!"

"Yes," said he. "It is in my heart, and it is most true and precious."

This is so true. You have not seen the twenty-third psalm to be a diamond of the purest water until you have seen its value to the saints in their departing moments.

I WILL NEVER FORSAKE YOU. *Hebrews 13:5*

Our translation does not convey the full force of the original. It is hardly possible in English to give the full weight of the Greek. We might freely translate it, "He has said, I will never, never, never leave you; I will never, never, never forsake you" (Heb. 13:5).

Put a traveler in a vast howling wilderness, where there is no trace of man, no footstep of a traveler. The solitary wretch cries for help, and the hollow echo of the rocks is his only reply. No bird in the air, not even a prowling jackal in the waste or a solitary blade of grass to remind him of God.

Yet, even there he is not alone. The barren rocks prove a God. Both the hot sand under his feet and the blazing sun above his head witness to a present Deity. What would be the loneliness of one forsaken by God? No migration could be so awful as this, thus he says, "If I take the wings of the morning, and dwell in the uttermost parts of the sea, even there Your hand shall lead me, and Your right hand shall hold me" (Ps. 139:9-10).

Loneliness is a feeling that none of us delight in. Solitude may have some charm, but those who are forced to be her captives have not discovered it. A transient solitude may give pleasure, but to be alone, utterly alone, is terrible. To be alone without God is such horrific loneliness that I defy the lip even of a damned spirit to express the horror and anguish that must be concentrated in it.

Thank God that you and I by this promise are taught that we never will know the desperate loneliness of being forsaken by God. Yet this is what it would be if He should forsake us.

WE MAY BOLDLY SAY. *Hebrews 13:6*

The fact that the Lord has constantly been our helper confirms our faith. If in looking back we could find a point where God failed, we might let our faith waiver. I speak from experience. I cannot find one example in all my life in which God was untrue or unkind. If we never doubt God until we have a reason, we will never doubt so long as we live.

Yesterday I looked at some birds in a cage. These poor little creatures are entirely dependent on those who feed them. They cannot help themselves. If seed and water is not supplied, they will die. Yet there they sit and sing with all their might. Their state of dependence never distresses them. They never think that their keeper will fail them.

That is my position. I am God's singing bird. Perhaps I wonder where I shall get my bread or my next sermons, and a great many cares and troubles come to me. But why should I be troubled? Instead of mistrusting my keeper, who has fed me these many years, I had best sit and sing as loudly as I can. That is the best thing to do. The birds do it, so why not you and me? We are suppose to have more intellect than a bird, but at times we do not seem to have half as much.

The Lord has constantly been true. Do not doubt. If some remarkable trial should waylay you between here and heaven, you will find extraordinary deliverance from Him who has been your helper. "For He Himself has said, 'I will never leave you nor forsake you.' So we may boldly say: 'The LORD is my helper; I will not fear'" (Heb. 13:5-6).

THE LORD IS MY HELPER. *Hebrews 13:6*

The God of the past has blotted out your sins (Acts 3:19). The God of the present makes all things work together for your good (Rom. 8:28). The God of the future will never leave you nor forsake you (Heb. 13:5). In God you are prepared for every emergency.

There is no point in having a God if you do not use Him, and yet many professing Christians would never dream of going to God for practical help. I believe that it is as well to have no God as to have an unreal God, one who cannot be found in the midnight of need. What a blessing to be able to go to God and pour out our hearts. God will be our Helper (Ps. 54:4), a near and dear Friend in joy and sorrow.

Dear friend, are you in trouble? Do you have a God? Then pray and spread your trial before Him. Do you have a troublesome letter in your house (2 Kin. 19:10-13)? Then go, like Hezekiah, and tell the Lord (2 Kin. 19:14). Is your child dying? Then cry to the Lord as David did (2 Sam. 12:16). Are you as low as Jonah? Then let your prayer rise from the bottom (Jon. 2:1). Are you bitter? Pour it out before the Lord.

Make good use of your God. Gain full advantage by pleading with Him. Tell Him your troubles. Search His promises, and then petition Him with holy boldness, for this is the surest and the fastest way to find relief.

What would we do if we could not speak with God, our ever-gracious Friend? We would die of a broken heart. Like Job, we would curse the day of our birth. We would wish that we had never been born (Job 3:3) and look forward to annihilation. But praise God, we can go to Him by faith and plead His promise. The dark clouds will withdraw, and we will come into the light.

COUNT IT ALL JOY. *James 1:2*

Think of the priceless virtue that is produced by various trials: patience! We all have a large supply of it until we need it, and then we have none. The one who truly possesses patience is one that has been tested.

What kind of patience do we get from the grace of God? It is a patience that accepts the trial as from God. Calm resignation does not come at once. Often, long years of physical pain, or mental depression, or career disappointment, or multiple deaths are needed to bring the soul into full submission to the Lord's will. After much crying, the child is weaned. After much chastening, the son is made obedient to the Father's will. By degrees, we learn to end our quarrels with God and to desire that there be not two wills between God and ourselves but one, that God's will may be our will. Believer, if your troubles work you to that, then you are a gainer, and I am sure that you may count them all joy.

Patience enables us to bear ill-treatment, slander, and injury without resentment. We feel it keenly, but bear it meekly. Like our Master, we do not open our mouths to reply; we refuse to return shout for shout. We give blessing in return for cursing, like the sandalwood tree that perfumes the axe that cuts it.

"Love suffers long and is kind; love does not envy; love does not parade itself, is not puffed up; does not behave rudely, does not seek its own, is not provoked, thinks no evil; does not rejoice in iniquity, but rejoices in the truth; bears all things, believes all things, hopes all things, endures all things. Love never fails" (1 Cor. 13: 4-8). If the grace of God by trial will work this in you, then you have gained a solid weight of character.

THE TESTING OF YOUR FAITH. *James 1:3*

The safest part of a Christian's life is during a trial. How we pray in adversity! We cannot live without prayer. We carry our burden to the mercy seat again and again.

When we are depressed, we read our Bibles; we do not care for deceiving light literature. We want the solid promise, the strong meat, of God's kingdom.

In adversity, we listen; we do not care for flowers and fine bits of rhetoric. We want the Word. We want the naked doctrine. We want Christ. We cannot be fed on whims and fancies now. We care less about theological speculation and ecclesiastical authority. We want to know something about eternal love, everlasting faithfulness, and the dealings of the Lord of hosts with the souls of His people.

We walk lightly in the world and hold it with a loose grip. We expect to be often in the way, and we hope to be out of the way, because the world has lost its attraction. I greatly question if we ever grow in grace unless we are in the furnace.

This is the way it should be: the joys and blessings that God gives in this life should make us increase in grace and gratitude. These joys should be sufficient motivation for the highest form of consecration. As a rule, however, most of us are only driven closer to Christ in a storm. There are blessed and favored exceptions, but most of us need the rod. We do not seem to learn obedience except through the Lord's chastening.

IF ANY OF YOU LACKS WISDOM. *James 1:5*

This verse has a special reference for people in trouble. Much tested and severely tried saints are frequently at their wits' end. Though they may be persuaded that in the long run good will come out of all their affliction, yet for the present they may be so distracted that they know not what to do.

A properly spoken word in season is this apostle's statement, "If any of you lacks wisdom, let him ask of God, who gives to all liberally and without reproach, and it will be given to him. But let him ask in faith, with no doubting, for he who doubts is like a wave of the sea driven and tossed by the wind" (James 1:5-6). This wisdom the Lord will give to His afflicted children.

"My brethren, count it all joy when you fall into various trials, knowing that the testing of your faith produces patience. But let patience have its perfect work, that you may be perfect and complete, lacking nothing" (James 1:2-4).

This promise, however, is not limited to any one particular application. The word, "if any of you," is so wide and so extensive that whatever may be our necessity, whatever the dilemma that perplexes, this verse consoles us with this counsel, "If any of you lack wisdom, let him ask of God, who gives to all liberally and without reproach, and it will be given to him" (James 1:5).

EVERY PERFECT GIFT. *James 1:17*

Take a great effort to know what God has promised and when He has promised it. Continually study God's Word to see if the promises have your name written on them. Many times God has brought a promise to my heart with such freshness that I felt it was given only to me. This promise contained private marks that exactly matched the counterpart of my soul's secrets. This proves that God meant me when He spoke.

When you pray, learn to take the promise and say, "My God, You have promised this blessing. You said that You will do it, and I know that you cannot lie! I am sure that You will give me this blessing because You are a God of truth. Your promises are a gracious bond. Your truthfulness cannot be questioned."

"Every good gift and every perfect gift . . . comes down from the Father of lights, with whom there is no variation or shadow of turning" (James 1:17). When the Lord made His promises, He foresaw every possible contingency, and He made His promises with a determination to keep them. Time makes no difference. His promises are as fresh and unfading as when they first delighted His chosen.

Fall on your knees and pray, "Lord, this is Your promise. Be gracious and grant it. You do not change. Your Word is not withdrawn. You have never run from your Word, and You never will. Therefore fulfill it, because this gives me reason to hope."

An unchanging God is the foundation of happiness for the believer.

NO VARIATION. *James 1:17*

Would you know yourself from twenty years ago if you were to meet that person in the street? I don't think you would, for you have undergone a marked change. Aches and pains of body have altered you. Your juvenile elasticity of spirit has vanished, and your outward appearance is the worse for wear.

You have changed, but your God has not. What a mercy, that, though eternal ages roll over His immutability, with Him "there is no variation or shadow of turning" (James 1:17). God stands firm like the great mountains, and we like clouds melt on the mountains' peaks. We come and go; we are, and we are not. We are the mists of an hour, but He is the same.

There is no end to His years. This is our consolation as we sing with Moses, "LORD, You have been our dwelling place in all generations. Before the mountains were brought forth, or even You had formed the earth and the world, even from everlasting to everlasting, You are God" (Ps. 90:1-2).

You do not ask. *James 4:2*

We have many cares—our children, our business, our homes. Frequently, we do not bring these cares to God, feeling that they are too little to mention to Him. This is absurd! Have nothing else to do with such a sinful silence. Tell it all to Jesus. The Lord tells you to cast all your care upon Him, for He cares for you (1 Pet. 5:7). Tell Him! Why carry your sin, your need, and your care? Why not have greater desires and broader expectations? After all, Jesus says, "According to your faith let it be to you" (Matt. 9:29).

There are times when the angel of mercy flies around the homes of God's people and brings an abundance of precious blessings. Sometimes while we sleep, the angel of mercy hovers on soft wings, but there is no empty container in which to pour the blessing. Later, the angel visits another home, where in their prayers the residents set out a number of empty containers. The angel fills the containers from the supply of overflowing mercy, and when the petitioners awake they find an abundant supply of rich grace.

Some have feeble wishes, small desires, and slender prayers, or hardly any prayer at all. "You do not have because you do not ask" (James 4:2). Others have large desires, earnest prayers, great faith, and large expectations. God gives according to your faith.

HE GIVES MORE GRACE. *James 4:6*

Periods of weakness will occur. A great strain may be placed on us. We become exhausted or severely depressed, and we may imagine that we are ready to die. At times like this, God will supply strength. Our extreme distress will be His opportunity; our famine, His hour of plenty. "His strength is made perfect in weakness" (2 Cor. 12:9). "He gives power to the weak, and to those who have no might He increases strength" (Is. 40:29).

David sung, "He satisfies your mouth with good things, so that your youth is renewed like the eagle's" (Ps. 103:5). David expected this to happen always. "He restores my soul" (Ps. 23:3), he says. Often, David's psalms start in painful depression but conclude with exultation because heavenly love has poured fresh life into his fainting soul. From much soul sickness, Jesse's son has recovered; from many a sinking, he has been lifted in holy joy.

Expect this, believer. God will give you strength as you need it. "As your days, so shall your strength be" (Deut. 33:25). "He gives more grace" (James 4:6). Revel in God's smile. Find a haven in His manifested love. Have faith and be of good cheer. There are even richer mercies to come. Therefore, lift up your head.

WHAT TOMORROW MAY BRING. *James 4:14*

God has given us a memory, that we may look back. It would be well if we used our memories better, to remember, reflect, and repent. God has not given us eyes to pry into the future. He unveils the past for our penitence, but He veils the future from our curiosity.

Dark days may be near at hand for some of us, but we do not perceive them. Let us be thankful that we do not, for our afflictions would be multiplied at the foresight of them. The prospect of evil to come might cast a gloom over pleasure near at hand. As we may feel a thousand deaths in fearing one, so we may faint under a single stroke in dreading a thousand.

It is good that God conceals our earthly joys until the time of their arrival. Great prosperity may await you, but you do not know it. It is just as well, for you might be none the better for the prospect. Earth's goods are like glue; they are apt to hold us to things below and prevent us from soaring toward heaven. If, then, we could know all the pleasurable events that may happen, we might become more worldly and more earthbound than we are. None of us should desire that this present evil world should have an increased influence over us. We are glad that it should have less. Thus, we rejoice that its future has such slight power over us because that future is unknown.

IT IS EVEN A VAPOR. *James 4:14*

St. Augustine used to say that he did not know whether to call it a dying life or a living death. I leave you the choice between those two expressions. This is certainly a dying life, for its march is marked by graves, and nothing but a continuous miracle keeps any of us from the tomb. Were Omnipotence to stay its power but for a moment, earth would return to earth and ashes to ashes.

It is a dying life, and equally true, it is a living death. We are always dying. Every beating pulse leaves the number less. The more years we count, the fewer that remain. While we are sitting still in this house, the earth is revolving around the sun, carrying us through space at an amazing rate. We are all moving, yet we do not realize it. At this moment, you are being carried toward eternity at lightning speed. Though we dream that we are constant, we never rest; the stream is carrying us onward. Ever must we obey the mandate, "Onward, onward, onward." From childhood to youth, from youth to manhood, from manhood to gray old age, we march in ranks from which none can retire. We do not linger, even when we sleep. Then what is our life?

Our verse gives us an instructive answer. It does not so much tell us what life actually is as what it is like: a vapor. James compares our life to a subtle, unsubstantial, flimsy thing: a vapor (James 4:14). If you live on a height, from which you can look down on a stretch of country, you see in the early morning a mist covering all the valleys. It marks the tops of the great elms, like islands in a sea of clouds, with perhaps a church spire rising like a pyramid from the mist. In a little time the vapor has vanished. It was so thin, so fine, that a breath of wind scattered it. Such is your life. This is the picture James presents to us. "What is your life? It is even a vapor that appears for a little time and then vanishes away."

WE COUNT THEM BLESSED. *James 5·11*

Between here and heaven, we have no guarantee that the road will be easy or the sea smooth. We have no promise that we will be kept like flowers in a hot house, safe from the breath of frost or veiled from the heat of the sun.

The voice of wisdom says, "Be patient, be patient, be patient, for you may need a triple measure of it to be ready for the trial." I suppose, also, that we are over and over exhorted to be patient because it is so high an attainment. It is not child's play to be silent like sheep before shearers, to lie still while the shears are taking away all that warmed and comforted us. The silent Christian under the afflicting rod is no common person. We kick like oxen that feel the goad for the first time; we are for years like a bullock unaccustomed to the yoke.

"Be patient, be patient, be patient," is the lesson to be repeated to our hearts many times. It is the Holy Spirit, ever patient under our provocations, who calls us to be patient. It is the long-suffering Father who commands us, "Be patient." You who are soon to be in heaven, be patient, for yet a little while and your reward will be revealed.

We may well be patient under trials, for it is the Lord who sends them. He is ruling in all our circumstances, and He is blessing us by them. He is waiting to end them, and He is pledged to bring us through. Shall we not gladly submit to the Father of our spirits? Is not this our deepest wish, "Your will be done" (Matt. 6:10)? Shall we quarrel with that which blesses us? Shall we worry when the end of the trouble is so near? No! We see that the Lord is full of tender mercy, and so we will be patient.

YOU GREATLY REJOICE. *1 Peter 1:6*

Mariners tell us that parts of the ocean have a strong surface current going one way but a strong undercurrent running the other way down in the depths. The Christian is like that. On the surface there may be a stream of heaviness rolling with dark waves, but in the depths may roll a strong undercurrent of great rejoicing, always flowing.

Even when the Christian is "grieved by various trials," what a mercy to know that we are the elect of God! Every believer is assured that "He chose us in Him before the foundation of the world" (Eph. 1:4).

Let me lie on a sickbed and revel in this one thought: before God made the heavens and the earth, before He laid the pillars of the firmament in their golden sockets, He set His love upon me. On the breast of the great High Priest, He wrote my name, and in His everlasting book it will never be erased: elect according to the foreknowledge of God. If this makes your soul leap, all the heaviness that the infirmities of the flesh lay on you will be as nothing. This tremendous current of his overflowing joy will sweep away the milldam of your grief. Bursting and leaping over every obstacle, joy will overflow your sorrows until they are drowned forever.

Come Christian, depressed and thrown down, think for a moment. You are chosen of God and precious. Let the bell of election ring in your ear, that ancient Sabbath bell of the covenant. Let your name be heard in its notes. "In this you greatly rejoice, though now for a little while, if need be, you have been grieved by various trials, that the genuineness of your faith, being more precious than gold that perishes, though it is tested by fire, may be found to praise, honor, and glory at the revelation of Jesus Christ" (1 Pet. 1:6-7).

FOR A LITTLE WHILE. *1 Peter 1:6*

I was lying on the couch this past week, and my spirits were so low that I cried like a child. I did not know why I wept, but a little thing will move me to tears. A kind friend was telling of some poor old soul who was suffering great pain and yet was full of joy and rejoicing. I was so distressed by that story and so ashamed of myself that I did not know what to do. Here was a poor woman with a terrible cancer, yet in the most frightful agony she could rejoice with "joy inexpressible and full of glory" (1 Pet. 1:8).

In a moment, 1 Peter 1:6 flashed on my mind with its real meaning. "Though now for a little while, if need be, you have been grieved by various trials." You have been made to weep, and you cannot bear your pain. You are brought to the very dust of death, and wish that you might die. Your faith seems as if it would fail you.

This is what the text declares: at times the Christian should endure suffering without a gallant and a joyous heart. Sometimes your spirit should sink. Sometimes you should become as a little child struck by the hand of God.

Beloved, we sometimes talk about the rod, but it is one thing to see it and another to feel it. The breaking down of the strong is the result of God striking. Many times we have said, "If I did not feel so low in spirit, I would not mind this affliction." What is that but saying, "If I did not feel the rod, I would not mind it?" It is how you feel that is, after all, the force and center of your affliction.

This one idea has been enough to feed me for many days. There may be some child of God here to whom it may bring some slight comfort. "Though now for a little while, if need be, you have been grieved by various trials."

YOU HAVE BEEN GRIEVED. *1 Peter 1:6*

The apostle Peter wrote, "Though now for a little while, if need be, you have been grieved by various trials" (1 Pet. 1:6). Not only do we have various trials; they also grieve and depress us. It happens to the best of God's servants. I know several people who love the Lord, and the Lord loves them. They are precious to Him. They are humble, gentle, and gracious people, but they have come into deep trouble or some heavy cloud rests on them. It is especially to them that I write.

Dear troubled friend, you may have a grief or sorrow that is not known to anybody. You do not want to reveal it. You would not whisper it to the dearest confidant that you have on earth. You keep it to yourself. Perhaps this is the reason that it becomes so bitter. Communicating to some Christian friend might be a real help. There is relief in shedding tears when you are in great anguish. If you can have a good cry, you can get over the trouble readily.

Yet sometimes you cannot find expression for grief and the pent-up flame becomes more fierce. If you have a grief that you cannot tell to any human being, let me affectionately invite you to look to Jesus. Tell the Lord all about your sorrow, and ask Him to give you help in time of need. Whatever your case, tell it to Him. As surely as Jesus lives, He will hear and answer, and you will go your way in peace.

I do not know the details of your situation. "The heart knows its own bitterness, and a stranger does not share its joy" (Prov. 14:10). There are depths and there are heights where we must be by ourselves. Do not be surprised if, as far as human beings are concerned, you sometimes have to sail alone. But if Christ is in the vessel, you cannot have better company.

VARIOUS TRIALS. *1 Peter 1:6*

Trials do not come by chance (1 Pet. 1:6-7). Trials are sent because God judges them necessary (James 1:2). Trials are weighed out with discretion and are given by cautious wisdom. "Trials" is a beautiful name for affliction.

I do not look on affliction as a judgment for my sin, for my sin has been punished in Christ (1 Pet. 2:24). Rather, I look at my affliction as coming from the all-wise judgment of a kind and infinitely wise Father. Afflictions are called judgments not because they are judicial but because they are judicious.

Some of God's industrious, energetic, honest, and wise servants are unable to prosper in business. They are thwarted in all their purposes. There seems to be an ongoing fatality connected with their enterprises. If they touch a business or a bargain that should turn into gold, it nevertheless melts into dross. We cannot discover the cause or always explain the reason. "Your judgments are a great deep" (Ps. 36:6), a matter perceived as a fact but not to be explained by reasoning. Why does the Lord send us an affliction that we cannot understand? Because He is the Lord. Regardless of your experience, you are only a child when compared with the divine mind. What intelligence do you have? How can you expect God to act in a way that you can understand? He is God. Therefore, it is good to sit in silence and feel and know that it must be right, even though we cannot understand it.

Genuine faith. *1 Peter 1:7*

We sometimes think that we have strong faith when our faith is weak. How are we to know if it is weak or strong until it is tried? If you were to lie in bed week after week and perhaps get the idea that you were strong, you would certainly be mistaken. Only when you do work that requires muscular strength will you discover how strong or how weak you are. God would not have us form a wrong estimate of ourselves. He does not want us to say that we are rich and increased in goods and have need of nothing when just the opposite is true. Therefore, He sends trials to test the genuineness of our faith (1 Pet. 1:7), that we may understand how strong or how weak we are.

"A week ago," says one, "I used to sing and think I had the full assurance of faith. Now I can hardly tell whether I am one of God's people." Now you know how much faith you really possess. Now you can tell how much was solid, how much was sham. For had that which failed you been genuine, it would not have been consumed by any trial through which it passed. You have lost the froth from the top of the cup, but all that was really worth having is still there.

Understand, dear friend, that for many necessary purposes there is a need for trials. You will get that trial because God in His wisdom will give faith what faith needs.

Tested by Fire. *1 Peter 1:7*

If we Christians did not sometimes suffer, we would begin to grow too proud and think too much of ourselves. Those of us who are elastic of spirit and are in health and full of everything that can make life happy, we are apt to forget the Most High God. Lest we would be satisfied and forget that all of our springs must be in Him, the Lord sometimes seems to sap the spring of life. He seems to drain the heart of all its spirit and leave us without soul or strength for laughter. It is then that we discover what we are made of, and out of the depths we cry to God, humbled by our adversities.

In heaviness, we learn lessons that we never could attain elsewhere. Do you know that God has beauties for every part of the world and for every place of experience? There are views from the top of the Alps that you can never see elsewhere. There are beauties in the depths of the valley that you could never see on the mountaintops. But there are also beauties to be seen in our Gethsemanes, and some marvelously sweet flowers are to be picked near the dens of leopards. We will never become great in divinity until we become great in suffering.

"Ah!" said Luther, "Affliction is the best book in my library." May I add that the best page in that book is the blackest one, the page called heaviness, when the spirit sinks within us and we cannot endure as we would wish.

Those who have been in the chamber of affliction know how to comfort those who are there. God—I speak with reverence of His Holy Name—cannot make ministers, cannot make a Barnabas, except in the fire. It is there and there alone that He makes His sons of consolation. He may make His sons of thunder anywhere, but His sons of consolation are made in the fire. Who shall speak to those whose hearts are broken? Who shall bind up their wounds? Those whose hearts have been broken, whose wounds have long run with the sore of grief.

THE LORD IS GRACIOUS. *1 Peter 2:3*

Y ou are depressed with heavy grief. Things have gone amiss. You do not prosper in business, or you are sick, or a loved one lies ill. No wonder you feel exceedingly burdened. Passing through this thick darkness, you will be strongly tempted to think badly of God and to blame Him for the troubles that surround you. This will only make matters worse and increase your sin and your sorrow.

You are ready to despair. You say, "There is no hope. I am caught in a net. There is no escape." You are ready to try some wrong method of help. Satan will suggest dishonest, impure, or reckless courses that seem to offer some shadow of relief.

The Lord assures you that there is a far wiser course: just turn to Him. When He hears your cry, He will be gracious. He will answer you. There is help in your present trial. Infinite wisdom understands it, and infinite power can help you through it. God can remove your suffering, or He can prevent the occurrence of what you dread.

Or if in His divine wisdom He sees fit to lay the rod on, He can enable you to bear it and make it turn to your everlasting good. Be well assured, "He does not afflict willingly, nor grieve the children of men" (Lam. 3:33). There is a need for the heavy trial that weighs you down. The Lord is not visiting you in wrath, for there is kindness in His severity. Your strength, your comfort, and your ultimate deliverance will come from knowing that this is true. Yield to God. Trust Him in your affliction, and you will obtain deliverance.

HE WHO BELIEVES ON HIM. *1 Peter 2:6*

Christians will be tested by the flesh. Natural desires will break into vehement lusts and shame will seek to throw them down. Will believers then perish? No! Those that believe in Christ will conquer themselves and readily overcome their besetting sins.

There will be losses and crosses, business trials and domestic bereavements. What then? We will not be put to shame; our Lord will sustain us under every trial.

At last death will come. People will wipe the cold sweat from our brows. We will gasp for breath, but we will not be put to shame. We may not be able to shout "Victory," and we may be too weak to sing triumphant hymns, but with our last breath we will whisper the precious name. They that watch will know by our peace that a Christian does not die but only melts into everlasting life.

Beloved, we will never be put to shame, even amid the grandeur of eternity. We will pass into the next state. After a while, the trumpet will sound and these bodies will rise, and then we will stand with the countless throng on that great day for which all other days were made (1 Thess. 4:14-18).

Those who have other foundations will cry to the rocks to hide them (Rev. 6:16), but we will stand calmly and quietly adoring our Lord the Judge. It will be a solemn day even for us. Assuredly the words of our hymn are true:

> Bold shall I stand in that great day,
> For who aught to my charge shall lay?
> While through His blood absolved I am
> From sin's tremendous curse and shame.

341

DO NOT THINK IT STRANGE. *1 Peter 4:12*

Fiery trials give new life to prayer. Do we ever pray so well as when we feel the pressure of our Father's sword? He never wounds so severely as to kill us, but He sometimes gently probes to wake us from our lethargy. What fervent prayers we offer in the furnace! What grateful songs we sing when we come out! I think that in times of sorrow there is more life in one's holiness than at any other season.

I do not wish to be set aside from preaching, but I must confess that I have often felt unusual spiritual power when preaching after a season of sickness. I have heard some say, "Our minister speaks more sweetly now than before he was set aside." Yes, the olives must go into the press if the oil is to be squeezed. The grapes must be trodden with loving feet before the wine flows. The file must be used to bring out the true quality of our metal. We will never be made into fine gold unless we are frequently put into the crucible of hot fire. We get much good from our trials. Trials make faith grow stronger.

Young people readily enlist in the Lord's army. They put the colors in their hats. They think that they are going to do great things: stir up the church and rout the world, the flesh, and the devil. Soon they find that they have to be drilled by Sergeant Affliction and march to the warrior's battle. Then after many conflicts, they become hardened veterans.

Were it not for our trials, we would turn our back on the enemy. But because of the trials, we become as bold as lions for the Lord our God.

THE FIERY TRIAL. *1 Peter 4:12*

Are you in trouble? Are you afraid? Your fear will be removed when you find that He who sent the trouble teaches you through the trouble. In our schools, much is learned from the chalkboard. In Christ's school, much is learned from affliction.

We are asked to pray for the lives of good people, but I have not always exercised faith while pleading. Often, it seems that Christ pulls one way and I pull the other. I pray, "Father, let them be here." But Jesus says, "Father, I desire that they also whom You gave Me may be with Me where I am, that they may behold My glory which You have given Me; for You loved Me before the foundation of the world" (John 17:24). Once you feel that Christ is drawing the other way, give up and let the Master have His way.

Our Master teaches us this lesson, "I thank You, Father, Lord of heaven and earth, that You have hidden these things from the wise and prudent and have revealed them to babes. Even so, Father, for it seemed good in Your sight" (Matt. 11:25-26). It pleased God to hide these things from the wise and the prudent, and therefore it pleased Christ.

It is well to have our hearts like the poor shepherd to whom a gentleman said, "I wish you a good day."

He replied, "I never knew a bad day."

"How is that, my friend?"

"The days are as God chooses to make them. Therefore they are all good."

Sweet simplicity that leaves everything with God is an attitude that makes Jesus not only your Savior, but also your Lord and Master.

GRACE TO THE HUMBLE.   *1 Peter 5:5*

Some of us are never long without affliction and trial. We seem to live in the flames, passing from fire to fire. Through a succession of shafts, we descend into the heart of the earth, going from woe to woe.

Frequently, our heavenly Father's plan in sending trials is to make and keep His children humble. Remember this and learn a lesson of wisdom. Peter's advice is, "All of you be submissive to one another, and be clothed with humility, for God resists the proud, but gives grace to the humble. Therefore humble yourselves under the mighty hand of God, that He may exalt you in due time, casting all your care upon Him, for He cares for you" (1 Pet. 5:5-7).

Many people have often been humbled, and yet they have not become humble. There is a great difference between the two. If God withdraws His grace and allows a Christian to fall into sin, that fall humbles him in the eyes of all good people, and yet he may not become humble. He may never give a true sense of how evil his actions have been. He may still persevere in his lofty spirit and be far from humility.

When this is the case, the proud spirit may expect a fall, for the rod will make wounds when pride is not abated with gentler blows. The most hopeful way of avoiding humbling affliction is to humble yourself. Be humble, that you may not be humbled. Put yourself into a humble attitude and draw near to God in a lowly spirit, and He will cease chiding.

HE MAY EXALT YOU. *1 Peter 5:6*

Have you been called by God to undertake a work far beyond your own visible power? Have you plunged into it by faith? You have! Then you will not be a stranger to these feelings. "Was I wise in doing this? Others have attempted great things and failed. Will I fail ridiculously? Am I a mere fanatic? Is my trust in God a superstition? Where will I be if I fail?" You must have been sifted in this sifter again and again.

It is indeed delightful when you can feel that God is with you as a refuge and a strength, as a very present help in time of trouble. Therefore you will not fear, even though the earth is removed or the mountains carried into the midst of the sea (Ps. 46:1-2).

My responsibilities are overwhelming, but my God is omnipotent. I cannot carry the load, but He can. "Therefore humble yourself under the mighty hand of God, that He may exalt you in due time, casting all your care upon Him, for He cares for you" (1 Pet. 5:6-7).

Cast your cares upon God. *1 Peter 5:7*

The Lord sends hard times. "You have laid me in the lowest pit, in darkness, in the depths. Your wrath lies heavy upon me, and You have afflicted me" (Ps. 88:6-7).

The Lord sends good times. His is the sun that cheers and the frost that chills. His is the deep calm and the fierce tornado. To dwell on second causes is frequently frivolous. The world says, "It might have been prevented if. . . . " Why conjecture about what would have been different if this or that had happened? This is folly.

As long as I trace my pain to accident, my bereavement to mistake, my loss to another's wrong, or my discomfort to an enemy, I am earthy and shall break my teeth with gravel (Lam. 3:16). Yet when I rise to my God and see His hand at work, I grow calm and stop complaining. "I did not open my mouth, because it was You who did it" (Ps. 39:9).

David preferred to fall into God's hands, and all believers know that they are safest and happiest in divine hands. Raising objections with man is poor work. Pleading with God brings help and comfort. "Casting all your care upon Him, for He cares for you" (1 Pet. 5:7). This is a precept that will be easy to practice when you see that the burden came originally from God.

HIS ETERNAL GLORY.   *1 Peter 5:10*

In the famous resurrection chapter, Paul speaks of the body as being "sown in dishonor," but he adds that "it is raised in glory" (1 Cor. 15:43). And in Philippians 3:21, he says that our divine Lord at His coming "will transform our lowly body that it may be conformed to His glorious body, according to the working by which He is able even to subdue all things to Himself." What a wonderful change that will be for this frail, feeble, suffering body! It is an unhandy body for a spirit. It fits a soul well enough, but a spirit wants something more ethereal and less earthbound, something more full of life than this poor flesh, blood, and bone can ever be.

Well, the body is to be changed. What alteration will it undergo? It will be fully developed. The dwarf will attain full stature. The blind will not be sightless in heaven. The lame will not limp, nor will the elderly tremble. The deaf will hear and the mute will sing God's praises. We will carry none of our deficiencies or infirmities to heaven. There, we will never know an aching brow, a weak knee, or a failing eye. "The inhabitant will not say, 'I am sick'" (Is. 33:24).

We will have a body that is incapable of any kind of suffering. No heart failure, no depression, no aching limbs, no lethargic soul will worry us there. We will be perfectly delivered from every evil of that kind. Our bodies will be immortal. Our risen bodies will not be capable of decay, much less death. There are no graves in glory. Blessed are the dead that die in the Lord, for their bodies will rise never to know death and decay a second time. The risen body will be greatly increased in power. "It is sown in weakness, it is raised in power" (1 Cor. 15:43).

STRENGTHEN AND SETTLE YOU. *1 Peter 5:10*

Thank God for hairbreadth escapes. Thank God for unknown mercies. You may have been within an inch of death and never knew it. Our gratitude to God is stirred when we perceive a danger and escape. Yet we are more in His debt when we do not perceive the peril. Without imagining mischief or nervously inventing perils, we may soberly judge that even in the calmest hours dangers have frequently hovered around us. It is the greatest comfort to feel the Holy Spirit making us strong. But it is no small joy to know that God is round about us, making us safe.

We know that our adversary, the devil, "walks about like a roaring lion, seeking whom he may devour" (1 Pet. 5:8). At this very moment, he may be trying to seize us with hostile attacks. Still, this is our security: "The LORD is our shield" (Ps. 28:7). Though earth and hell should blend their malice, we are safe when God protects.

"Where would you hide," someone asked Luther, "if the elector of Saxony should withdraw his protection?"

Luther smiled and answered, "I put no trust in the prince of Saxony. Under the broad shield of heaven, I stand secure." So he did, and so do we.

In many emergencies, I would be weakness itself if the power of the Eternal had not upheld me. I would be drifting near madness if He had not interposed and kept my heart in the hour of trouble. Is it the same with you? Have you waded through trouble and escaped from a dilemma? Do you ascribe your deliverance to the Lord who strengthened you?

Perhaps your own fault has placed you in predicaments out of which you could never have extricated yourself had He not stretched His hand and picked you up. This is not fiction; this is the finger of God.

GREAT PROMISES. *2 Peter 1:4*

For every trial that God's people have, there are exceedingly great and precious promises of help. Some of you have laid awake worrying about things that God has already answered in His Word. You are like a person in the dark who is dying of hunger while locked in a kitchen. There is food all around if only you would put out your hand and take it. Child of God, if you search the Scriptures, you will find that the Master has opened the pantry of promise.

At times, food appears in the form of someone else's experience. Perhaps nothing is more comforting under the blessing of God than the discovery that another believer has been through a similar experience. When we see the footsteps of the flock, we are in the Shepherd's path.

If you are in deep trouble, read David's prayer in Psalm 88. Was anyone ever cast from God's sight and banished from all hope like David? Still there was no brighter saint. If you are depressed, read the entire book of Job. Some of Job's remarks were terrible, but who could doubt Job's salvation or his redemption for all adversity. Today his name is one of the most illustrious of those who have overcome the world by faith. Turn to the sigh of King Hezekiah (2 Kin. 20:3) or to the lamentation of Jeremiah, surely in one of these you will find your circumstances.

If your problem is inner contention, read Romans 7:15-24. Here Paul, in wonderful paradox, says, "What I am doing, I do not understand. For what I will to do, that I do not practice; but what I hate, that I do. O wretched man that I am! Who will deliver me from this body of death?"

Be of good cheer. The experiences of others and the promises that abound in God's Word will refresh you.

PRECIOUS PROMISES. *2 Peter 1:4*

The promises are precious. They comfort us in distress. Give children of God a divine promise and let them appropriate it, and you cannot make their house or their heart dark. A promise believed is a sun in the soul, a song in the heart. It is marrow to the bones and rejoicing to the spirit. You that have the promises have heaven and earth as your heritage. You will ride in the heights of the earth. You will draw honey from the rock and oil from the flinty rock (Deut. 32:13). The eternal God is your refuge and underneath are the everlasting arms (Deut. 33:27). You shall dwell in safety, in a land of grain and new wine, and the heavens shall drop down dew (Deut. 33:28).

The promises of God not only comfort believers in adversity, but also strengthen them in service. Let the worker who is serving God, but who is depressed under personal weakness, receive this cheering promise, "I will certainly be with you" (Ex. 3:12). "Fear not, for I am with you; be not dismayed, for I am your God. I will strengthen you, yes, I will help you, I will uphold you with My righteous right hand" (Is. 41:10).

These promises elevate the soul. People who do not have God's promises to enrich them may accumulate gold and silver, but they are earthbound with their possessions. They try to be content with corn, wine, and oil, but these things only satisfy our animal nature. Too often, people grovel and hoard all the more as they increase in wealth. But those who grasp the promises are uplifted, for their minds rise to the hand from which every good gift and every perfect gift is poured (James 1:17). Walking by faith in the promise of an unseen God, we are elevated in judgment and taste and become a better people.

DELIVERANCE. *2 Peter 2:9*

I will deliver you" (Ps. 50:15). This text is plain enough, but whether deliverance will be tomorrow, next week, or next year is not clear. You are in a great hurry, but the Lord is not. Your trial may not have produced all the good that it was sent to do, and thus it must last longer.

When gold is thrown into the refining pot, it might cry to the goldsmith, "Let me out."

"No," says the goldsmith. "You still have dross. You must remain in the fire until I have purified you."

God may subject you to many trials, but when He says, "I will deliver you," depend on it. God keeps His Word! The Lord's promise is like a check from a well-financed company; it may be dated three months ahead, but anyone will accept it since it carries a trusted name. When you have God's "I will," you may always cash it by faith, and no discount is taken, for it is current money even when it is only, "I will."

"Call upon Me in the day of trouble; I will deliver you." This is tantamount to deliverance already received. It means, "If I do not deliver you now, I will deliver you at a time that is better than now."

The Lord is always punctual. You will never be kept waiting by Him. You have kept Him waiting, but He is prompt to the second. He never keeps His servants waiting one single tick of the clock beyond His own appointed, wise, and proper moment. Therefore, be of good courage. God Himself will rescue those who call on Him. "The Lord knows how to deliver the godly" (2 Pet. 2:9).

351

NOT YET REVEALED. *1 John 3:2*

God has a motive! His thoughts are working to give you a future and a hope (Jer. 29:11). All things are working for good to those who love God, to those who are the called according to His purpose (Rom. 8:28). We see only the beginning; God sees the end from the beginning. We spell the alphabet—alpha, beta, gamma . . . But from alpha to omega, God reads all at once. He knows every letter in the Book of Providence. He sees not only what He is doing, but also the final results.

God sees your present pain and grief. He also sees the future joy and the usefulness that will come from this affliction. He observes not only the plow tearing the soil, but also a golden harvest clothing that soil. He sees the consequences of affliction and knows that it will lead to much blessed happiness.

"Beloved, now are we the children of God; and it has not yet been revealed what we shall be" (1 John 3:2). You never see the Great Artist's masterpiece. You only see the rough marble and mark the chips that fall to the ground. You have felt the edge of His chisel; you know the weight of His hammer. If you could see the glorious image as it will be when He has put the finishing blows to it, you would better understand the chisel, the hammer, and the Artist.

WE SHALL SEE HIM. *1 John 3:2*

The apostle said, "It has not yet been revealed what we shall be, but we know that when He is revealed, we shall be like Him, for we shall see Him as He is" (1 John 3:2). We cannot see it now; we can only discern it by faith, but in His time His coming shall appear. His appearance is drawing near. We will reign with Christ Jesus (Rev. 20:6). We will wear the crown (Rev. 2:10), and this world, which now despises us, will know us as judges and kings (1 Cor. 6:20; Rev. 1:6).

When Jesus comes, we will judge angels with Him (1 Cor. 6:3), giving our verdict and adding our "Amen" to all His sentences. Then in heaven, angels will minister to the heirs of salvation, and we will sit on thrones (Rev. 20:4). Christian, all this will be yours.

Jesus said, "Father, I desire that they also whom You gave Me may be with Me where I am, that they may behold My glory which You have given Me" (John 17:24). You will be with the Savior. You will see His glory and have a share of it.

Why then should you be afraid, dejected, or depressed? Pluck up your courage! An hour with God will make up for it all; one glimpse of Him and your trials will seem nothing. You have been called ugly names, and ill words have been thrown at you. But those trials will be nothing when you hear Him say, "Come, you blessed of My Father, inherit the kingdom prepared for you from the foundation of the world" (Matt. 25:34).

Cheered by this reward, I urge you to press on. Greater riches than all the treasures of Egypt will be yours. "Be faithful unto death, and I will give you the crown of life" (Rev. 2:10).

God grant that we may be found numbered among the election of grace, that none of us will be lost. His shall be the praise forever and ever. Amen.

WE HAVE PASSED. *1 John 3:14*

Life is like a parade that passes before our eyes. It comes. Hear the people shouting. It is here. In a few minutes, people crowd the streets. Then it vanishes and is gone. Does life strike you as being just that?

I remember, ah I remember, so many in the parade. I have stood, as it were, at a window, even though I have also been in the procession. I recall the hearty men of my boyhood, whom I use to hear pray. They are now singing up yonder.

I remember a long parade of saints who have passed before me and have gone into glory. What a host of friends we have in the unseen world, who are "gone over to the majority." As we grow older, they really are the majority, for our friends on earth are outnumbered by our friends in heaven.

Some of you will fondly remember loved ones who have passed away in the parade. But please remember that you also are in the parade. Though they seem to have passed before you, you have been passing along with them, and soon you will reach the vanishing point. We are all walking in the procession. We are all passing away to the land of substance and reality.

We expect good things to come. We are not inhabitants of this country; we are citizens of the New Jerusalem. We are only shipwrecked here for a while, exiled from home until the boat comes to ferry us across the stream to the land where our true possessions lie.

Life, light, love, and everything is He who has gone before. Jesus is our Forerunner to the place that He has prepared for them that love Him (John 14:2).

NO GREATER JOY.   *3 John 4*

No cross is so heavy to carry as a living cross. Next to a woman who is bound to an ungodly husband or a man who is unequally yoked with a graceless wife, I pity the parents whose children are not walking in the truth. Must it always be that the father goes to the house of God and his son to the alehouse? Must we come to the communion table alone and our children be separated from us? God grant that it may not be so. It is a solemn reflection.

More solemn is the vision if we look across the river of death into the eternity beyond. What if our children should not walk in the truth and die unsaved? There cannot be tears in heaven, but if there were, the celestial would look over the wall of the New Jerusalem and weep their fill at the sight of their children in the flames of hell. What if those to whom we gave birth should be weeping and gnashing their teeth in torment while we are looking into the face of our Father in heaven?

I pray that it may never be the lot of anyone to weep over sons and daughters dead and twice dead. Better that they had never been born. Better that they had perished like untimely fruit than they should dishonor their father's God and their mother's Savior. It is terrible to die and receive, "Depart, you cursed," from the same lips that will say to their parents, "Come, you blessed of My Father, inherit the kingdom prepared for you from the foundation of the world" (Matt. 25:34).

Proportionate to the greatness of the joy before us is the terror of the contrast. I pray that such an overwhelming calamity may never happen to anyone connected with any of our families.

"I have no greater joy than to hear that my children walk in truth" (3 John 4).

YOUR MOST HOLY FAITH. *Jude 20*

Are you so deep in trouble that you are sinking? That is a great position, provided your faith proves equal to the occasion and leads you to throw yourself on God and swim to the shore. Leaning on God's invisible arm is great work. If you can walk where there is no visible path, you belong to the immortals. A God-given faith proves your lineage to be divine.

Perhaps you have a task that is much too heavy. Then you have the honor of being placed where you can display your trust in God. What you can do you must do, but what you cannot do and must do, you may confidently expect the Lord to enable you to perform. He will elevate your weakness into a platform for His power. When you reach the end of your resources, you get to the beginning of God's resources.

You may look at your trouble until your spirits sinks. You may watch God's adversaries until your soul is heavy with despair. Lift your eyes to Him who works all things according to His will. Across His face no cloud can ever pass. He speaks and it is done. He commands and it stands still. He bears up the arch of heaven and, unaided, wheels the planets along their trackless courses (Heb. 1:10). When you lift up your eyes to Him, difficulties vanish, impossibilities end, and perils and dangers cease.

ALPHA AND OMEGA. *Revelation 1:8*

Nothing will happen that God has not foreseen. No unexpected event will destroy His plans. No emergency will transpire for which He has not provided. No peril will occur against which He has not guarded. No remarkable need will take Him by surprise. He declares the end from the beginning, from ancient times things that are not yet done (Is. 46:10). God fills His own eternal now. He sees everything, the past, the present, the future. All, all, all of the future is foreseen and fixed by Him. Derive great comfort from this fact.

Suppose you go to sea with the most skillful captain. That captain cannot possibly know what may occur during the voyage. Even with the greatest foresight, he can never promise an absolutely safe passage. There are dangers. Hurricanes or tremendous waves could sink the ship.

When you come to the ship of Providence, however, He who is at the helm is Master of every wind that blows and of every wave that breaks its force on the ship. He foresees both the events that will happen at the destination and those at the starting port. He knows every wave, its height, width, and force. He knows every wind in all its connections. We are safe with a Captain who has forearranged and foreordained all things from the beginning to the end. It is to our advantage to put implicit confidence in His guidance:

> Be this my joy, that evermore
> Thou rulest all things at Thy will:
> Thy sovereign wisdom I adore,
> And calmly, sweetly, trust Thee still.

DO NOT BE AFRAID. *Revelation 1:17*

This "do not be afraid" may be specifically applied to the grave. We need not fear death, because Jesus has the key to the grave. Jesus will come to our dying bed in all the glory of His supernal splendor and say, "Come with me from Lebanon, my spouse, with me from Lebanon. Look from the top of Amana" (Song 4:8). Come with me "until the day breaks and the shadows flee away" (Song 4:6). The sight of Jesus as He thrusts in the key and opens that gate of death will make you forget the supposed terrors of the grave. They are only suppositions; you will find it sweet to die.

Since Jesus has the sepulcher's key, never fear it again, never again. Depend on it. Your dying hour will be the best hour you have ever known. Your last moment will be your richest. Better than the day of your birth will be the day of your death. It will be the beginning of heaven, the rising of a sun that will never go down forever. Let the fear of death be banished by faith in a living Savior.

We have stood and peered as best we could through the mist that gathers over the black river. We have wondered what it must be like to have left the body and be flitting through that land from which no traveler has ever returned. It is not as if you crossed the channel from England to France and were among people speaking another language under another sovereignty. You do not pass from one province of your Lord's empire to another. In that spirit-land above, they speak the same language, the language of New Jerusalem, which you have already begun to speak. They acknowledge the King that you obey here. When you enter heaven, you will find them singing the praise of the same glorious One whom you adore. You will find them triumphing in the love of Him who was your Savior here below.

BE FAITHFUL UNTIL DEATH. *Revelation 2:10*

Are you worried about dying? Do you fear the last hour of this life? Beloved, there is a peril more perilous than death, and that is to live life well. Live it well; that is the point! If you succeed in this, you will find that to die is nothing more than closing life's story. If your main concern is to run the race with honor, you will finish the course with joy. You can leave the dying until the time comes, if you see to the living while the time to live lasts.

There is one grace we do not need today while we are alive, and that is dying grace. We will not require that comfort until our departure is at hand. You cannot know what sort of summons you will get to quit your fleshly tabernacle, or what sharp pain you may have to bear, or what sweet comfort may be provided when heart and flesh fail. So serve God now with all your strength. Rest in His precious blood. Seek fellowship with your living, loving Lord, and He will supply grace sufficient for all your future needs.

You do not know the good that He has in store for you. As time and space contract, your mind will expand to survey the eternity beyond. As film covers these dull organs of sight, the eyes of your understanding will be opened. Many who depart this life hear the songs of angels long before their ears are closed to the sounds of earth. And how precious Christ becomes to them then. They hardly knew the moment they entered heaven, for as they left earth the radiance of that bright realm dawned in a vision of glory.

Perhaps you will never die! Christ may return before you die, and therefore you will be changed, in a moment, in the twinkling of an eye (1 Cor. 15:51-52). Your Father's good pleasure will not be frustrated; your hope of heaven will not be disappointed.

THE CROWN OF LIFE. *Revelation 2:10*

Carlyle, in his History of the French Revolution, tells of the Duke of Orleans who did not believe in death. One day his secretary stumbled on the words, "The late king of Spain," and the duke angrily demanded what he meant by that remark. The secretary responded, "My Lord, it is a title that some of the kings have taken."

We are immortal. God has endowed us with a spiritual nature that will outlive the sun, outlast the stars, and exist throughout eternity. When the righteous soul leaves the body, it appears before God. "Assuredly, I say to you, today you will be with Me in Paradise" (Luke 23:43).

Christ, however, has not only bought His people's souls, but also their bodies. Our bodies will be raised, and our souls will re-enter our bodies. Here we are a shriveled grain, sown in the earth, but our next body will have all the loveliness that heaven can give. It will be a glorious body, raised in honor, raised in power, raised to die no more (1 Cor. 16:54). "I know that my Redeemer lives, and He shall stand at last on the earth; and after my skin is destroyed, this I know, that in my flesh I shall see God, whom I shall see for myself, and my eyes shall behold, and not another" (Job 19:25-27).

Let me wave the palm of victory (Rev. 7:9). Let me wear the crown of life (Rev. 2:10). Let me wear the fine white linen of immaculate perfection (Rev. 19:8). Let me cast my crown before Jehovah's throne (Rev. 4:10). Let me sing the everlasting song. Let my voice join the eternal chorus, "Alleluia! For the Lord God Omnipotent reigns!" (Rev. 19:6). My voice will be sweetly tuned to the notes of gratitude, and my heart will dance with ecstasy before the throne.

"He who testifies to these things says, 'Surely I am coming quickly.' Amen. Even so, come, Lord Jesus" (Rev. 22:20).

THAT YOU MAY BE RICH. *Revelation 3.18*

Tested child of God, your daughter is sick, or your gold has melted in the fire, or you are sick of yourself. Your heart is sad. Christ counsels, "Cast your burden on the LORD, and He shall sustain you; He shall never permit the righteous to be moved" (Ps. 55:22).

Young person, seeking great things for yourself, Christ counsels, "Do not seek them." I remember that as a young man I was ambitious. I was seeking to go to college, to leave my congregation in the wilderness that I might become something great. As I was out walking, this text came with power to my heart, "Do you seek great things for yourself? Do not seek them" (Jer. 45:5).

"Lord," 1 said, "I will follow Your counsel and not my own plans." I have never had cause to regret that decision. Always take the Lord for your guide, and you will never be wrong.

Backslider, you that have a name to live but are nearly dead, Christ gives you counsel, "Because you say, 'I am rich, have become wealthy, and have need of nothing'—and do not know that you are wretched, miserable, poor, blind and naked—I counsel you to buy from Me gold refined in the fire, that you may be rich; and white garments, that you may be clothed" (Rev. 3:17-18).

Sinner, Christ's counsel is, "Come to Me, all you who labor and are heavy laden, and I will give you rest" (Matt. 11:28). Depend on it, for it is loving counsel. Take it, go home, get on your knees, seek Christ, listen to His voice, and hear it and live.

AS MANY AS I LOVE. *Revelation 3:19*

God chastens in pure love when He sees that it is absolutely necessary. "He does not afflict willingly, nor grieve the children of men" (Lam. 3:33). Our parents too often corrected according to their pleasure, yet we respected them. Our heavenly Father, however, corrects only when necessary. Shall we not pay greater reverence to Him and live?

I find that life and health often come to the saints through briny tears or through the bruising of the flesh and the oppression of the spirit. I bear willing witness that sickness has brought me health and that loss has conferred gain, and I do not doubt that one day death will bring me fuller life.

Be wise then, dear child of God. Look on your present affliction as a chastening. "What son is there whom a father does not chasten?" (Heb. 12:7). "As many as I love, I rebuke and chasten" (Rev. 3:19). There is not a more profitable instrument in all God's house than the rod. Our brightest joys are given birth by our bitterest griefs.

A chastened spirit is a gracious spirit, and how shall we obtain it unless we are chastened? Like our Lord Jesus, we learn obedience by the things we suffer. God had one son without sin, but He never had a son without sorrow. And He never will while the world remains. Therefore, bless God for all His dealings, and as a child of His, confess, "You, Lord, have chastened me."

I REBUKE AND CHASTEN. *Revelation 3:19*

God's dealings toward the sons of men have always puzzled the wise of the earth. Apart from the revelation of God, the dealings of Jehovah toward His creatures in this world seem inexplicable. Who can understand why the wicked flourish and are in great power? "I have seen the wicked in great power, and spreading himself like a native green tree" (Ps. 37:35). The ungodly prosper and are filled with riches. They pile up gold like dust. They add field to field and acre to acre.

On the other hand, the righteous are thrown down. Often, virtue is dressed in the rags of poverty. Frequently, the most holy ones suffer from hunger, thirst, and nakedness. We have sometimes heard Christians say, "Surely, I have served God in vain. I have fasted for nothing. How can this be?"

The heathen says, "The man that prospers is favored by the gods; the man who is unsuccessful is obnoxious to the Most High." They do not know any better. Those more enlightened easterners who talked with Job during his affliction got but little further. They believed that all who serve God have hedges around them and that God multiplies their wealth and increases their happiness. They saw in Job's affliction a sign that he was a hypocrite. Thus they thought that God had quenched his candle and put out his light.

Unfortunately, even Christians have fallen into the same error. They have been apt to think that if God lifts one up there must be some excellence in him. If He chastens and afflicts, they generally think that it must be an exhibition of wrath. Listen to the text and the riddle will be unriddled. Listen to the words of Jesus speaking to His servant John, and the mystery is all unmysteried. "As many as I love, I rebuke and chasten. Therefore be zealous and repent" (Rev. 3:19).

An end to tears. *Revelation 7:17*

The ancients were accustomed to use bottles to catch the tears of mourners. I see a bottle that contains grief common to all, for believers suffer like the rest of the human race. Physical pain does not spare the servants of God. Their nerves, blood vessels, limbs, and organs are as susceptible to disease as those of the unregenerate. Some of the finest saints have lain long on beds of sickness. The dearest to the heart of God have felt the heaviest blows of the chastening rod. Great pain forces tears to wet the cheeks. The human body is capable of a fearful degree of agony, and few there are who have not at some time watered their bed with tears because of pain.

Coupled with this are the losses and crosses of daily life. What Christian among you lives without occasional difficulty and serious losses? Can you travel from the first of January to the last of December without feeling the weariness of the way?

No ship can navigate the Atlantic of earth without meeting with storms; only on the Pacific of heaven is all calm, and that forever. If Jesus wept (John 11:35), do not expect that you will be without tears of bereavement. Parents will go before us; infants will be taken, and brothers and sisters will fall before the scythe of death.

You cannot, dear friend, travel the wilderness of this world without discovering that thorns and thistles grow in it. Step as you may, your feet must sometimes feel the power of the thorn to wound. We may forget to laugh, but we will always know how to weep.

The surest method of getting rid of present tears is communion and fellowship with God. When I can creep under the wing of my dear God and nestle close to His bosom. I am safe, content, happy, peaceful, and rejoicing.

NO MORE PAIN. *Revelation 21:4*

I owe everything to the furnace, hammer, and file. The best piece of furniture in my house has been the cross. My greatest enricher has been personal pain, and for that I thank God. I can sing with the poet:

> God in Israel sows the seeds
> Of affliction, pain, and toil;
> These spring up and choke the weeds
> Which would else overspread the soil.
>
> Trials make the promise sweet;
> Trials give new life to prayer;
> Trials bring me to His feet,
>   Lay me low, and keep me there.

THE BOOK OF LIFE. *Revelation 21:27*

Fame is a transient blessing, and yet our humanity fondly covets and eagerly pursues it. We want to be more illustrious than our peers and outstrip all our competitors. It is natural to want to make a name, or to gain some note in our circle, or to widen that circle whenever possible.

Yet fame does bring an equal measure of dissatisfaction. When you work for fame or honor, there is a degree of pleasure in the search that is not possessed when the object is gained. Some of the most famous have also been the most wretched.

If you have fame and honor, accept it. But let this be your prayer, "My God, bless me indeed. For what profit is there if my name is in a thousand mouths and You vomit it out of Your mouth? (Rev. 3:16). What value is it if my name is written in marble and not written in the Lamb's Book of Life? (Rev. 21:27). These blessings are only shadows and wind that mock me. Give me Your blessing. The honor that comes from You will make me blest indeed."

If you live in obscurity and have never obtained any degree of fame, be content to run your own course and fulfill your own vocation. Being unknown is not the most serious illness. It is far worse to have fame that whitens the ground like snow in the morning but disappears in the heat of the day. Does it make any difference to the dead if people are talking about them?

Make sure that you indeed get God's blessing.

UNTIL THE DAY BREAKS. *Song of Solomon 4:6*

What a place heaven must be to those whose bones have worn through their skin from extended stays on sickbeds. I have stood at the bedsides of suffering saints and wept at their pain.

What a change from the nursing home or the hospital to the New Jerusalem (Rev. 3:12)! What a transition from agony to bliss! Track the chosen's glorious flight from the sickbed to the crown (Rev. 2:10), to the harp (Rev. 14:2), to the palm branch (Rev. 7:9), and to the King in His beauty (Rev. 19:16).

It will be well when the spirit breaks from the body's worn, dilapidated hovel and rises to heaven. "For we know that if our earthly house, this tent, is destroyed, we have a building from God, a house not made with hands eternal in the heavens. For we who are in this tent groan, being burdened. We are confident, yes, well pleased rather to be absent from the body and to be present with the Lord" (2 Cor. 5:1, 4, 8).

Let me live, if God will be with me in life. Let me die, if He will be with me in death. So long as I am "forever with the Lord," what else matters? What God decrees is my delight. I feel no abhorrence to anything He appoints in life or in death.

If you have chosen Christ, mercy, and eternal life, and if by faith these are yours, enjoy them. Rehearse the music of the skies. Taste the delights of God's fellowship. Rejoice in the victory that has overcome the world: our faith (1 John 5:4). You and I will be in Gloryland before long, and some of us much sooner than we think.

As this meditation ends, under a sense of my own frailty, I wish you a sincere farewell "until the day breaks and the shadows flee away" (Song 4:6). Goodbye.

Topical Index

DIFFICULTIES:
4, 26, 65, 67, 131, 153, 154, 166, 184, 196, 200, 208, 209, 226, 246, 272, 304, 345.

DOUBT:
20, 26, 53, 154, 155, 160, 191, 274, 281, 327, 345, 346, 347, 350.

DUTY:
4, 103, 125, 126, 178, 346, 347.

FEAR:
1, 8, 20, 24, 40, 53, 61, 68, 86, 93, 124, 179, 216, 251.

GRIEF:
6, 39, 81, 84, 104, 109, 158, 203, 218, 352.

LONELINESS:
5, 76, 77, 81, 88, 93, 119, 144, 153, 158, 198, 206, 219, 233, 271, 305, 311.

LOSS:
1, 5, 22, 34, 53, 55, 59, 60, 165, 197, 216, 222, 242, 244, 251, 270, 311, 321.

NERVOUSNESS:
4, 98, 112, 158, 180, 242.

OLD AGE:
2, 30, 32, 47, 57, 92, 142, 165, 270, 317, 318, 364.

PAIN—PHYSICAL:
7, 11, 24, 30, 39, 45, 47, 49, 59, 65, 66, 72, 79, 99, 105, 106, 114, 193, 218, 241, 275, 283, 305, 312, 317, 318, 352, 359, 362, 365.

PEACE:
33, 54, 70, 180, 181, 213, 257, 258, 276, 319, 321, 364.

POVERTY:
3, 4, 12, 14, 27, 36, 41, 47, 50, 53, 57, 60, 61, 65, 71, 76, 86, 87, 88,

92, 93, 97, 102, 110, 114, 115, 121, 129, 133, 138, 144, 150, 162,
163, 172, 178, 181, 183, 188, 205, 211, 212, 214, 225, 236, 256,
258, 267, 271, 275, 282, 284, 297, 305, 307, 310, 319, 362, 363.

SHUT-IN:
24, 30, 38, 78, 110, 127, 149, 300, 334, 338, 342, 367.

SICKNESS:
4, 11, 37, 38, 39, 53, 55, 57, 61, 64, 65, 74, 76, 78, 79, 97, 99, 100,
102, 110, 112, 129, 132, 133, 139, 162, 164, 167, 176, 222, 225,
230, 240, 241, 250, 271, 289, 297, 301, 317, 318, 342, 359.

SORROW:
3, 6, 8, 11, 14, 16, 49, 51, 52, 76, 81, 83, 97, 100, 114, 122, 128,
134, 139, 143, 149, 157, 251, 285, 314, 362.

SUFFERING:
3, 7, 11, 30, 47, 49, 51, 66, 74, 80, 86, 127, 132, 135, 143, 167, 203,
269, 314, 338, 340, 347.

TEMPTATION:
5, 150, 172, 185, 315, 324.

TRIALS:
1, 2, 3, 10, 16, 19, 20, 32, 34, 37, 38, 40, 42, 43, 44, 45, 47, 49, 58,
59, 63, 71, 72, 75, 77, 80, 83, 90, 93, 100, 104, 107, 108, 115, 116,
117, 132, 134, 139, 161, 163, 172, 177, 182, 184, 187, 190, 191,
199, 203, 209, 212, 228, 230, 234, 237, 238, 240, 248, 252, 266,
269, 273, 277, 278, 283, 296, 301, 306, 314, 315, 322, 324, 325,
326, 333, 334, 335, 336, 337, 338, 340, 341, 342, 348, 349, 351.

TROUBLES:
5, 13, 14, 16, 23, 34, 37, 48, 52, 56, 65, 71, 72, 73, 75, 77, 82, 83,
85, 87, 90, 95, 100, 105, 108, 117, 128, 129, 132, 135, 139, 140,
162, 164, 166, 178, 182, 183, 184, 187, 189, 191, 204, 205, 210,
215, 219, 228, 230, 232, 243, 252, 254, 267, 281, 290, 291, 294,
296, 301, 308, 310, 314, 316, 323, 326, 330, 349.

TRUSTING:
15, 34, 35, 40, 41, 44, 48, 108, 113, 140, 147, 148, 155, 163, 173, 180, 202, 210, 218, 230, 231, 239, 243, 248, 251, 253, 265, 270, 284, 292, 293, 304, 309, 327, 328.

WEAKNESS:
5, 17, 21, 24, 30, 69, 89, 105, 109, 127, 135, 136, 140, 142, 146, 176, 183, 193, 202, 245, 254, 266, 268, 279, 280, 298, 313, 319, 330.

WEARINESS:
3, 25, 109, 127, 135, 144, 145, 149, 153, 156, 160, 185, 193, 194, 242, 247, 256, 265, 268, 288, 298, 361, 364.